J. W. Powell

Exploration of the Colorado River of the West and its Tributaries

J. W. Powell

Exploration of the Colorado River of the West and its Tributaries

ISBN/EAN: 9783741123191

Manufactured in Europe, USA, Canada, Australia, Japa

Cover: Foto ©Lupo / pixelio.de

Manufactured and distributed by brebook publishing software
(www.brebook.com)

J. W. Powell

Exploration of the Colorado River of the West and its Tributaries

EXPLORATION

OF THE

COLORADO RIVER OF THE WEST

AND

ITS TRIBUTARIES.

EXPLORED IN

1869, 1870, 1871, and 1872,

UNDER THE

DIRECTION OF THE SECRETARY OF THE SMITHSONIAN INSTITUTION.

WASHINGTON:
GOVERNMENT PRINTING OFFICE.
1875.

REPORT

OF

J. W. POWELL.

Figure 1.— Grand Cañon of the Colorado. (6,000 feet deep.)

SMITHSONIAN INSTITUTION,
Washington, D. C., June 18, 1874.

SIR: I have the honor to submit herewith the report of the exploration of the Colorado River of the West and its tributaries, by Prof. J. W. Powell.

This exploration was placed under the direction of the Smithsonian Institution by Congress.

Very respectfully, your obedient servant,

JOSEPH HENRY,
Secretary Smithsonian Institution.

Hon. J. G. BLAINE,
Speaker of the House of Representatives.

WASHINGTON, D. C., *June* 16, 1874.

SIR: I have the honor to submit herewith my report of the exploration of the Colorado River of the West and its tributaries, and respectfully request that the same may be forwarded to Congress.

I am, with great respect, your obedient servant,

J. W. POWELL.

Prof. JOSEPH HENRY,
  Secretary Smithsonian Institution,
    Washington, D. C.

CONTENTS.

PART FIRST.

HISTORY OF THE EXPLORATION OF THE CAÑONS OF THE COLORADO.

PART SECOND.

ON THE PHYSICAL FEATURES OF THE VALLEY OF THE COLORADO.

PART THIRD.

ZOOLOGY.

LIST OF ILLUSTRATIONS.

PREFACE.

In the summer of 1867, with a small party of naturalists, students, and amateurs like myself, I visited the mountain region of Colorado Territory. While in Middle Park, I explored a little cañon, through which the Grand River runs, immediately below the well-known watering-place, "Middle Park Hot Springs." Later in the fall I passed through Cedar Cañon, the gorge by which the Grand leaves the park. The result of the summer's study was to kindle a desire to explore the cañons of the Grand, Green, and Colorado Rivers, and the next summer I organized an expedition with the intention of penetrating still farther into that cañon country.

As soon as the snows were melted, so that the main range could be crossed, I went over into Middle Park, and proceeded thence down the Grand to the head of Cedar Cañon, then across the Park range by Gore's Pass, and in October found myself and party encamped on the White River, about a hundred and twenty miles above its mouth. At that point I built cabins, and established winter quarters, intending to occupy the cold season, as far as possible, in exploring the adjacent country. The winter of 1868–'69 proved favorable to my purposes, and several excursions were made, southward to the Grand, down the White to the Green River, northward to the Yampa, and around the Uinta Mountains.

During these several excursions, I seized every opportunity to study the cañons through which these upper streams run, and, while thus engaged, formed plans for the exploration of the cañons of the Colorado. Since that time I have been engaged in executing these plans, sometimes employed in the field, sometimes in the office. Begun originally as an exploration, the work has finally developed into a survey embracing the geography, geology, ethnography, and natural history of the country, and a number of gentlemen have, from time to time, assisted me in the work.

II COL

It is expected that the results of these labors will, as soon as practicable, be published by the General Government, in a series of volumes, and such publication commences with the present, which, in Part First, gives a history of the original exploration through a region practically unknown prior to the time it was made. It has not been thought best to give a history of all our travels, but only those portions which were original explorations.

Accompanying the volume will be found a map of the "Green River from the Union Pacific Railroad to the mouth of the White River," including the eastern portion of the Uinta Mountains, and a "Profile of the Green River and Colorado River of the West, from the crossing of the Union Pacific Railroad to the mouth of the Colorado, compared with the profile of the Ohio and Mississippi Rivers from Pittsburgh to Vicksburgh." It has been prepared from barometric data collected at different times during the exploration and survey. That portion below the mouth of the Rio Virgen has been taken from Lieutenant Ives's "Report upon the Colorado River of the West."

The altitude of the mouth of the Rio Virgen is represented on the profile with this volume as somewhat less than it appears on that made by Lieutenant Ives. Our own determinations fix it as we represent it. Lieutenant Ives's data for the upper portion of his line are indefinite, but can be interpreted to agree with the results which we have obtained; perhaps better than with his own profile.

As far as possible we have adopted the names of geographic features used by the settlers of the adjacent country, but many of the mountains, plateaus, valleys, cañons, and streams were unknown and unnamed. In such cases we have accepted the Indian names, whenever they could be determined with accuracy. I intend, finally, to publish a glossary of all these new names, giving their significance.

I am greatly indebted to many gentlemen living in Utah, Wyoming, and Colorado Territories for their assistance and co-operation in this enterprise. To mention them severally would inordinately swell this preface.

Professor A. H. Thompson has been my companion and collaborator during the greater part of the time, and has had entire charge of the geographic work; the final maps will exhibit the results of his learning and executive ability.

Professor Joseph Henry, the Secretary of the Smithsonian Institution, under whose direction the work was performed, prior to the 1st of July, 1874, has contributed greatly to any success which we may have had, by his instructions and advice, and by his most earnest sympathy; and I have taken the liberty to express my gratitude for his kindness, and reverence for his profound attainments, by attaching his name to a group of lofty mountains.

To the officers of the Union Pacific, the Chicago, Burlington and Quincy, the Utah Central, and other railroads, I am indebted for many valuable favors; but for their co-operation the work could not have been accomplished with the means at my command. Many thousands of dollars, in the aggregate, have been contributed by them to the enterprise in the form of free transportation. I earnestly hope that the final result of the work, as a contribution to American science, will not disappoint their expectations.

J. W. P.

Washington, D. C., 1875.

PART FIRST.

HISTORY

EXPLORATION OF THE CAÑONS OF THE COLORADO.

1 COL

CHAPTER 1.

The Colorado River is formed by the junction of the Grand and Green. The Grand River has its source in the Rocky Mountains, five or six miles west of Long's Peak, in latitude 40° 17′ and longitude 105° 43′ approximately. A group of little alpine lakes, that receive their waters directly from perpetual snow-banks, discharge into a common reservoir, known as Grand Lake, a beautiful sheet of water. Its quiet surface reflects towering cliffs and crags of granite on its eastern shore; and stately pines and firs stand on its western margin.

The Green River heads near Frémont's Peak, in the Wind River Mountains, in latitude 43° 15′ and longitude 109° 45′ approximately. This river, like the last, has its sources in alpine lakes, fed by everlasting snows. Thousands of these little lakes, with deep, cold, emerald waters, are embosomed among the crags of the Rocky Mountains. These streams, born in the cold, gloomy solitudes of the upper mountain-region, have a strange, eventful history as they pass down through gorges, tumbling in cascades and cataracts, until they reach the hot, arid plains of the Lower Colorado, where the waters that were so clear above empty as turbid floods into the Gulf of California.

The mouth of the Colorado is in latitude 31° 53′ and longitude 115°.

The Green River is larger than the Grand, and is the upper continuation of the Colorado. Including this river, the whole length of the stream is about two thousand miles. The region of country drained by the Colorado and its tributaries is about eight hundred miles in length, and varies from three hundred to five hundred in width, containing about three hundred thousand square miles, an area larger than all the New England and Middle States, with Maryland and Virginia added, or as large as Minnesota, Wisconsin, Iowa, Illinois, and Missouri.

There are two distinct portions of the basin of the Colorado. The lower third is but little above the level of the sea, though here and there ranges of mountains rise to an altitude of from two to six thousand feet. This part of the valley is bounded on the north by a line of cliffs, which present a bold, often vertical step, hundreds or thousands of feet to the table-lands above.

The upper two-thirds of the basin rises from four to eight thousand feet above the level of the sea. This high region, on the east, north, and west, is set with ranges of snow-clad mountains, attaining an altitude above the sea varying from eight to fourteen thousand feet. All winter long, on its mountain-crested rim, snow falls, filling the gorges, half burying the forests, and covering the crags and peaks with a mantle woven by the winds from the waves of the sea—a mantle of snow. When the summer-sun comes, this snow melts, and tumbles down the mountain-sides in millions of cascades. Ten million cascade brooks unite to form ten thousand torrent creeks; ten thousand torrent creeks unite to form a hundred rivers beset with cataracts; a hundred roaring rivers unite to form the Colorado, which rolls, a mad, turbid stream, into the Gulf of California.

Consider the action of one of these streams: its source in the mountains, where the snows fall; its course through the arid plains. Now, if at the river's flood storms were falling on the plains, its channel would be cut but little faster than the adjacent country would be washed, and the general level would thus be preserved; but, under the conditions here mentioned, the river deepens its bed, as there is much through corrasion and but little lateral degradation.

So all the streams cut deeper and still deeper until their banks are towering cliffs of solid rock. These deep, narrow gorges are called cañons.

For more than a thousand miles along its course, the Colorado has cut for itself such a cañon; but at some few points, where lateral streams join it, the cañon is broken, and narrow, transverse valleys divide it properly into a series of cañons.

The Virgen, Kanab, Paria, Escalante, Dirty Devil, San Rafael, Price, and Uinta on the west, the Grand, Yampa, San Juan, and Colorado Chiquito on the east, have also cut for themselves such narrow, winding gorges, or deep cañons. Every river entering these has cut another cañon;

Figure 2.—Lower Cañon of the Kanab. (3,000 feet deep.)

Figure 3.—Pa-ru′-nu-weap Cañon.

every lateral creek has cut a cañon; every brook runs in a cañon; every rill born of a shower, and born again of a shower, and living only during these showers, has cut for itself a cañon; so that the whole upper portion of the basin of the Colorado is traversed by a labyrinth of these deep gorges.

Owing to a great variety of geological conditions, these cañons differ much in general aspect. The Rio Virgen, between Long Valley and the Mormon town of Schunesburgh, runs through Pa-rn'-nu-weap Cañon, often not more than twenty or thirty feet in width, and from six hundred to one thousand five hundred feet deep.

Away to the north, the Yampa empties into the Green by a cañon that I essayed to cross in the fall of 1868, and was baffled from day to day until the fourth had nearly passed before I could find my way down to the river. But thirty miles above its mouth, this cañon ends, and a narrow valley, with a flood-plain, is found. Still farther up the stream, the river comes down through another cañon, and beyond that a narrow valley is found, and its upper course is now through a cañon and now a valley.

All these cañons are alike changeable in their topographic characteristics.

The longest cañon through which the Colorado runs is that between the mouth of the Colorado Chiquito and the Grand Wash, a distance of two hundred and seventeen and a half miles. But this is separated from another above, sixty-five and a half miles in length, only by the narrow cañon-valley of the Colorado Chiquito.

All the scenic features of this cañon-land are on a giant scale, strange and weird. The streams run at depths almost inaccessible; lashing the rocks which beset their channels; rolling in rapids, and plunging in falls, and making a wild music which but adds to the gloom of the solitude.

The little valleys nestling along the streams are diversified by bordering willows, clumps of box-elder, and small groves of cottonwood.

Low mesas, dry and treeless, stretch back from the brink of the cañon, often showing smooth surfaces of naked, solid rock. In some places, the country rock being composed of marls, the surface is a bed of loose, disintegrated material, and you walk through it as in a bed of ashes. Often these marls are richly colored and variegated. In other places, the country rock is a loose sandstone, the disintegration of which has left broad stretches of drifting sand, white, golden, and vermilion.

Where this sandstone is a conglomerate, a paving of pebbles has been left, a mosaic of many colors, polished by the drifting sands, and glistening in the sunlight.

After the cañons, the most remarkable features of the country are the long lines of cliffs. These are bold escarpments, often hundreds or thousands of feet in altitude, great geographic steps, scores or hundreds of miles in length, presenting steep faces of rock, often quite vertical.

Having climbed one of these steps, you may descend by a gentle, sometimes imperceptible, slope to the foot of another. They will thus present a series of terraces, the steps of which are well-defined escarpments of rock. The lateral extension of such a line of cliffs is usually very irregular; sharp salients are projected on the plains below, and deep recesses are cut into the terraces above.

Intermittent streams coming down the cliffs have cut many cañons or cañon valleys, by which the traveler may pass from the plain below to the terrace above By these gigantic stairways, you may ascend to high plateaus, covered with forests of pine and fir.

The region is further diversified by short ranges of eruptive mountains. A vast system of fissures—huge cracks in the rocks to the depths below—extends across the country. From these crevices, floods of lava have poured, covering mesas and table lands with sheets of black basalt. The expiring energies of these volcanic agencies have piled up huge cinder-cones, that stand along the fissures, red, brown, and black, naked of vegetation, and conspicuous landmarks, set, as they are, in contrast to the bright, variegated rocks of sedimentary origin.

These cañon gorges, obstructing cliffs and desert wastes, have prevented the traveler from penetrating the country, so that, until the Colorado River Exploring Expedition was organized, it was almost unknown. Yet enough had been seen to foment rumor, and many wonderful stories have been told in the hunter's cabin and prospector's camp. Stories were related of parties entering the gorge in boats, and being carried down with fearful velocity into whirlpools, where all were overwhelmed in the abyss of waters; others, of underground passages for the great river, into which boats had passed never to be seen again. It was currently believed that the river was lost under the rocks for several hundred miles. There were other accounts of great falls, whose roaring music could be heard on the distant mountain-summits. There were many stories current of parties wandering on the brink of the cañon, vainly endeavoring to reach the waters below, and perishing with thirst at last in sight of the river which was roaring its mockery into dying ears.

The Indians, too, have woven the mysteries of the cañons into the myths of their religion. Long ago, there was a great and wise chief, who mourned the death of his wife, and would not be comforted until Ta-vwoats, one of the Indian gods, came to him, and told him she was in a happier land, and offered to take him there, that he might see for himself, if, upon his return, he would cease to mourn. The great chief promised Then Ta-vwoats made a trail through the mountains that intervene between that beautiful land, the balmy region in the great west, and this, the desert home of the poor Nu'-ma.

This trail was the cañon gorge of the Colorado. Through it he led him; and, when they had returned, the deity exacted from the chief a promise that he would tell no one of the joys of that land, lest, through discontent with the circumstances of this world, they should desire to go to heaven. Then he rolled a river into the gorge, a mad, raging stream, that should engulf any that might attempt to enter thereby.

More than once have I been warned by the Indians not to enter this cañon. They considered it disobedience to the gods and contempt for their authority, and believed that it would surely bring upon me their wrath.

For two years previous to the exploration, I had been making some geological studies among the heads of the cañons leading to the Colorado, and a desire to explore the Grand Cañon itself grew upon me. Early in the spring of 1869, a small party was organized for this purpose. Boats were built in Chicago, and transported by rail to the point where the Union Pacific Railroad crosses the Green River. With these we were to descend the Green into the Colorado, and the Colorado down to the foot of the Grand Cañon.

CHAPTER II.

May 24, 1869.—The good people of Green River City turn out to see us start. We raise our little flag, push the boats from shore, and the swift current carries us down.

Our boats are four in number. Three are built of oak; stanch and firm; doubled-ribbed, with double stem and stern posts, and further strengthened by bulkheads, dividing each into three compartments.

Two of these, the fore and aft, are decked, forming water-tight cabins. It is expected these will buoy the boats should the waves roll over them in rough water. The little vessels are twenty-one feet long, and, taking out the cargoes, can be carried by four men.

The fourth boat is made of pine, very light, but sixteen feet in length, with a sharp cut-water, and every way built for fast rowing, and divided into compartments as the others.

We take with us rations deemed sufficient to last ten months; for we expect, when winter comes on and the river is filled with ice, to lie over at some point until spring arrives; so we take with us abundant supplies of clothing. We have also a large quantity of ammunition and two or three dozen traps. For the purpose of building cabins, repairing boats, and meeting other exigencies, we are supplied with axes, hammers, saws, augers, and other tools, and a quantity of nails and screws. For scientific work, we have two sextants, four chronometers, a number of barometers, thermometers, compasses, and other instruments.

The flour is divided into three equal parts; the meat and all other articles of our rations in the same way. Each of the larger boats has an ax, hammer, saw, auger, and other tools, so that all are loaded alike. We distribute the cargoes in this way, that we may not be entirely destitute of some important article should any one of the boats be lost. In the small boat, we

Figure 4.—The start from Green River Station.

pack a part of the scientific instruments, three guns, and three small bundles of clothing only. In this, I proceed in advance, to explore the channel.

J. C. Sumner and William H. Dunn are my boatmen in the "Emma Dean;" then follows "Kitty Clyde's Sister," manned by W. H. Powell and G. Y. Bradley; next, the "No Name," with O. G. Howland, Seneca Howland, and Frank Goodman; and last comes the "Maid of the Cañon," with W. R. Hawkins and Andrew Hall.

Our boats are heavily loaded, and only with the utmost care is it possible to float in the rough river without shipping water.

A mile or two below town, we run on a sand-bar. The men jump into the stream, and thus lighten the vessels, so that they drift over; and on we go. In trying to avoid a rock, an oar is broken on one of the boats, and, thus crippled, she strikes. The current is swift, and she is sent reeling and rocking into the eddy. In the confusion, two others are lost overboard and the men seem quite discomfited, much to the amusement of the other members of the party.

Catching the oars and starting again, the boats are once more borne down the stream until we land at a small cottonwood grove on the bank, and camp for noon.

During the afternoon, we run down to a point where the river sweeps the foot of an overhanging cliff, and here we camp for the night. The sun is yet two hours high, so I climb the cliffs, and walk back among the strangely carved rocks of the Green River bad-lands. These are sandstones and shales, gray and buff, red and brown, blue and black strata in many alternations, lying nearly horizontal, and almost without soil and vegetation. They are very friable, and the rain and streams have carved them into quaint shapes. Barren desolation is stretched before me; and yet there is a beauty in the scene. The fantastic carving, imitating architectural forms, and suggesting rude but weird statuary, with the bright and varied colors of the rocks, conspire to make a scene such as the dweller in verdure-clad hills can scarcely appreciate.

Standing on a high point, I can look off in every direction over a vast landscape, with salient rocks and cliffs glittering in the evening sun. Dark shadows are settling in the valleys and gulches, and the heights are made

2 COL

higher and the depths deeper by the glamour and witchery of light and shade.

Away to the south, the Uinta Mountains stretch in a long line; high peaks thrust into the sky, and snow-fields glittering like lakes of molten silver; and pine-forests in somber green; and rosy clouds playing around the borders of huge, black masses; and heights and clouds, and mountains and snow-fields, and forests and rock-lands, are blended into one grand view. Now the sun goes down, and I return to camp.

May 25.—We start early this morning, and run along at a good rate until about nine o'clock, when we are brought up on a gravelly bar. All jump out, and help the boats over by main strength. Then a rain comes on, and river and clouds conspire to give us a thorough drenching. Wet, chilled, and tired to exhaustion, we stop at a cottonwood grove on the bank, build a huge fire, make a cup of coffee, and are soon refreshed and quite merry. When the clouds "get out of our sunshine," we start again. A few miles farther down, a flock of mountain-sheep are seen on a cliff to the right. The boats are quietly tied up, and three or four men go after them. In the course of two or three hours, they return. The cook has been successful in bringing down a fat lamb. The unsuccessful hunters taunt him with finding it dead; but it is soon dressed, cooked, and eaten, making a fine four o'clock dinner.

"All aboard," and down the river for another dozen miles. On the way, we pass the mouth of Black's Fork, a dirty little stream that seems somewhat swollen. Just below its mouth, we land and camp.

May 26.—To-day, we pass several curiously-shaped buttes, standing between the west bank of the river and the high bluffs beyond. These buttes are outliers of the same beds of rocks exposed on the faces of the bluffs; thinly laminated shales and sandstones of many colors, standing above in vertical cliffs, and buttressed below with a water-carved talus; some of them attain an altitude of nearly a thousand feet above the level of the river.

We glide quietly down the placid stream past the carved cliffs of the *mauvaises terres*, now and then obtaining glimpses of distant mountains.

Figure 5.—Indian camp on Henry's Fork.

Occasionally, deer are started from the glades among the willows; and several wild geese, after a chase through the water, are shot.

After dinner, we pass through a short, narrow cañon into a broad valley; from this, long, lateral valleys stretch back on either side as far as the eye can reach.

Two or three miles below, Henry's Fork enters from the right. We land a short distance above the junction, where a *cache* of instruments and rations was made several months ago, in a cave at the foot of the cliff, a distance back from the river. Here it was safe from the elements and wild beasts, but not from man. Some anxiety is felt, as we have learned that a party of Indians have been camped near it for several weeks. Our fears are soon allayed, for we find it all right. Our chronometer wheels are not taken for hair ornaments; our barometer tubes, for beads; nor the sextant thrown into the river as "bad medicine," as had been predicted.

Taking up our *cache*, we pass down to the foot of the Uinta Mountains, and, in a cold storm, go into camp.

The river is running to the south; the mountains have an easterly and westerly trend directly athwart its course, yet it glides on in a quiet way as if it thought a mountain range no formidable obstruction to its course. It enters the range by a flaring, brilliant, red gorge, that may be seen from the north a score of miles away.

The great mass of the mountain-ridge through which the gorge is cut is composed of bright vermilion rocks; but they are surmounted by broad bands of mottled buff and gray, and these bands come down with a gentle curve to the water's edge on the nearer slope of the mountain.

This is the head of the first cañon we are about to explore—an introductory one to a series made by the river through this range. We name it Flaming Gorge. The cliffs or walls we find, on measurement, to be about one thousand two hundred feet high.

May 27.—To-day it rains, and we employ the time in repairing one of our barometers, which was broken on the way from New York. A new tube has to be put in; that is, a long glass tube has to be filled with mercury four or five inches at a time, and each installment boiled over a spirit-lamp. It is a delicate task to do this without breaking the glass; but we have success, and are ready to measure mountains once more.

May 28.—To-day we go to the summit of the cliff on the left and take observations for altitude, and are variously employed in topographic and geological work.

May 29.—This morning, Bradley and I cross the river, and climb more than a thousand feet to a point where we can see the stream sweeping in a long, beautiful curve through the gorge below. Turning and looking to the west, we can see the valley of Henry's Fork, through which, for many miles, the little river flows in a tortuous channel. Cottonwood groves are planted here and there along its course, and between them are stretches of grass land. The narrow mountain valley is inclosed on either side by sloping walls of naked rock of many bright colors. To the south of the valley are the Uintas, and the peaks of the Wasatch Mountains can be faintly seen in the far west. To the north, desert plains, dotted here and there with curiously carved hills and buttes, extend to the limit of vision.

For many years, this valley has been the home of a number of mountaineers, who were originally hunters and trappers, living with the Indians. Most of them have one or more Indian wives. They no longer roam with the nomadic tribes in pursuit of buckskin or beaver, but have accumulated herds of cattle and horses, and consider themselves quite well-to-do. Some of them have built cabins; others still live in lodges.

John Baker is one of the most famous of these men; and, from our point of view, we can see his lodge three or four miles up the river.

The distance from Green River City to Flaming Gorge is sixty-two miles. The river runs between bluffs, in some places standing so close to each other that no flood-plain is seen. At such a point, the river might properly be said to run through a cañon. The bad-lands on either side are interrupted here and there by patches of *Artemesia*, or sage-brush. Where there is a flood-plain along either side of the river, a few cottonwoods may be seen.

.

Figure 6.—Camp at Flaming Gorge.

CHAPTER III.

You must not think of a mountain-range as a line of peaks standing on a plain, but as a broad platform many miles wide, from which mountains have been carved by the waters. You must conceive, too, that this plateau is cut by gulches and cañons in many directions, and that beautiful valleys are scattered about at different altitudes. The first series of cañons we are about to explore constitutes a river channel through such a range of mountains. The cañon is cut nearly half-way through the range, then turns to the east, and is cut along the central line, or axis, gradually crossing it to the south. Keeping this direction for more than fifty miles, it then turns abruptly to a southwest course, and goes diagonally through the southern slope of the range.

This much we knew before entering, as we made a partial exploration of the region last fall, climbing many of its peaks, and in a few places reaching the brink of the cañon walls, and looking over precipices, many hundreds of feet high, to the water below.

Here and there the walls are broken by lateral cañons, the channels of little streams entering the river; through two or three of these, we found our way down to the Green in early winter, and walked along the low water-beach at the foot of the cliffs for several miles. Where the river has this general easterly direction, the western part only has cut for itself a cañon, while the eastern has formed a broad valley, called, in honor of an old-time trapper, Brown's Park, and long known as a favorite winter resort for mountain men and Indians.

May 30.—This morning we are ready to enter the mysterious cañon, and start with some anxiety. The old mountaineers tell us that it cannot be run; the Indians say, "Water heap catch 'em," but all are eager for the trial, and off we go.

Entering Flaming Gorge, we quickly run through it on a swift current, and emerge into a little park. Half a mile below, the river wheels sharply to the left, and we turned into another cañon cut into the mountain. We enter the narrow passage. On either side, the walls rapidly increase in altitude. On the left are overhanging ledges and cliffs five hundred—a thousand—fifteen hundred feet high.

On the right, the rocks are broken and ragged, and the water fills the channel from cliff to cliff. Now the river turns abruptly around a point to the right, and the waters plunge swiftly down among great rocks; and here we have our first experience with cañon rapids. I stand up on the deck of my boat to seek a way among the wave beaten rocks. All untried as we are with such waters, the moments are filled with intense anxiety. Soon our boats reach the swift current; a stroke or two, now on this side, now on that, and we thread the narrow passage with exhilarating velocity, mounting the high waves, whose foaming crests dash over us, and plunging into the troughs, until we reach the quiet water below; and then comes a feeling of great relief. Our first rapid is run. Another mile, and we come into the valley again.

Let me explain this cañon. Where the river turns to the left above, it takes a course directly into the mountain, penetrating to its very heart, then wheels back upon itself, and runs out into the valley from which it started only half a mile below the point at which it entered; so the cañon is in the form of an elongated letter U, with the apex in the center of the mountain. We name it Horseshoe Cañon.

Soon we leave the valley, and enter another short cañon, very narrow at first, but widening below as the cañon walls increase in height. Here we discover the mouth of a beautiful little creek, coming down through its narrow water worn cleft. Just at its entrance there is a park of two or three hundred acres, walled on every side by almost vertical cliffs, hundreds of feet in altitude, with three gateways through the walls—one up, another down the river, and a third passage through which the creek comes in. The river is broad, deep, and quiet, and its waters mirror towering rocks.

Kingfishers are playing about the streams, and so we adopt as names

Kingfisher Creek, Kingfisher Park, and Kingfisher Cañon. At night, we camp at the foot of this cañon.

Our general course this day has been south, but here the river turns to the east around a point which is rounded to the shape of a dome, and on its sides little cells have been carved by the action of the water; and in these pits, which cover the face of the dome, hundreds of swallows have built their nests. As they flit about the cliffs, they look like swarms of bees, giving to the whole the appearance of a colossal beehive of the old time form, and so we name it Beehive Point.

The opposite wall is a vast amphitheater, rising in a succession of terraces to a height of 1,200 or 1,500 feet. Each step is built of red sandstone, with a face of naked, red rock, and a glacis clothed with verdure. So the amphitheater seems banded red and green, and the evening sun is playing with roseate flashes on the rocks, with shimmering green on the cedars' spray, and iridescent gleams on the dancing waves. The landscape revels in the sunshine.

May 31.—We start down another cañon, and reach rapids made dangerous by high rocks lying in the channel; so we run ashore, and let our boats down with lines. In the afternoon we come to more dangerous rapids, and stop to examine them. I find we must do the same work again, but, being on the wrong side of the river to obtain a foothold, must first cross over—no very easy matter in such a current, with rapids and rocks below. We take the pioneer boat "Emma Dean" over, and unload her on the bank; then she returns and takes another load. Running back and forth, she soon has half our cargo over; then one of the larger boats is manned and taken across, but carried down almost to the rocks in spite of hard rowing. The other boats follow and make the landing, and we go into camp for the night.

At the foot of the cliff on this side, there is a long slope covered with pines ; under these we make our beds, and soon after sunset are seeking rest and sleep. The cliffs on either side are of red sandstone, and stretch up toward the heavens 2,500 feet. On this side, the long, pine clad slope is surmounted by perpendicular cliffs, with pines on their summits. The wall on the other side is bare rock from the water's edge up 2,000 feet, then slopes back, giving footing to pines and cedars.

As the twilight deepens, the rocks grow dark and somber; the threat-

ening roar of the water is loud and constant, and I lie awake with thoughts
of the morrow and the cañons to come, interrupted now and then by characteristics of the scenery that attract my attention. And here I make a
discovery. On looking at the mountain directly in front, the steepness of
the slope is greatly exaggerated, while the distance to its summit and its true
altitude are correspondingly diminished. I have heretofore found that to
properly judge of the slope of a mountain side, you must see it in profile.
In coming down the river this afternoon, I observed the slope of a particular
part of the wall, and made an estimate of its altitude. While at supper, I
noticed the same cliff from a position facing it, and it seemed steeper, but
not half as high. Now lying on my side and looking at it, the true proportions appear. This seems a wonder, and I rise up to take a view of it standing. It is the same cliff as at supper time. Lying down again, it is the
cliff as seen in profile, with a long slope and distant summit. Musing on
this, I forget "the morrow and the cañons to come." I find a way to estimate the altitude and slope of an inclination as I can judge of distance along
the horizon. The reason is simple. A reference to the stereoscope will
suggest it. The distance between the eyes forms a base-line for optical
triangulation.

June 1.—To-day we have an exciting ride. The river rolls down the
cañon at a wonderful rate, and, with no rocks in the way, we make almost
railroad speed. Here and there the water rushes into a narrow gorge; the
rocks on the side roll it into the center in great waves, and the boats go
leaping and bounding over these like things of life. They remind me of
scenes witnessed in Middle Park; herds of startled deer bounding through
forests beset with fallen timber. I mention the resemblance to some of the
hunters, and so striking is it that it comes to be a common expression, "See
the black-tails jumping the logs." At times the waves break and roll over
the boats, which necessitates much bailing, and obliges us to stop occasionally for that purpose. At one time, we run twelve miles in an hour, stop-
pages included.

Last spring, I had a conversation with an old Indian named Pa′-ri-ats,
who told me about one of his tribe attempting to run this cañon. "The
rocks," he said, holding his hands above his head, his arms vertical, and

Figure 7.—Pa'-ri-ats.

looking between them to the heavens, "the rocks h-e-a-p, h-e-a-p high; the water go h-oo-woogh, h-oo-woogh; water-pony (boat) h-e-a-p buck; water catch 'em; no see 'em Injun any more! no see 'em squaw any more! no see 'em pappoose any more!"

Those who have seen these wild Indian ponies rearing alternately before and behind, or "bucking," as it is called in the vernacular, will appreciate his description.

At last we come to calm water, and a threatening roar is heard in the distance. Slowly approaching the point whence the sound issues, we come near to falls, and tie up just above them on the left. Here we will be compelled to make a portage; so we unload the boats, and fasten a long line to the bow, and another to the stern, of the smaller one, and moor her close to the brink of the fall. Then the bow-line is taken below, and made fast; the stern line is held by five or six men, and the boat let down as long as they can hold her against the rushing waters; then, letting go one end of the line, it runs through the ring; the boat leaps over the fall, and is caught by the lower rope.

Now we rest for the night.

June 2.—This morning we make a trail among the rocks, transport the cargoes to a point below the falls, let the remaining boats over, and are ready to start before noon.

On a high rock by which the trail passes we find the inscription: "Ashley 18-5." The third figure is obscure—some of the party reading it 1835, some 1855.

James Baker, an old time mountaineer, once told me about a party of men starting down the river, and Ashley was named as one. The story runs that the boat was swamped, and some of the party drowned in one of the cañons below. The word "Ashley" is a warning to us, and we resolve on great caution.

Ashley Falls is the name we give to the cataract.

The river is very narrow; the right wall vertical for two or three hundred feet, the left towering to a great height, with a vast pile of broken rocks lying between the foot of the cliff and the water. Some of the rocks broken down from the ledge above have tumbled into the channel and caused this

3 COL

fall. One great cubical block, thirty or forty feet high, stands in the middle of the stream, and the waters, parting to either side, plunge down about twelve feet, and are broken again by the smaller rocks into a rapid below. Immediately below the falls, the water occupies the entire channel, there being no talus at the foot of the cliffs.

We embark, and run down a short distance, where we find a landing-place for dinner.

On the waves again all the afternoon. Near the lower end of this cañon, to which we have given the name Red Cañon, is a little park, where streams come down from distant mountain summits, and enter the river on either side; and here we camp for the night under two stately pines.

June 3.—This morning we spread our rations, clothes, &c., on the ground to dry, and several of the party go out for a hunt. I take a walk of five or six miles up to a pine grove park, its grassy carpet bedecked with crimson, velvet flowers, set in groups on the stems of pear shaped cactus plants; patches of painted cups are seen here and there, with yellow blossoms protruding through scarlet bracts; little blue-eyed flowers are peeping through the grass; and the air is filled with fragrance from the white blossoms of a *Spiræa*. A mountain brook runs through the midst, ponded below by beaver dams. It is a quiet place for retirement from the raging waters of the cañon.

It will be remembered that the course of the river, from Flaming Gorge to Beehive Point, is in a southerly direction, and at right angles to the Uinta Mountains, and cuts into the range until it reaches a point within five miles of the crest, where it turns to the east, and pursues a course not quite parallel to the trend of the range, but crosses the axis slowly in a direction a little south of east. Thus there is a triangular tract between the river and the axis of the mountain, with its acute angle extending eastward. I climb a mountain overlooking this country. To the east, the peaks are not very high, and already most of the snow has melted; but little patches lie here and there under the lee of ledges of rock. To the west, the peaks grow higher and the snow fields larger. Between the brink of the cañon and the foot of these peaks, there is a high bench. A number of creeks have their sources in the snow banks to the south, and run north into the cañon, tumbling down from 3,000 to 5,000 feet in a distance of five or six miles. Along their upper courses, they run through grassy valleys; but, as they approach Red Cañon, they rapidly disappear under the general surface of the country, and emerge into the cañon below in deep, dark gorges of their own. Each of these short lateral cañons is marked by a succession of cascades and a wild confusion of rocks and trees and fallen timber and thick undergrowth.

The little valleys above are beautiful parks; between the parks are stately pine forests, half hiding ledges of red sandstone. Mule-deer and elk abound; grizzly bears, too, are abundant; wild cats, wolverines. and mountain lions are here at home. The forest aisles are filled with the music of birds, and the parks are decked with flowers. Noisy brooks meander through them; ledges of moss covered rocks are seen; and gleaming in the distance are the snow fields, and the mountain tops are away in the clouds.

June 4.—We start early and run through to Brown's Park. Half way down the valley, a spur of a red mountain stretches across the river, which cuts a cañon through it. Here the walls are comparatively low, but vertical. A vast number of swallows have built their *adobe* houses on the face of the cliffs, on either side of the river. The waters are deep and quiet, but the swallows are swift and noisy enough, sweeping by in their curved paths through the air, or chattering from the rocks. The young birds stretch their little heads on naked necks through the doorways of their mud houses, clamoring for food. They are a noisy people.

We call this Swallow Cañon.

Still down the river we glide, until an early hour in the afternoon, when we go into camp under a giant cottonwood, standing on the right bank, a little way back from the stream. The party had succeeded in killing a fine lot of wild ducks, and during the afternoon a mess of fish is taken.

June 5.—With one of the men, I climb a mountain, off on the right. A long spur, with broken ledges of rock, puts down to the river; and along its course, or up the "hog-back," as it is called, I make the ascent. Dunn, who is climbing to the same point, is coming up the gulch. Two hours' hard work has brought us to the summit. These mountains are all verdure clad; pine and cedar forests are set on green terraces; snow clad mountains

are seen in the distance, to the west; the plains of the upper Green stretch
out before us, to the north, until they are lost in the blue heavens; but half
of the river cleft range intervenes, and the river itself is at our feet.

This half range, beyond the river, is composed of long ridges, nearly
parallel with the valley. On the farther ridge, to the north, four creeks
have their sources. These cut through the intervening ridges, one of which
is much higher than that on which they head, by cañon gorges; then they
run, with gentle curves, across the valley, their banks set with willows, box-
elders, and cottonwood groves.

To the east, we look up the valley of the Vermilion, through which Frémont found his path on his way to the great parks of Colorado.

The reading of the barometer taken, we start down in company, and
reach camp tired and hungry, which does not abate one bit our enthusiasm,
as we tell of the day's work, with its glory of landscape.

June 6.—At daybreak, I am awakened by a chorus of birds. It seems
as if all the feathered songsters of the region have come to the old tree.
Several species of warblers, woodpeckers, and flickers above, meadow-larks
in the grass, and wild geese in the river. I recline on my elbow, and watch
a lark near by, and then awaken my bed fellow, to listen to my Jenny Lind.
A morning concert for me; none of your "*matinées.*"

Our cook has been an ox-driver, or "bull-whacker," on the plains, in
one of those long trains now no longer seen, and he hasn't forgotten his old
ways. In the midst of the concert, his voice breaks in: "Roll out! roll out!
bulls in the corral! chain up the gaps! Roll out! roll out! roll out!" And
this is our breakfast bell.

To-day we pass through the park, and camp at the head of another
cañon.

June 7.—To day, two or three of us climb to the summit of the cliff,
on the left, and find its altitude, above camp, to be 2,086 feet. The rocks
are split with fissures, deep and narrow, sometimes a hundred feet, or more,
to the bottom. Lofty pines find root in the fissures that are filled with
loose earth and decayed vegetation. On a rock we find a pool of clear,
cold water, caught from yesterday evening's shower. After a good drink,
we walk out to the brink of the cañon, and look down to the water

below. I can do this now, but it has taken several years of mountain climbing to cool my nerves, so that I can sit, with my feet over the edge, and calmly look down a precipice 2,000 feet. And yet I cannot look on and see another do the same. I must either bid him come away, or turn my head.

The cañon walls are buttressed on a grand scale, with deep alcoves intervening; columned crags crown the cliffs, and the river is rolling below.

When we return to camp, at noon, the sun shines in splendor on vermilion walls, shaded into green and gray, where the rocks are lichened over; the river fills the channel from wall to wall, and the cañon opens, like a beautiful portal, to a region of glory.

This evening, as I write, the sun is going down, and the shadows are settling in the cañon. The vermilion gleams and roseate hues, blending with the green and gray tints, are slowly changing to somber brown above, and black shadows are creeping over them below; and now it is a dark portal to a region of gloom—the gateway through which we are to enter on our voyage of exploration to-morrow. What shall we find?

The distance from Flaming Gorge to Beehive Point is nine and two-thirds miles. Besides, passing through the gorge, the river runs through Horseshoe and Kingfisher Cañons, separated by short valleys. The highest point on the walls, at Flaming Gorge, is 1,300 feet above the river. The east wall, at the apex of Horseshoe Cañon, is about 1,600 feet above the water's edge, and, from this point, the walls slope both to the head and foot of the cañon.

Kingfisher Cañon, starting at the water's edge above, steadily increases in altitude to 1,200 feet at the foot.

Red Cañon is twenty-five and two-thirds miles long, and the highest walls are about 2,500 feet.

Brown's Park is a valley, bounded on either side by a mountain range, really an expansion of the cañon. The river, through the park, is thirty-five and a half miles long, but passes through two short cañons, on its way, where spurs, from the mountains on the south, are thrust across its course.

CHAPTER IV.

June 8.—We enter the cañon, and, until noon, find a succession of rapids, over which our boats have to be taken.

Here I must explain our method of proceeding at such places. The "Emma Dean" goes in advance; the other boats follow, in obedience to signals. When we approach a rapid, or what, on other rivers, would often be called a fall, I stand on deck to examine it, while the oarsmen back water, and we drift on as slowly as possible. If I can see a clear chute between the rocks, away we go; but if the channel is beset entirely across, we signal the other boats, pull to land, and I walk along the shore for closer examination. If this reveals no clear channel, hard work begins. We drop the boats to the very head of the dangerous place, and let them over by lines, or make a portage, frequently carrying both boats and cargoes over the rocks, or, perhaps, only the cargoes, if it is safe to let the boats down.

The waves caused by such falls in a river differ much from the waves of the sea. The water of an ocean wave merely rises and falls; the form only passes on, and form chases form unceasingly. A body floating on such waves merely rises and sinks—does not progress unless impelled by wind or some other power. But here, the water of the wave passes on, while the form remains. The waters plunge down ten or twenty feet, to the foot of a fall; spring up again in a great wave; then down and up, in a series of billows, that gradually disappear in the more quiet waters below; but these waves are always there, and you can stand above and count them.

A boat riding such, leaps and plunges along with great velocity. Now, the difficulty in riding over these falls, when the rocks are out of the way, is in the first wave at the foot. This will sometimes gather for a moment, heaping up higher and higher, until it breaks back. If the boat strikes it the instant after it breaks, she cuts through, and the mad breaker dashes its spray over the boat, and would wash us overboard did we not cling tight.

Figure 8.—Gate of Lodore.

If the boat, in going over the falls, chances to get caught in some side current, and is turned from its course, so as to strike the wave "broadside on," and the wave breaks at the same instant, the boat is capsized. Still, we must cling to her, for, the water tight compartments acting as buoys, she cannot sink; and so we go, dragged through the waves, until still waters are reached. We then right the boat, and climb aboard. We have several such experiences to day.

At night, we camp on the right bank, on a little shelving rock, between the river and the foot of the cliff; and with night comes gloom into these great depths.

After supper, we sit by our camp fire, made of drift wood caught by the rocks, and tell stories of wild life; for the men have seen such in the mountains, or on the plains, and on the battle fields of the South. It is late before we spread our blankets on the beach.

Lying down, we look up through the cañon, and see that only a little of the blue heaven appears overhead—a crescent of blue sky, with two or three constellations peering down upon us.

I do not sleep for some time, as the excitement of the day has not worn off. Soon I see a bright star, that appears to rest on the very verge of the cliff overhead to the east. Slowly it seems to float from its resting place on the rock over the cañon. At first, it appeared like a jewel set on the brink of the cliff; but, as it moves out from the rock, I almost wonder that it does not fall. In fact, it does seem to descend in a gentle curve, as though the bright sky in which the stars are set was spread across the cañon, resting on either wall, and swayed down by its own weight. The stars appear to be in the cañon. I soon discover that it is the bright star Vega, so it occurs to me to designate this part of the wall as the "Cliff of the Harp."

June 9.—One of the party suggests that we call this the Cañon of Lodore, and the name is adopted. Very slowly we make our way, often climbing on the rocks at the edge of the water for a few hundred yards, to examine the channel before running it.

During the afternoon, we come to a place where it is necessary to make a portage. The little boat it landed, and the others are signaled to come up.

When these rapids or broken falls occur, usually the channel is suddenly narrowed by rocks which have been tumbled from the cliffs or have been washed in by lateral streams. Immediately above the narrow, rocky channel, on one or both sides, there is often a bay of quiet water, in which we can land with ease. Sometimes the water descends with a smooth, unruffled surface, from the broad, quiet spread above, into the narrow, angry channel below, by a semicircular sag. Great care must be taken not to pass over the brink into this deceptive pit, but above it we can row with safety. I walk along the bank to examine the ground, leaving one of my men with a flag to guide the other boats to the landing-place. I soon see one of the boats make shore all right and feel no more concern; but a minute after, I hear a shout, and looking around, see one of the boats shooting down the center of the sag. It is the "No Name," with Captain Howland, his brother, and Goodman. I feel that its going over is inevitable, and run to save the third boat. A minute more, and she turns the point and heads for the shore. Then I turn down stream again, and scramble along to look for the boat that has gone over. The first fall is not great, only ten or twelve feet, and we often run such; but below, the river tumbles down again for forty or fifty feet, in a channel filled with dangerous rocks that break the waves into whirlpools and beat them into foam. I pass around a great crag just in time to see the boat strike a rock, and, rebounding from the shock, careen and fill the open compartment with water. Two of the men lose their oars; she swings around, and is carried down at a rapid rate, broadside on, for a few yards, and strikes amidships on another rock with great force, is broken quite in two, and the men are thrown into the river; the larger part of the boat floating buoyantly, they soon seize it, and down the river they drift, past the rocks for a few hundred yards to a second rapid, filled with huge boulders, where the boat strikes again, and is dashed to pieces, and the men and fragments are soon carried beyond my sight. Running along, I turn a bend, and see a man's head above the water, washed about in a whirlpool below a great rock.

It is Frank Goodman, clinging to it with a grip upon which life depends. Coming opposite, I see Howland trying to go to his aid from an island on which he has been washed. Soon, he comes near enough to reach Frank with a pole, which he extends toward him. The latter lets go the rock,

Figure 9.—Winnie's Grotto, a side cañon.
(Walls 2,000 feet high.)

grasps the pole, and is pulled ashore. Seneca Howland is washed farther down the island, and is caught by some rocks, and, though somewhat bruised, manages to get ashore in safety. This seems a long time, as I tell it, but it is quickly done.

And now the three men are on an island, with a swift, dangerous river on either side, and a fall below. The "Emma Dean" is soon brought down, and Sumner, starting above as far as possible, pushes out. Right skillfully he plies the oars, and a few strokes set him on the island at the proper point. Then they all pull the boat up stream, as far as they are able, until they stand in water up to their necks. One sits on a rock, and holds the boat until the others are ready to pull, then gives the boat a push, clings to it with his hands, and climbs in as they pull for mainland, which they reach in safety. We are as glad to shake hands with them as though they had been on a voyage around the world, and wrecked on a distant coast.

Down the river half a mile we find that the after cabin of the wrecked boat, with a part of the bottom, ragged and splintered, has floated against a rock, and stranded. There are valuable articles in the cabin; but, on examination, we determine that life should not be risked to save them. Of course, the cargo of rations, instruments, and clothing is gone.

We return to the boats, and make camp for the night. No sleep comes to me in all those dark hours. The rations, instruments, and clothing have been divided among the boats, anticipating such an accident as this; and we started with duplicates of everything that was deemed necessary to success. But, in the distribution, there was one exception to this precaution, and the barometers were all placed in one boat, and they are lost. There is a possibility that they are in the cabin lodged against the rock, for that is where they were kept. But, then, how to reach them! The river is rising. Will they be there to-morrow? Can I go out to Salt Lake City, and obtain barometers from New York?

June 10.—I have determined to get the barometers from the wreck, if they are there. After breakfast, while the men make the portage, I go down again for another examination. There the cabin lies, only carried fifty or sixty feet farther on.

Carefully looking over the ground, I am satisfied that it can be reached

4 COL

with safety, and return to tell the men my conclusion. Sumner and Dunn volunteer to take the little boat and make the attempt. They start, reach it, and out come the barometers; and now the boys set up a shout, and I join them, pleased that they should be as glad to save the instruments as myself. When the boat lands on our side, I find that the only things saved from the wreck were the barometers, a package of thermometers, and a three gallon keg of whisky, which is what the men were shouting about. They had taken it aboard, unknown to me, and now I am glad they did, for they think it will do them good, as they are drenched every day by the melting snow, which runs down from the summits of the Rocky Mountains.

Now we come back to our work at the portage. We find that it is necessary to carry our rations over the rocks for nearly a mile, and let our boats down with lines, except at a few points, where they also must be carried.

Between the river and the eastern wall of the cañon there is an immense talus of broken rocks. These have tumbled down from the cliffs above, and constitute a vast pile of huge angular fragments. On these we build a path for a quarter of a mile, to a small sand beach covered with drift-wood, through which we clear a way for several hundred yards, then continue the trail on over another pile of rocks, nearly half a mile farther down, to a little bay. The greater part of the day is spent in this work. Then we carry our cargoes down to the beach and camp for the night.

While the men are building the camp fire, we discover an iron bake oven, several tin plates, a part of a boat, and many other fragments, which denote that this is the place where Ashley's party was wrecked.

June 11.—This day is spent in carrying our rations down to the bay— no small task to climb over the rocks with sacks of flour or bacon. We carry them by stages of about 5(0 yards each, and when night comes, and the last sack is on the beach, we are tired, bruised, and glad to sleep.

June 12.—To-day we take the boats down to the bay. While at this work, we discover three sacks of flour from the wrecked boat, that have lodged in the rocks. We carry them above high-water mark, and leave them, as our cargoes are already too heavy for the three remaining boats. We also find two or three oars, which we place with them.

Figure 10.—Wreck at Disaster Falls.

As Ashley and his party were wrecked here, and as we have lost one of our boats at the same place, we adopt the name Disaster Falls for the scene of so much peril and loss.

Though some of his companions were drowned, Ashley and one other survived the wreck, climbed the cañon wall, and found their way across the Wasatch Mountains to Salt Lake City, living chiefly on berries, as they wandered through an unknown and difficult country. When they arrived at Salt Lake, they were almost destitute of clothing, and nearly starved. The Mormon people gave them food and clothing, and employed them to work on the foundation of the Temple, until they had earned sufficient to enable them to leave the country. Of their subsequent history, I have no knowledge. It is possible they returned to the scene of the disaster, as a little creek entering the river below is known as Ashley's Creek, and it is reported that he built a cabin and trapped on this river for one or two winters; but this may have been before the disaster.

June 13.—Still rocks, rapids, and portages.

We camp to-night at the foot of the left wall on a little patch of flood-plain covered with a dense growth of box-elders, stopping early in order to spread the clothing and rations to dry. Everything is wet and spoiling.

June 14.—Howland and I climb the wall, on the west side of the cañon, to an altitude of 2,000 feet. Standing above, and looking to the west, we discover a large park, five or six miles wide and twenty or thirty long. The cliff we have climbed forms a wall between the cañon and the park, for it is 800 feet, down the western side, to the valley. A creek comes winding down, 1,200 feet above the river, and, entering the intervening wall by a cañon, it plunges down, more than a thousand feet, by a broken cascade, into the river below.

June 15.—To-day, while we make another portage, a peak, standing on the east wall, is climbed by two of the men, and found to be 2,700 feet above the river. On the east side of the cañon, a vast amphitheater has been cut, with massive buttresses, and deep, dark alcoves, in which grow beautiful mosses and delicate ferns, while springs burst out from the further recesses, and wind, in silver threads, over floors of sand rock. Here we have three falls in close succession. At the first, the water is compressed into a very narrow channel, against the right-hand cliff, and falls fifteen feet in ten yards; at the second, we have a broad sheet of water, tumbling down twenty feet over a group of rocks that thrust their dark heads through the foaming waters. The third is a broken fall, or short, abrupt rapid, where the water makes a descent of more than twenty feet among huge, fallen fragments of the cliff. We name the group Triplet Falls.

We make a portage around the first; past the second and third we let down with lines.

During the afternoon, Dunn and Howland, having returned from their climb, we run down, three-quarters of a mile, on quiet water, and land at the head of another fall. On examination, we find that there is an abrupt plunge of a few feet, and then the river tumbles, for half a mile, with a descent of a hundred feet, in a channel beset with great numbers of huge bowlders. This stretch of the river is named Hell's Half-Mile.

The remaining portion of the day is occupied in making a trail among the rocks to the foot of the rapid.

June 16.—Our first work this morning is to carry our cargoes to the foot of the falls. Then we commence letting down the boats. We take two of them down in safety, but not without great difficulty; for, where such a vast body of water, rolling down an inclined plane, is broken into eddies and cross currents by rocks projecting from the cliffs and piles of boulders in the channel, it requires excessive labor and much care to prevent their being dashed against the rocks or breaking away. Sometimes we are compelled to hold the boat against a rock, above a chute, until a second line, attached to the stem, is carried to some point below, and, when all is ready, the first line is detached, and the boat given to the current, when she shoots down, and the men below swing her into some eddy.

At such a place, we are letting down the last boat, and, as she is set free, a wave turns her broadside down the stream, with the stem, to which the line is attached, from shore, and a little up. They haul on the line to bring the boat in, but the power of the current, striking obliquely against her, shoots her out into the middle of the river. The men have their hands burned with the friction of the passing line; the boat breaks away, and speeds, with great velocity, down the stream.

The "Maid of the Cañon" is lost, so it seems; but she drifts some distance, and swings into an eddy, in which she spins about, until we arrive with the small boat, and rescue her.

Soon we are on our way again, and stop at the mouth of a little brook, on the right, for a late dinner. This brook comes down from the distant mountains, in a deep side cañon. We set out to explore it, but are soon cut off from farther progress up the gorge by a high rock, over which the brook glides in a smooth sheet. The rock is not quite vertical, and the water does not plunge over in a fall.

Then we climb up to the left for an hour, and are a thousand feet above the river, and six hundred above the brook. Just before us, the cañon divides, a little stream coming down on the right, and another on the left, and we can look away up either of these cañons, through an ascending vista, to cliffs and crags and towers, a mile back, and two thousand feet overhead. To the right, a dozen gleaming cascades are seen. Pines and firs stand on the rocks, and aspens overhang the brooks. The rocks below are red and brown, set in deep shadows, but above, they are buff and vermilion, and stand in the sunshine. The light above, made more brilliant by the bright-tinted rocks, and the shadows below more gloomy by the somber hues of the brown walls, increase the apparent depths of the cañons, and it seems a long way up to the world of sunshine and open sky, and a long way down to the bottom of the cañon glooms. Never before have I received such an impression of the vast heights of these cañon walls; not even at the Cliff of the Harp, where the very heavens seemed to rest on their summits.

We sit on some overhanging rocks, and enjoy the scene for a time, listening to the music of falling waters away up the cañons. We name this Rippling Brook.

Late in the afternoon we make a short run to the mouth of another little creek, coming down from the left into an alcove filled with luxuriant vegetation. Here camp is made with a group of cedars on one side and a dense mass of box-elders and dead willows on the other.

I go up to explore the alcove. While away a whirlwind comes, scattering the fire among the dead willows and cedar-spray, and soon there is a conflagration. The men rush for the boats, leaving all they cannot readily seize at the moment, and even then they have their clothing burned and hair singed, and Bradley has his ears scorched. The cook fills his arms with the mess-kit, and, jumping into a boat, stumbles and falls, and away go our cooking utensils into the river. Our plates are gone; our spoons are gone; our knives and forks are gone. "Water catch 'em; h-e-a-p catch 'em."

When on the boats, the men are compelled to cut loose, as the flames, running out on the overhanging willows, are scorching them. Loose on the stream, they must go down, for the water is too swift to make headway against it. Just below is a rapid, filled with rocks. On they shoot, no channel explored, no signal to guide them. Just at this juncture I chance to see them, but have not yet discovered the fire, and the strange movements of the men fill me with astonishment. Down the rocks I clamber, and run to the bank. When I arrive, they have landed. Then we all go back to the late camp to see if anything left behind can be saved. Some of the clothing and bedding taken out of the boats is found, also a few tin cups, basins, and a camp kettle, and this is all the mess kit we now have. Yet we do just as well as ever.

June 17.—We run down to the mouth of Yampa River. This has been a chapter of disasters and toils, notwithstanding which the cañon of Lodore was not devoid of scenic interest, even beyond the power of pen to tell. The roar of its waters was heard unceasingly from the hour we entered it until we landed here. No quiet in all that time. But its walls and cliffs, its peaks and crags, its amphitheaters and alcoves, tell a story of beauty and grandeur that I hear yet—and shall hear.

The cañon of Lodore is twenty and three-quarter miles in length. It starts abruptly at what we have called the Gate of Lodore, with walls nearly two thousand feet high, and they are never lower than this until we reach Alcove Brook, about three miles above the foot. They are very irregular, standing in vertical or overhanging cliffs in places, terraced in others, or receding in steep slopes, and are broken by many side gulches and cañons.

The highest point on the wall is at Dunn's Cliff, near Triplet Falls, where the rocks reach an altitude of 2,700 feet, but the peaks a little way back rise nearly a thousand feet higher. Yellow pines, nut pines, firs, and cedars stand in extensive forests on the Uinta Mountains, and, clinging to the rocks and growing in the crevices, come down the walls to the water's edge from Flaming Gorge to Echo Park. The red sandstones are lichened over; delicate mosses grow in the moist places, and ferns festoon the walls.

CHAPTER V.

The Yampa enters the Green from the east. At a point opposite its mouth, the Green runs to the south, at the foot of a rock, about seven hundred feet high and a mile long, and then turns sharply around it to the right, and runs back in a northerly course, parallel to its former direction, for nearly another mile, thus having the opposite sides of a long, narrow rock for its bank. The tongue of rock so formed is a peninsular precipice, with a mural escarpment along its whole course on the east, but broken down at places on the west.

On the east side of the river, opposite the rock, and below the Yampa, there is a little park, just large enough for a farm, already fenced with high walls of gray homogeneous sandstone. There are three river entrances to this park: one down the Yampa; one below, by coming up the Green; and another down the Green. There is also a land entrance down a lateral cañon. Elsewhere the park is inaccessible. Through this land-entrance by the side cañon there is a trail made by Indian hunters, who come down here in certain seasons to kill mountain sheep.

Great hollow domes are seen in the eastern side of the rock, against which the Green sweeps; willows border the river; clumps of box-elder are seen; and a few cottonwoods stand at the lower end. Standing opposite the rock, our words are repeated with startling clearness, but in a soft, mellow tone, that transforms them into magical music. Scarcely can you believe it is the echo of your own voice. In some places two or three echoes come back; in other places they repeat themselves, passing back and forth across the river between this rock and the eastern wall.

To hear these repeated echoes well, you must shout. Some of the party aver that ten or twelve repetitions can be heard. To me, they seem to rapidly diminish and merge by multiplicity, like telegraph poles on an

Figure 11.— Echo Rock.

outstretched plain. I have observed the same phenomenon once before in the cliffs near Long's Peak, and am pleased to meet with it again.

During the afternoon, Bradley and I climb some cliffs to the north. Mountain sheep are seen above us, and they stand out on the rocks, and eye us intently, not seeming to move. Their color is much like that of the gray sandstone beneath them, and, immovable as they are, they appear like carved forms. Now a fine ram beats the rock with his fore foot, and, wheeling around, they all bound away together, leaping over rocks and chasms, and climbing walls where no man can follow, and this with an ease and gracefulness most wonderful. At night we return to our camp, under the box-elders, by the river side. Here we are to spend two or three days, making a series of astronomic observations for latitude and longitude.

June 18.—We have named the long peninsular rock on the other side Echo Rock. Desiring to climb it, Bradley and I take the little boat and pull up stream as far as possible, for it cannot be climbed directly opposite. We land on a talus of rocks at the upper end, to reach a place where it seems practicable to make the ascent; but we must go still farther up the river. So we scramble along, until we reach a place where the river sweeps against the wall. Here we find a shelf, along which we can pass, and now are ready for the climb.

We start up a gulch; then pass to the left, on a bench, along the wall; then up again, over broken rocks; then we reach more benches, along which we walk, until we find more broken rocks and crevices, by which we climb, still up, until we have ascended six or eight hundred feet; then we are met by a sheer precipice.

Looking about, we find a place where it seems possible to climb. I go ahead; Bradley hands the barometer to me, and follows. So we proceed, stage by stage, until we are nearly to the summit. Here, by making a spring, I gain a foothold in a little crevice, and grasp an angle of the rock overhead. I find I can get up no farther, and cannot step back, for I dare not let go with my hand, and cannot reach foot-hold below without. I call to Bradley for help. He finds a way by which he can get to the top of the rock over my head, but cannot reach me. Then he looks around for some stick or limb of a tree, but finds none. Then he suggests that he had better

5 COL

help me with the barometer case; but I fear I cannot hold on to it. The moment is critical. Standing on my toes, my muscles begin to tremble. It is sixty or eighty feet to the foot of the precipice. If I lose my hold I shall fall to the bottom, and then perhaps roll over the bench, and tumble still farther down the cliff. At this instant it occurs to Bradley to take off his drawers, which he does, and swings them down to me. I hug close to the rock, let go with my hand, seize the dangling legs, and, with his assistance, I am enabled to gain the top.

Then we walk out on a peninsular rock, make the necessary observations for determining its altitude above camp, and return, finding an easy way down.

June 19.—To-day, Howland, Bradley, and I take the "Emma Dean," and start up the Yampa River. The stream is much swollen, the current swift, and we are able to make but slow progress against it. The cañon in this part of the course of the Yampa is cut through light gray sandstone. The river is very winding, and the swifter water is usually found on the outside of the curve, sweeping against vertical cliffs, often a thousand feet high. In the center of these curves, in many places, the rock above overhangs the river. On the opposite side, the walls are broken, craggy, and sloping, and occasionally side cañons enter. When we have rowed until we are quite tired we stop, and take advantage of one of these broken places to climb out of the cañon. When above, we can look up the Yampa for a distance of several miles.

From the summit of the immediate walls of the cañon the rocks rise gently back for a distance of a mile or two, having the appearance of a valley, with an irregular, rounded sandstone floor, and in the center of the valley a deep gorge, which is the cañon. The rim of this valley on the north is from two thousand five hundred to three thousand feet above the river; on the south, it is not so high. A number of peaks stand on this northern rim, the highest of which has received the name Mount Dawes.

Late in the afternoon we descend to our boat, and return to camp in Echo Park, gliding down in twenty minutes on the rapid river a distance of four or five miles, which was only made up stream by several hours' hard rowing in the morning.

June 20.—This morning two of the men take me up the Yampa for a short distance, and I go out to climb. Having reached the top of the cañon, I walk over long stretches of naked sandstone, crossing gulches now and then, and by noon reach the summit of Mount Dawes. From this point I can look away to the north, and see in the dim distance the Sweetwater and Wind River Mountains, more than a hundred miles away. To the north-west, the Wasatch Mountains are in view and peaks of the Uinta. To the east, I can see the western slopes of the Rocky Mountains, more than a hundred and fifty miles distant.

. The air is singularly clear to day; mountains and buttes stand in sharp outline, valleys stretch out in the perspective, and I can look down into the deep cañon gorges and see gleaming waters.

Descending, I cross to a ridge near the brink of the cañon of Lodore, the highest point of which is nearly as high as the last mentioned mountain.

Late in the afternoon I stand on this elevated point, and discover a monument that has evidently been built by human hands. A few plants are growing in the joints between the rocks, and all are lichened over to a greater or less extent, showing evidences that the pile was built a long time ago. This line of peaks, the eastern extension of the Uinta Mountains, has received the name of Sierra Escalanti, in honor of a Spanish priest, who traveled in this region of country nearly a century ago; and, perchance, the reverend father built this monument.

Now I return to the river and discharge my gun, as a signal for the boat to come and take me down to camp. While we have been in the park, the men have succeeded in catching quite a number of fish, and we have an abundant supply. This is quite an addition to our *cuisine.*

June 21.—We float around the long rock, and enter another cañon. The walls are high and vertical; the cañon is narrow; and the river fills the whole space below, so that there is no landing-place at the foot of the cliff. The Green is greatly increased by the Yampa, and we now have a much larger river. All this volume of water, confined, as it is, in a narrow chan-nel, and rushing with great velocity, is set eddying and spinning in whirl-pools by projecting rocks and short curves, and the waters waltz their way through the cañon, making their own rippling, rushing, roaring music. The cañon is much narrower than any we have seen. With difficulty we manage our boats. They spin about from side to side, and we know not where we are going, and find it impossible to keep them headed down the stream. At first, this causes us great alarm, but we soon find there is but little danger, and that there is a general movement of progression down the river, to which this whirling is but an adjunct; and it is the merry mood of the river to dance through this deep, dark gorge; and right gaily do we join in the sport.

Soon our revel is interrupted by a cataract; its roaring command is heeded by all our power at the oars, and we pull against the whirling current. The "Emma Dean" is brought up against a cliff, about fifty feet above the brink of the fall. By vigorously plying the oars on the side opposite the wall, as if to pull up stream, we can hold her against the rock. The boats behind are signaled to land where they can. The "Maid of the Cañon" is pulled to the left wall, and, by constant rowing, they can hold her also. The "Sister" is run into an alcove on the right, where an eddy is in a dance, and in this she joins. Now my little boat is held against the wall only by the utmost exertion, and it is impossible to make headway against the current. On examination, I find a horizontal crevice in the rock, about ten feet above the water, and a boat's length below us, so we let her down to that point. One of the men clambers into the crevice, in which he can just crawl; we toss him the line, which he makes fast in the rocks, and now our boat is tied up. Then I follow into the crevice, and we crawl along a distance of fifty feet, or more, up stream, and find a broken place, where we can climb about fifty feet higher. Here we stand on a shelf, that passes along down stream to a point above the falls, where it is broken down, and a pile of rocks, over which we can descend to the river, is lying against the foot of the cliff.

It has been mentioned that one of the boats is on the other side. I signal for the men to pull her up alongside of the wall, but it cannot be done; then to cross. This they do, gaining the wall on our side just above where the "Emma Dean" is tied.

The third boat is out of sight, whirling in the eddy of a recess. Looking about, I find another horizontal crevice, along which I crawl to a point just over the water, where this boat is lying, and, calling loud and long, I finally succeed in making the crew understand that I want them to bring the boat down, hugging the wall. This they accomplish, by taking advantage of every crevice and knob on the face of the cliff, so that we have the three boats together at a point a few yards above the falls. Now, by passing a line up on the shelf, the boats can be let down to the broken rocks below. This we do, and, making a short portage, our troubles here are over.

Below the falls, the cañon is wider, and there is more or less space between the river and the walls; but the stream, though wide, is rapid, and rolls at a fearful rate among the rocks. We proceed with great caution, and run the large boats altogether by signal.

At night we camp at the mouth of a small creek, which affords us a good supper of trout. In camp, to-night, we discuss the propriety of several different names for this cañon. At the falls, encountered at noon, its characteristics change suddenly. Above, it is very narrow, and the walls are almost vertical; below, the cañon is much wider, and more flaring; and, high up on the sides, crags, pinnacles, and towers are seen. A number of wild, narrow side cañons enter, and the walls are much broken. After many suggestions, our choice rests between two names, Whirlpool Cañon and Craggy Cañon, neither of which is strictly appropriate for both parts of it; but we leave the discussion at this point, with the understanding that it is best, before finally deciding on a name, to wait until we see what the cañon is below.

June 22.—Still making short portages and letting down with lines. While we are waiting for dinner to-day, I climb a point that gives me a good view of the river for two or three miles below, and I think we can make a long run. After dinner, we start; the large boats are to follow in fifteen minutes, and look out for the signal to land. Into the middle of the stream we row, and down the rapid river we glide, only making strokes enough with the oars to guide the boat. What a headlong ride it is! shooting past rocks and islands! I am soon filled with exhilaration only experienced before in riding a fleet horse over the outstretched prairie. One, two, three, four miles we go, rearing and plunging with the waves, until we wheel to the right into a beautiful park, and land on an island, where we go into camp.

An hour or two before sunset, I cross to the mainland, and climb a point of rocks where I can overlook the park and its surroundings. On the east it is bounded by a high mountain ridge. A semicircle of naked hills bounds it on the north, west, and south. The broad, deep river meanders through the park, interrupted by many wooded islands; so I name it Island Park, and decide to call the cañon above Whirlpool Cañon.

June 23.—We remain in camp to-day to repair our boats, which have had hard knocks, and are leaking. Two of the men go out with the barometer to climb the cliff at the foot of Whirlpool Cañon and measure the walls; another goes on the mountain to hunt; and Bradley and I spend the day among the rocks, studying an interesting geological fold and collecting fossils. Late in the afternoon, the hunter returns, and brings with him a fine, fat deer, so we give his name to the mountain—Mount Hawkins. Just before night we move camp to the lower end of the park, floating down the river about four miles

June 24.—Bradley and I start early to climb the mountain ridge to the east; find its summit to be nearly three thousand feet above camp, and it has required some labor to scale it; but on its top, what a view! There is a long spur running out from the Uinta Mountains toward the south, and the river runs lengthwise through it. Coming down Lodore and Whirlpool Cañons, we cut through the southern slope of the Uinta Mountains; and the lower end of this latter cañon runs into the spur, but, instead of splitting it the whole length, the river wheels to the right at the foot of Whirlpool Cañon, in a great curve to the northwest, through Island Park. At the lower end of the park, the river turns again to the southeast, and cuts into the mountain to its center, and then makes a detour to the southwest, splitting the mountain ridge for a distance of six miles nearly to its foot, and then turns out of it to the left. All this we can see where we stand on the summit of Mount Hawkins, and so we name the gorge below Split Mountain Cañon.

We are standing three thousand feet above its waters, which are troubled with billows, and white with foam. Its walls are set with crags and peaks, and buttressed towers, and overhanging domes. Turning to the right, the park is below us, with its island groves reflected by the deep, quiet

Figure 12.—Swallow Cave.

waters. Rich meadows stretch out on either hand, to the verge of a sloping plain, that comes down from the distant mountains. These plains are of almost naked rock, in strange contrast to the meadows; blue and lilac colored rocks, buff and pink, vermilion and brown, and all these colors clear and bright. A dozen little creeks, dry the greater part of the year, run down through the half circle of exposed formations, radiating from the island-center to the rim of the basin. Each creek has its system of side streams, and each side stream has its system of laterals, and, again, these are divided, so that this outstretched slope of rock is elaborately embossed. Beds of different colored formations run in parallel bands on either side. The perspective, modified by the undulations, gives the bands a waved appearance, and the high colors gleam in the midday sun with the luster of satin. We are tempted to call this Rainbow Park. Away beyond these beds are the Uinta and Wasatch Mountains, with their pine forests and snow fields and naked peaks. Now we turn to the right, and look up Whirlpool Cañon, a deep gorge, with a river in the bottom—a gloomy chasm, where mad waves roar; but, at this distance and altitude, the river is but a rippling brook, and the chasm a narrow cleft. The top of the mountain on which we stand is a broad, grassy table, and a herd of deer is feeding in the distance. Walking over to the southeast, we look down into the valley of White River, and beyond that see the far distant Rocky Mountains, in mellow, perspective haze, through which snow fields shine.

June 25.—This morning, we enter Split Mountain Cañon, sailing in through a broad, flaring, brilliant gateway. We run two or three rapids after they have been carefully examined. Then we have a series of six or eight, over which we are compelled to pass by letting the boats down with lines. This occupies the entire day, and we camp at night at the mouth of a great cave.

The cave is at the foot of one of these rapids, and the waves dash in nearly to its very end. We can pass along a little shelf at the side until we reach the back part. Swallows have built their nests in the ceiling, and they wheel in, chattering and scolding at our intrusion; but their clamor is almost drowned by the noise of the waters. Looking out of the cave, we can see, far up the river, a line of crags standing sentinel on either side, and Mount Hawkins in the distance.

June 26.—The forenoon is spent in getting our large boats over the rapids. This afternoon, we find three falls in close succession. We carry our rations over the rocks, and let our boats shoot over the falls, checking and bringing them to land with lines in the eddies below. At three o'clock we are all aboard again. Down the river we are carried by the swift waters at great speed, sheering around a rock now and then with a timely stroke or two of the oars. At one point, the river turns from left to right, in a direction at right angles to the cañon, in a long chute, and strikes the right, where its waters are heaped up in great billows, that tumble back in breakers. We glide into the chute before we see the danger, and it is too late to stop. Two or three hard strokes are given on the right, and we pause for an instant, expecting to be dashed against the rock. The bow of the boat leaps high on a great wave; the rebounding waters hurl us back, and the peril is past. The next moment, the other boats are hurriedly signaled to land on the left. Accomplishing this, the men walk along the shore, holding the boats near the bank, and let them drift around. Starting again, we soon debouch into a beautiful valley, and glide down its length for ten miles, and camp under a grand old cottonwood. This is evidently a frequent resort for Indians. Tent poles are lying about, and the dead embers of late camp fires are seen. On the plains, to the left, antelope are feeding. Now and then a wolf is seen, and after dark they make the air resound with their howling.

June 27.—Now our way is along a gently flowing river, beset with many islands; groves are seen on either side, and natural meadows, where herds of antelope are feeding. Here and there we have views of the distant mountains on the right.

During the afternoon, we make a long detour to the west, and return again, to a point not more than half a mile from where we started at noon, and here we camp, for the night, under a high bluff.

June 28.—To day, the scenery on either side of the river is much the same as that of yesterday, except that two or three lakes are discovered, lying in the valley to the west. After dinner, we run but a few minutes, when we discover the mouth of the Uinta, a river coming in from the west. Up the valley of this stream, about forty miles, the reservation of the Uinta Indians is situated. We propose to go there, and see if we can replenish our mess kit, and, perhaps, send letters to friends. We also desire to establish an astronomic station here; and hence this will be our stopping place for several days.

Some years ago, Captain Berthoud surveyed a stage route from Salt Lake City to Denver, and this is the place where he crossed the Green River. His party was encamped here for some time, constructing a ferry boat and opening a road.

A little above the mouth of the Uinta, on the west side of the Green, there is a lake of several thousand acres. We carry our boat across the divide between this and the river, have a row on its quiet waters, and succeed in shooting several ducks.

June 29.—A mile and three quarters from here is the junction of the White River with the Green. The White has its source far to the east, in the Rocky Mountains. This morning, I cross the Green, and go over into the valley of the White, and extend my walk several miles along its winding way, until, at last, I come in sight of some strangely carved rocks, named by General Hughes, in his journal, "Goblin City." Our last winter's camp was situated a hundred miles above the point reached to day. The course of the river, for much of the distance, is through cañons; but, at some places, valleys are found. Excepting these little valleys, the region is one of great desolation: arid, almost treeless, bluffs, hills, ledges of rock, and drifting sands. Along the course of the Green, however, from the foot of Split Mountain Cañon to a point some distance below the mouth of the Uinta, there are many groves of cottonwood, natural meadows, and rich lands. This arable belt extends some distance up the White River, on the east, and the Uinta, on the west, and the time must soon come when settlers will penetrate this country, and make homes.

June 30.—We have a row up the Uinta to day, but are not able to make much headway against the swift current, and hence conclude we must walk all the way to the agency.

July 1.—Two days have been employed in obtaining the local time,

6 COL

taking observations for latitude and longitude, and making excursions into the adjacent country. This morning, with two of the men, I start for the Agency. It is a toilsome walk, twenty miles of the distance being across a sand desert. Occasionally, we have to wade the river, crossing it back and forth. Toward evening, we cross several beautiful streams, which are tributaries of the Uinta, and we pass through pine groves and meadows, arriving just at dusk at the Reservation. Captain Dodds, the agent, is away, having gone to Salt Lake City, but his assistants receive us very kindly. It is rather pleasant to see a house once more, and some evidences of civilization, even if it is on an Indian reservation, several days' ride from the nearest home of the white man.

July 2.—I go, this morning, to visit *Tsau'-wi-at.* This old chief is but the wreck of a man, and no longer has influence. Looking at him, you can scarcely realize that he is a man. His skin is shrunken, wrinkled, and dry, and seems to cover no more than a form of bones. He is said to be more than a hundred years old. I talk a little with him, but his conversation is incoherent, though he seems to take pride in showing me some medals, that must have been given him many years ago. He has a pipe which, he says, he has used a long time. I offer to exchange with him, and he seems to be glad to accept; so I add another to my collection of pipes. His wife, "The Bishop," as she is called, is a very garrulous old woman; she exerts a great influence, and is much revered. She is the only Indian woman I have known to occupy a place in the council ring. She seems very much younger than her husband, and, though wrinkled and ugly, is still vigorous. She has much to say to me concerning the condition of the people, and seems very anxious that they should learn to cultivate the soil, own farms, and live like white men. After talking a couple of hours with these old people, I go to see the farms. They are situated in a very beautiful district, where many fine streams of water meander across alluvial plains and meadows. These creeks have quite a fall, and it is very easy to take their waters out above, and, with them, overflow the lands.

It will be remembered that irrigation is necessary, in this dry climate, to successful farming. Quite a number of Indians have each a patch of ground, of two or three acres, on which they are raising wheat, potatoes, turnips,

Figure 13.—Saï'-ar, the interpreter, and his family.

Figure 14.—Indian Lodge in the Uinta Valley.

pumpkins, melons, and other vegetables. Most of the crops are looking well, and it is rather surprising with what pride they show us that they are able to cultivate crops like white men. They are still occupying lodges, and refuse to build houses, assigning as a reason that when any one dies in a lodge it is always abandoned, and very often burned with all the effects of the deceased, and when houses have been built for them they have been treated in the same way. With their unclean habits, a fixed residence would doubtless be no pleasant place. This beautiful valley has been the home of a people of a higher grade of civilization than the present Utes. Evidences of this are quite abundant; on our way here yesterday we discovered, in many places along the trail, fragments of pottery; and wandering about the little farms to day, I find the foundations of ancient houses, and mealing stones that were not used by nomadic people, as they are too heavy to be transported by such tribes, and are deeply worn. The Indians, seeing that I am interested in these matters, take pains to show me several other places where these evidences remain, and tell me that they know nothing about the people who formerly dwelt here. They further tell me that up in the cañon the rocks are covered with pictures.

July 5.—The last two days have been spent in studying the language of the Indians, and making collections of articles illustrating the state of arts among them.

Frank Goodman informs me, this morning, that he has concluded not to go on with the party, saying that he has seen danger enough. It will be remembered that he was one of the crew on the "No Name," when she was wrecked. As our boats are rather heavily loaded, I am content that he should leave, although he has been a faithful man.

We start early on our return to the boats, taking horses with us from the reservation, and two Indians, who are to bring the animals back.

Whirlpool Cañon is fourteen and a quarter miles in length, the walls varying from one thousand eight hundred to two thousand four hundred feet in height. The course of the river through Island Park is nine miles,

Split Mountain Cañon is eight miles long. The highest crags on its walls reach an altitude above the river of from two thousand five hundred to two thousand seven hundred feet. In these cañons, cedars only are found on the walls.

The distance by river from the foot of Split Mountain Cañon to the mouth of the Uinta is sixty-seven miles. The valley through which it runs is the home of many antelope, and we have adopted the Indian name, *Won'-sits Yu-av*—Antelope Valley.

Figure 15.—The Warrior and his Bride.

CHAPTER VI.

July 6.—Start early this morning. A short distance below the mouth of the Uinta, we come to the head of a long island. Last winter, a man named Johnson, a hunter and Indian trader, visited us at our camp in White River Valley. This man has an Indian wife, and, having no fixed home, usually travels with one of the Ute bands. He informed me it was his intention to plant some corn, potatoes, and other vegetables on this island in the spring, and, knowing that we would pass it, invited us to stop and help ourselves, even if he should not be there; so we land and go out on the island. Looking about, we soon discover his garden, but it is in a sad condition, having received no care since it was planted. It is yet too early in the season for corn, but Hall suggests that potato tops are good greens, and, anxious for some change from our salt meat fare, we gather a quantity and take them aboard. At noon we stop and cook our greens for dinner; but soon, one after another of the party is taken sick; nausea first, and then severe vomiting, and we tumble around under the trees, groaning with pain, and I feel a little alarmed, lest our poisoning be severe. Emetics are administered to those who are willing to take them, and about the middle of the afternoon we are all rid of the pain. Jack Sumner records in his diary that "Potato tops are not good greens on the sixth day of July."

This evening we enter another cañon, almost imperceptibly, as the walls rise very gently.

July 7.—We find quiet water to day, the river sweeping in great and beautiful curves, the cañon walls steadily increasing in altitude. The escarpment formed by the cut edges of the rock are often vertical, sometimes terraced, and in some places the treads of the terraces are sloping. In these quiet curves vast amphitheaters are formed, now in vertical rocks, now in steps.

The salient point of rock within the curve is usually broken down in a steep slope, and we stop occasionally to climb up, at such a place, where, on looking down, we can see the river sweeping the foot of the opposite cliff, in a great, easy curve, with a perpendicular or terraced wall rising from the water's edge many hundreds of feet.   One of these we find very symmetrical, and name it Summer's Amphitheater.   The cliffs are rarely broken by the entrance of side cañons, and we sweep around curve after curve, with almost continuous walls, for several miles.

Late in the afternoon, we find the river much rougher, and come upon rapids, not dangerous, but still demanding close attention.

We camp at night on the right bank, having made to day twenty six miles.

July 8.—This morning, Bradley and I go out to climb, and gain an altitude of more than two thousand feet above the river, but still do not reach the summit of the wall.

After dinner, we pass through a region of the wildest desolation.   The cañon is very tortuous, the river very rapid, and many lateral cañons enter on either side.   These usually have their branches, so that the region is cut into a wilderness of gray and brown cliffs.   In several places, these lateral cañons are only separated from each other by narrow walls, often hundreds of feet high, but so narrow in places that where softer rocks are found below, they have crumbled away, and left holes in the wall, forming passages from one cañon into another.   These we often call natural bridges; but they were never intended to span streams.   They had better, perhaps, be called side doors between cañon chambers.

Piles of broken rock lie against these walls; crags and tower shaped peaks are seen everywhere; and away above them, long lines of broken cliffs, and above and beyond the cliffs are pine forests, of which we obtain occasional glimpses, as we look up through a vista of rocks.

The walls are almost without vegetation; a few dwarf bushes are seen here and there, clinging to the rocks, and cedars grow from the crevices— not like the cedars of a land refreshed with rains, great cones bedecked with spray, but ugly clumps, like war clubs, beset with spines.   We are minded to call this the Cañon of Desolation.

Figure 16.—Sumner's Ampitheater.

The wind annoys us much to day. The water, rough by reason of the rapids, is made more so by head gales. Wherever a great face of rock has a southern exposure, the rarified air rises, and the wind rushes in below, either up or down the cañon, or both, causing local currents.

Just at sunset, we run a bad rapid, and camp at its foot.

July 9.—Our run to day is through a cañon, with ragged, broken walls, many lateral gulches or cañons entering on either side. The river is rough, and occasionally it becomes necessary to use lines in passing rocky places. During the afternoon, we come to a rather open cañon valley, stretching up toward the west, its farther end lost in the mountains. From a point to which we climb, we obtain a good view of its course, until its angular walls are lost in the vista.

July 10.—Sumner, who is a fine mechanist, is learning to take observations for time with the sextant. To day, he remains in camp to practice.

Howland and myself determine to climb out, and start up a lateral cañon, taking a barometer with us, for the purpose of measuring the thickness of the strata over which we pass. The readings of a barometer below are recorded every half hour, and our observations must be simultaneous. Where the beds, which we desire to measure, are very thick, we must climb with the utmost speed, to reach their summits in time. Again, where there are thinner beds, we wait for the moment to arrive; and so, by hard and easy stages, we make our way to the top of the cañon wall, and reach the plateau above about two o'clock.

Howland, who has his gun with him, sees deer feeding a mile or two back, and goes off for a hunt. I go to a peak, which seems to be the highest one in this region, about half a mile distant, and climb, for the purpose of tracing the topography of the adjacent country. From this point, a fine view is obtained. A long plateau stretches across the river, in an easterly and westerly direction, the summit covered by pine forests, with intervening elevated valleys and gulches. The plateau itself is cut in two by the cañon. Other side cañons head away back from the river, and run down into the Green. Besides these, deep and abrupt cañons are seen to head back on the plateau, and run north toward the Uinta and White Rivers. Still other cañons head in the valleys, and run toward the south. The elevation of the plateau being about eight thousand feet above the level of the sea, brings it into a region of moisture, as is well attested by the forests and grassy valleys. The plateau seems to rise gradually to the west, until it merges into the Wasatch Mountains. On these high table lands, elk and deer abound; and they are favorite hunting grounds for the Ute Indians.

A little before sunset, Howland and I meet again at the head of the side cañon, and down we start. It is late, and we must make great haste, or be caught by the darkness; so we go, running where we can; leaping over the ledges; letting each other down on the loose rocks, as long as we can see. When darkness comes, we are still some distance from camp, and a long, slow, anxious descent we make, toward the gleaming camp fire.

After supper, observations for latitude are taken, and only two or three hours for sleep remain, before daylight.

July 11.—A short distance below camp we run a rapid, and, in doing so, break an oar, and then lose another, both belonging to the "Emma Dean." So the pioneer boat has but two oars.

We see nothing of which oars can be made, so we conclude to run on to some point, where it seems possible to climb out to the forests on the plateau, and there we will procure suitable timber from which to make new ones.

We soon approach another rapid. Standing on deck, I think it can be run, and on we go. Coming nearer, I see that at the foot it has a short turn to the left, where the waters pile up against the cliff. Here we try to land, but quickly discover that, being in swift water, above the fall, we cannot reach shore, crippled, as we are, by the loss of two oars; so the bow of the boat is turned down stream. We shoot by a big rock; a reflex wave rolls over our little boat and fills her. I see the place is dangerous, and quickly signal to the other boats to land where they can. This is scarcely completed when another wave rolls our boat over, and I am thrown some distance into the water. I soon find that swimming is very easy, and I cannot sink. It is only necessary to ply strokes sufficient to keep my head out of the water, though now and then, when a breaker rolls over me, I close my mouth, and am carried through it. The boat is drifting ahead of me twenty or thirty feet, and, when the great waves are passed, I overtake it,

Figure 17.—Light-House Rock in the Cañon of Desolation.

and find Summer and Dunn clinging to her. As soon as we reach quiet water, we all swim to one side and turn her over. In doing this, Dunn loses his hold and goes under; when he comes up, he is caught by Summer and pulled to the boat. In the mean time we have drifted down stream some distance, and see another rapid below. How bad it may be we cannot tell, so we swim toward shore, pulling our boat with us, with all the vigor possible, but are carried down much faster than distance toward shore is gained. At last we reach a huge pile of drift wood. Our rolls of blankets, two guns, and a barometer were in the open compartment of the boat, and, when it went over, these were thrown out. The guns and barometer are lost, but I succeeded in catching one of the rolls of blankets, as it drifted by, when we were swimming to shore; the other two are lost, and sometimes hereafter we may sleep cold.

A huge fire is built on the bank, our clothing is spread to dry, and then from the drift logs we select one from which we think oars can be made, and the remainder of the day is spent in sawing them out.

July 12.—This morning, the new oars are finished, and we start once more. We pass several bad rapids, making a short portage at one, and before noon we come to a long, bad fall, where the channel is filled with rocks on the left, turning the waters to the right, where they pass under an overhanging rock. On examination, we determine to run it, keeping as close to the left hand rocks as safety will permit, in order to avoid the over hanging cliff. The little boat runs over all right; another follows, but the men are not able to keep her near enough to the left bank, and she is carried, by a swift chute, into great waves to the right, where she is tossed about, and Bradley is knocked over the side, but his foot catching under the seat, he is dragged along in the water, with his head down; making great exertion, he seizes the gunwale with his left hand, and can lift his head above water now and then. To us who are below, it seems impossible to keep the boat from going under the overhanging cliff; but Powell, for the moment, heedless of Bradley's mishap, pulls with all his power for half a dozen strokes, when the danger is past; then he seizes Bradley, and pulls him in. The men in the boat above, seeing this, land, and she is let down by lines.

Just here we emerge from the Cañon of Desolation, as we have named it, into a more open country, which extends for a distance of nearly a mile, when we enter another cañon, cut through gray sandstone.

About three o'clock in the afternoon we meet with a new difficulty. The river fills the entire channel; the walls are vertical on either side, from the water's edge, and a bad rapid is beset with rocks. We come to the head of it, and land on a rock in the stream; the little boat is let down to another rock below, the men of the larger boat holding to the line; the second boat is let down in the same way, and the line of the third boat is brought with them. Now, the third boat pushes out from the upper rock, and, as we have her line below, we pull in and catch her, as she is sweeping by at the foot of the rock on which we stand. Again the first boat is let down stream the full length of her line, and the second boat is passed down by the first to the extent of her line, which is held by the men in the first boat; so she is two lines' length from where she started. Then the third boat is let down past the second, and still down, nearly to the length of her line, so that she is fast to the second boat, and swinging down three lines' lengths, with the other two boats intervening. Held in this way, the men are able to pull her into a cove, in the left wall, where she is made fast. But this leaves a man on the rock above, holding to the line of the little boat. When all is ready, he springs from the rock, clinging to the line with one hand, and swimming with the other, and we pull him in as he goes by. As the two boats, thus loosened, drift down, the men in the cove pull us all in, as we come opposite; then we pass around to a point of rock below the cove, close to the wall, land, and make a short portage over the worst places in the rapid, and start again.

At night we camp on a sand beach; the wind blows a hurricane; the drifting sand almost blinds us; and nowhere can we find shelter. The wind continues to blow all night; the sand sifts through our blankets, and piles over us, until we are covered as in a snow-drift. We are glad when morning comes.

July 13.—This morning, we have an exhilarating ride. The river is swift, and there are many smooth rapids. I stand on deck, keeping careful watch ahead, and we glide along, mile after mile, plying strokes now on the right, and then on the left, just sufficient to guide our boats past the rocks into

Figure 18.—Gunnison's Butte at the foot of Gray Cañon.
(2,700 feet high.)

smooth water. At noon we emerge from Gray Cañon, as we have named it, and camp, for dinner, under a cottonwood tree, standing on the left bank.

Extensive sand plains extend back from the immediate river valley, as far as we can see, on either side These naked, drifting sands gleam brilliantly in the midday sun of July. The reflected heat from the glaring surface, produces a curious motion of the atmosphere; little currents are generated, and the whole seems to be trembling and moving about in many directions, or, failing to see that the movement is in the atmosphere, it gives the impression of an unstable land. Plains, and hills, and cliffs, and distant mountains seem vaguely to be floating about in a trembling, wave rocked sea, and patches of landscape will seem to float away, and be lost, and then re-appear.

Just opposite, there are buttes, that are outliers of cliffs to the left. Below, they are composed of shales and marls of light blue and slate colors; and above, the rocks are buff and gray, and then brown. The buttes are buttressed below, where the azure rocks are seen, and terraced above through the gray and brown beds. A long line of cliffs or rock escarpments separate the table lands, through which Gray Cañon is cut, from the lower plain. The eye can trace these azure beds and cliffs, on either side of the river, in a long line, extending across its course, until they fade away in the perspective. These cliffs are many miles in length, and hundreds of feet high; and all these buttes—great mountain-masses of rock—are dancing and fading away, and re-appearing, softly moving about, or so they seem to the eye, as seen through the shifting atmosphere.

This afternoon, our way is through a valley, with cottonwood groves on either side. The river is deep, broad, and quiet.

About two hours from noon camp, we discover an Indian crossing, where a number of rafts, rudely constructed of logs and bound together by withes, are floating against the bank. On landing, we see evidences that a party of Indians have crossed within a very few days. This is the place where the lamented Gunnison crossed, in the year 1853, when making an exploration for a railroad route to the Pacific coast.

An hour later, we run a long rapid, and stop at its foot to examine some

curious rocks, deposited by mineral springs that at one time must have
existed here, but which are no longer flowing.

July 14.—This morning, we pass some curious black bluffs on the right,
then two or three short cañons, and then we discover the mouth of the San
Rafael, a stream which comes down from the distant mountains in the west.
Here we stop for an hour or two, and take a short walk up the valley, and
find it is a frequent resort for Indians. Arrow heads are scattered about,
many of them very beautiful. Flint chips are seen strewn over the ground
in great profusion, and the trails are well worn.

Starting after dinner, we pass some beautiful buttes on the left, many
of which are very symmetrical. They are chiefly composed of gypsum of
many hues, from light gray to slate color; then pink, purple, and brown
beds.

Now, we enter another cañon. Gradually the walls rise higher and
higher as we proceed, and the summit of the cañon is formed of the same
beds of orange colored sandstone. Back from the brink, the hollows of the
plateau are filled with sands disintegrated from these orange beds. They
are of rich cream color, shaded into maroon, everywhere destitute of vegetation, and drifted into long, wave like ridges.

The course of the river is tortuous, and it nearly doubles upon itself
many times. The water is quiet, and constant rowing is necessary to make
much headway. Sometimes, there is a narrow flood plain between the river
and the wall, on one side or the other. Where these long, gentle curves
are found, the river washes the very foot of the outer wall. A long peninsula of willow bordered meadow projects within the curve, and the talus, at
the foot of the cliff, is usually covered with dwarf oaks. The orange colored
sandstone is very homogeneous in structure, and the walls are usually vertical, though not very high. Where the river sweeps around a curve under
a cliff, a vast hollow dome may be seen, with many caves and deep alcoves,
that are greatly admired by the members of the party, as we go by.

We camp at night on the left bank.

July 15.—Our camp is in a great bend of the cañon. The perimeter
of the curve is to the west, and we are on the east side of the river. Just
opposite, a little stream comes down through a narrow side cañon. We cross,

and go up to explore it.   Just at its mouth, another lateral cañon enters, in
the angle between the former and the main cañon above.   Still another
enters in the angle between the cañon below and the side cañon first mentioned, so that three side cañons enter at the same point.   These cañons
are very tortuous, almost closed in from view, and, seen from the opposite
side of the river, they appear like three alcoves; and we name this Trin-
Alcove Bend.

Going up the little stream, in the central cove, we pass between high
walls of sandstone, and wind about in glens.   Springs gush from the rocks
at the foot of the walls; narrow passages in the rocks are threaded, caves
are entered, and many side cañons are observed.

The right cove is a narrow, winding gorge, with overhanging walls,
almost shutting out the light.

The left is an amphitheater, turning spirally up, with overhanging
shelves.   A series of basins, filled with water, are seen at different altitudes,
as we pass up; huge rocks are piled below on the right, and overhead there
is an arched ceiling.   After exploring these alcoves, we recross the river,
and climb the rounded rocks on the point of the bend.   In every direction,
as far as we are able to see, naked rocks appear.   Buttes are scattered on
the landscape, here rounded into cones, there buttressed, columned, and
carved in quaint shapes, with deep alcoves and sunken recesses.   All about
us are basins, excavated in the soft sandstones; and these have been filled by
the late rains.

Over the rounded rocks and water pockets we look off on a fine stretch
of river, and beyond are naked rocks and beautiful buttes to the Azure
Cliffs, and beyond these, and above them, the Brown Cliffs, and still beyond,
mountain peaks; and clouds piled over all.

On we go, after dinner, with quiet water, still compelled to row, in
order to make fair progress.   The cañon is yet very tortuous.

About six miles below noon camp, we go around a great bend to the
right, five miles in length, and come back to a point within a quarter of a
mile of where we started.   Then we sweep around another great bend to
the left, making a circuit of nine miles, and come back to a point within
six hundred yards of the beginning of the bend.   In the two circuits, we

describe almost the figure 8. The men call it a bow-knot of river; so we name it Bow-knot Bend. The line of the figure is fourteen miles in length.

There is an exquisite charm in our ride to-day down this beautiful cañon. It gradually grows deeper with every mile of travel; the walls are symmetrically curved, and grandly arched; of a beautiful color, and reflected in the quiet waters in many places, so as to almost deceive the eye, and suggest the thought, to the beholder, that he is looking into profound depths. We are all in fine spirits, feel very gay, and the badinage of the men is echoed from wall to wall. Now and then we whistle, or shout, or discharge a pistol, to listen to the reverberations among the cliffs.

At night we camp on the south side of the great Bow-knot, and, as we eat our supper, which is spread on the beach, we name this Labyrinth Cañon.

July 16.—Still we go down, on our winding way. We pass tower cliffs, then we find the river widens out for several miles, and meadows are seen on either side, between the river and the walls. We name this expansion of the river Tower Park.

At two o'clock we emerge from Labyrinth Cañon, and go into camp.

July 17.—The line which separates Labyrinth Cañon from the one below is but a line, and at once, this morning, we enter another cañon. The water fills the entire channel, so that nowhere is there room to land. The walls are low, but vertical, and, as we proceed, they gradually increase in altitude. Running a couple of miles, the river changes its course many degrees, toward the east. Just here, a little stream comes in on the right, and the wall is broken down; so we land, and go out to take a view of the surrounding country. We are now down among the buttes, and in a region, the surface of which is naked, solid rock—a beautiful red sandstone, forming a smooth, undulating pavement. The Indians call this the *"Toom'-pin Tu-weap'*,*"* or *"*Rock Land,*"* and sometimes the *"Toom'-pin wu-near' Tu-weap'*,*"* or *"*Land of Standing Rock.*"*

Off to the south we see a butte, in the form of a fallen cross. It is several miles away, still it presents no inconspicuous figure on the landscape, and must be many hundreds of feet high, probably more than two thousand. We note its position on our map, and name it *"*The Butte of the Cross.*"*

We continue our journey. In many places the walls, which rise from

Figure 19.—Buttes of the Cross in the Toom'-pin Wu-near' Tu-weap'.

the water's edge, are overhanging on either side. The stream is still quiet, and we glide along, through a strange, weird, grand region. The landscape everywhere, away from the river, is of rock—cliffs of rock; tables of rock; plateaus of rock; terraces of rock; crags of rock—ten thousand strangely carved forms. Rocks everywhere, and no vegetation; no soil; no sand. In long, gentle curves, the river winds about these rocks.

When speaking of these rocks, we must not conceive of piles of boulders, or heaps of fragments, but a whole land of naked rock, with giant forms carved on it: cathedral shaped buttes, towering hundreds or thousands of feet; cliffs that cannot be scaled, and cañon walls that shrink the river into insignificance, with vast, hollow domes, and tall pinnacles, and shafts set on the verge overhead, and all highly colored—buff, gray, red, brown, and chocolate; never lichened; never moss-covered; but bare, and often polished.

We pass a place, where two bends of the river come together, an intervening rock having been worn away; and a new channel formed across. The old channel ran in a great circle around to the right, by what was once a circular peninsula; then an island; then the water left the old channel entirely, and passed through the cut, and the old bed of the river is dry. So the great circular rock stands by itself, with precipitous walls all about it, and we find but one place where it can be scaled. Looking from its summit, a long stretch of river is seen, sweeping close to the overhanging cliffs on the right, but having a little meadow between it and the wall on the left. The curve is very gentle and regular. We name this Bonita Bend.

And just here we climb out once more, to take another bearing on The Butte of the Cross. Reaching an eminence, from which we can overlook the landscape, we are surprised to find that our butte, with its wonderful form, is indeed two buttes, one so standing in front of the other that, from our last point of view, it gave the appearance of a cross.

Again, a few miles below Bonita Bend, we go out a mile or two along the rocks, toward the Orange Cliffs, passing over terraces paved with jasper.

The cliffs are not far away, and we soon reach them, and wander in some deep, painted alcoves, which attracted our attention from the river; then we return to our boats.

Late in the afternoon, the water becomes swift, and our boats make great speed. An hour of this rapid running brings us to the junction of the Grand and Green, the foot of Stillwater Cañon, as we have named it.

These streams unite in solemn depths, more than one thousand two hundred feet below the general surface of the country. The walls of the lower end of Stillwater Cañon are very beautifully curved, as the river sweeps in its meandering course. The lower end of the cañon through which the Grand comes down, is also regular, but much more direct, and we look up this stream, and out into the country beyond, and obtain glimpses of snow clad peaks, the summits of a group of mountains known as the Sierra La Sal. Down the Colorado, the cañon walls are much broken.

We row around into the Grand, and camp on its northwest bank; and here we propose to stay several days, for the purpose of determining the latitude and longitude, and the altitude of the walls. Much of the night is spent in making observations with the sextant.

The distance from the mouth of the Uinta to the head of the Cañon of Desolation is twenty and three quarters miles. The Cañon of Desolation is ninety seven miles long; Gray Cañon thirty six. The course of the river through Gunnison's Valley is twenty seven and a quarter miles; Labyrinth Cañon, sixty two and a half miles.

In the Cañon of Desolation, the highest rocks immediately over the river are about two thousand four hundred feet. This is at Log Cabin Cliff. The highest part of the terrace is near the brink of the Brown Cliffs. Climbing the immediate walls of the cañon, and passing back to the cañon terrace, and climbing that, we find the altitude, above the river, to be 3,300 feet. The lower end of Gray Cañon is about two thousand feet; the lower end of Labyrinth Cañon, 1,300 feet.

Stillwater Cañon is forty two and three quarters miles long; the highest walls, 1,300 feet.

CHAPTER VII.

July 18.—The day is spent in obtaining the time, and spreading our rations, which, we find, are badly injured. The flour has been wet and dried so many times that it is all musty, and full of hard lumps. We make a sieve of mosquito netting, and run our flour through it, losing more than two hundred pounds by the process. Our losses, by the wrecking of the "No Name," and by various mishaps since, together with the amount thrown away to day, leave us little more than two months' supplies, and, to make them last thus long, we must be fortunate enough to lose no more.

We drag our boats on shore, and turn them over to recalk and pitch them, and Sumner is engaged in repairing barometers.· While we are here, for a day or two, resting, we propose to put everything in the best shape for a vigorous campaign.

July 19.—Bradley and I start this morning to climb the left wall below the junction. The way we have selected is up a gulch. Climbing for an hour over and among the rocks, we find ourselves in a vast amphitheater, and our way cut off. We clamber around to the left for half an hour, until we find that we cannot go up in that direction. Then we try the rocks around to the right, and discover a narrow shelf, nearly half a mile long. In some places, this is so wide that we pass along with ease; in others, it is so narrow and sloping that we are compelled to lie down and crawl. We can look over the edge of the shelf, down eight hundred feet, and see the river rolling and plunging among the rocks. Looking up five hundred feet, to the brink of the cliff, it seems to blend with the sky. We continue along, until we come to a point where the wall is again broken down. Up we climb. On the right, there is a narrow, mural point of rocks, extending toward the river, two or three hundred feet high, and six or eight hundred

8 COL

feet long. · We come back to where this sets in, and find it cut off from the main wall by a great crevice. Into this we pass. And now, a long, narrow rock is between us and the river. The rock itself is split longitudinally and transversely; and the rains on the surface above have run down through the crevices, and gathered into channels below, and then run off into the river. The crevices are usually narrow above, and, by erosion of the streams, wider below, forming a net work of caves; but each cave having a narrow, winding sky-light up through the rocks. We wander among these corridors for an hour or two, but find no place where the rocks are broken down, so that we can climb up. At last, we determine to attempt a passage by a crevice, and select one which we think is wide enough to admit of the passage of our bodies, and yet narrow enough to climb out by pressing our hands and feet against the walls. So we climb as men would out of a well. Bradley climbs first; I hand him the barometer, then climb over his head, and he hands me the barometer. So we pass each other alternately, until we emerge from the fissure, out on the summit of the rock. And what a world of grandeur is spread before us! Below is the cañon, through which the Colorado runs. We can trace its course for miles, and at points catch glimpses of the river. From the northwest comes the Green, in a narrow, winding gorge. From the northeast comes the Grand, through a cañon that seems bottomless from where we stand. Away to the west are lines of cliffs and ledges of rock—not such ledges as you may have seen where the quarry-man splits his blocks, but ledges from which the gods might quarry mountains, that, rolled out on the plain below, would stand a lofty range; and not such cliffs as you may have seen where the swallow builds its nest, but cliffs where the soaring eagle is lost to view ere he reaches the summit. Between us and the distant cliffs are the strangely carved and pinnacled rocks of the *Toom′-pin wu-near′ Tu-weap′*. On the summit of the opposite wall of the cañon are rock forms that we do not understand. Away to the east a group of eruptive mountains are seen—the Sierra La Sal. Their slopes are covered with pines, and deep gulches are flanked with great crags, and snow fields are seen near the summits. So the mountains are in uniform, green, gray, and silver. Wherever we look there is but a wilderness of rocks; deep gorges, where the rivers are lost below cliffs and towers and pinnacles; and ten thousand strangely carved forms in every direction; and beyond them, mountains blending with the clouds.

Now we return to camp. While we are eating supper, we very naturally speak of better fare, as musty bread and spoiled bacon are not pleasant. Soon I see Hawkins down by the boat, taking up the sextant, rather a strange proceeding for him, and I question him concerning it. He replies that he is trying to find the latitude and longitude of the nearest pie.

July 20.—This morning, Captain Powell and I go out to climb the west wall of the cañon, for the purpose of examining the strange rocks seen yesterday from the other side. Two hours bring us to the top, at a point between the Green and Colorado, overlooking the junction of the rivers. A long neck of rock extends toward the mouth of the Grand. Out on this we walk, crossing a great number of deep crevices. Usually, the smooth rock slopes down to the fissure on either side. Sometimes it is an interesting question to us whether the slope is not so steep that we cannot stand on it. Sometimes, starting down, we are compelled to go on, and we are not always sure that the crevice is not too wide for a jump, when we measure it with our eye from above. Probably the slopes would not be difficult if there was not a fissure at the lower end; nor would the fissures cause fear if they were but a few feet deep. It is curious how a little obstacle becomes a great obstruction, when a misstep would land a man in the bottom of a deep chasm. Climbing the face of a cliff, a man will walk along a step or shelf, but a few inches wide, without hesitancy, if the landing is but ten feet below, should he fall; but if the foot of the cliff is a thousand feet down, he will crawl. At last our way is cut off by a fissure so deep and wide that we cannot pass it. Then we turn and walk back into the country, over the smooth, naked sandstone, without vegetation, except that here and there dwarf cedars and piñon pines have found a footing in the huge cracks. There are great basins in the rock, holding water; some but a few gallons, others hundreds of barrels.

The day is spent in walking about through these strange scenes. A narrow gulch is cut into the wall of the main cañon. Follow this up, and you climb rapidly, as if going up a mountain side, for the gulch heads but a few hundred or a few thousand yards from the wall. But this gulch has its side gulches, and, as you come near to the summit, a group of radiating cañons is found. The spaces drained by these little cañons are terraced, and are, to a greater or less extent, of the form of amphitheaters, though some are oblong and some rather irregular. Usually, the spaces drained by any two of these little side cañons are separated by a narrow wall, one, two, or three hundred feet high, and often but a few feet in thickness. Sometimes the wall is broken into a line of pyramids above, and still remains a wall below. Now, there are a number of these gulches which break the wall of the main cañon of the Green, each one having its system of side cañons and amphitheaters, inclosed by walls, or lines of pinnacles. The course of the Green, at this point, is approximately at right angles to that of the Colorado, and on the brink of the latter cañon we find the same system of terraced and walled glens. The walls, and pinnacles, and towers are of sandstone, homogeneous in structure, but not in color, as they show broad bands of red, buff, and gray. This painting of the rocks, dividing them into sections, increases their apparent height. In some places, these terraced and walled glens, along the Colorado, have coalesced with those along the Green; that is, the intervening walls are broken down. It is very rarely that a loose rock is seen. The sand is washed off so that the walls, terraces, and slopes of the glens are all of smooth sandstone.

In the walls themselves, curious caves and channels have been carved. In some places, there are little stairways up the walls; in others, the walls present what are known as royal arches; and so we wander through glens, and among pinnacles, and climb the walls from early morn until late in the afternoon.

July 21.—We start this morning on the Colorado. The river is rough, and bad rapids, in close succession, are found. Two very hard portages are made during the forenoon. After dinner, in running a rapid, the "Emma Dean" is swamped, and we are thrown into the river, we cling to her, and in the first quiet water below she is righted and bailed out; but three oars are lost in this mishap. The larger boats land above the dangerous place, and we make a portage, that occupies all the afternoon. We camp at night, on the rocks on the left bank, and can scarcely find room to lie down.

Figure 20.—The Heart of Cataract Cañon.

July 22.—This morning, we continue our journey, though short of oars. There is no timber growing on the walls within our reach, and no drift wood along the banks, so we are compelled to go on until something suitable can be found. A mile and three quarters below, we find a huge pile of drift wood, among which are some cottonwood logs. From these we select one which we think the best, and the men are set at work sawing oars. Our boats are leaking again, from the strains received in the bad rapids yesterday, so, after dinner, they are turned over, and some of the men are engaged in calking them.

Captain Powell and I go out to climb the wall to the east, for we can see dwarf pines above, and it is our purpose to collect the resin which oozes from them, to use in pitching our boats. We take a barometer with us, and find that the walls are becoming higher, for now they register an altitude, above the river, of nearly fifteen hundred feet.

July 23.—On starting, we come at once to difficult rapids and falls, that, in many places, are more abrupt than in any of the cañons through which we have passed, and we decide to name this Cataract Cañon.

From morning until noon, the course of the river is to the west; the scenery is grand, with rapids and falls below, and walls above, beset with crags and pinnacles. Just at noon we wheel again to the south, and go into camp for dinner.

While the cook is preparing it, Bradley, Captain Powell, and myself go up into a side cañon, that comes in at this point. We enter through a very narrow passage, having to wade along the course of a little stream until a cascade interrupts our progress. Then we climb to the right, for a hundred feet, until we reach a little shelf, along which we pass, walking with great care, for it is narrow, until we pass around the fall. Here the gorge widens into a spacious, sky roofed chamber. In the farther end is a beautiful grove of cottonwoods, and between us and the cottonwoods the little stream widens out into three clear lakelets, with bottoms of smooth rock. Beyond the cottonwoods, the brook tumbles, in a series of white, shining cascades, from heights that seem immeasurable. Turning around, we can look through the cleft through which we came, and see the river, with towering walls beyond. What a chamber for a resting place is this! hewn from the solid rock; the heavens for a ceiling; cascade fountains within; a grove in the conservatory, clear lakelets for a refreshing bath, and an outlook through the doorway on a raging river, with cliffs and mountains beyond.

Our way, after dinner, is through a gorge, grand beyond description. The walls are nearly vertical; the river broad and swift, but free from rocks and falls. From the edge of the water to the brink of the cliffs it is one thousand six hundred to one thousand eight hundred feet. At this great depth, the river rolls in solemn majesty. The cliffs are reflected from the more quiet river, and we seem to be in the depths of the earth, and yet can look down into waters that reflect a bottomless abyss. We arrive, early in the afternoon, at the head of more rapids and falls, but, wearied with past work, we determine to rest, so go into camp, and the afternoon and evening are spent by the men in discussing the probabilities of successfully navigating the river below. The barometric records are examined, to see what descent we have made since we left the mouth of the Grand, and what descent since we left the Pacific Railroad, and what fall there yet must be to the river, ere we reach the end of the great cañons. The conclusion to which the men arrive seems to be about this: that there are great descents yet to be made, but, if they are distributed in rapids and short falls, as they have been heretofore, we will be able to overcome them. But, may be, we shall come to a fall in these cañons which we cannot pass, where the walls rise from the water's edge, so that we cannot land, and where the water is so swift that we cannot return. Such places have been found, except that the falls were not so great but that we could run them with safety. How will it be in the future! So they speculate over the serious probabilities in jesting mood, and I hear Sumner remark, "My idea is, we had better go slow, and learn to peddle."

July 24.—We examine the rapids below. Large rocks have fallen from the walls—great, angular blocks, which have rolled down the talus, and are strewn along the channel. We are compelled to make three portages in succession, the distance being less than three fourths of a mile, with a fall of seventy five feet. Among these rocks, in chutes, whirlpools, and great waves, with rushing breakers and foam, the water finds its way, still tumbling down. We stop for the night, only three fourths of a mile below the last camp. A very hard day's work has been done, and at evening I sit on a rock by the edge of the river, to look at the water, and listen to its roar. Hours ago, deep shadows had settled into the cañon as the sun passed behind the cliffs. Now, doubtless, the sun has gone down, for we can see no glint of light on the crags above. Darkness is coming on. The waves are rolling, with crests of foam so white they seem almost to give a light of their own. Near by, a chute of water strikes the foot of a great block of lime-stone, fifty feet high, and the waters pile up against it, and roll back. Where there are sunken rocks, the water heaps up in mounds, or even in cones. At a point where rocks come very near the surface, the water forms a chute above, strikes, and is shot up ten or fifteen feet, and piles back in gentle curves, as in a fountain; and on the river tumbles and rolls.

July 25.—Still more rapids and falls to day. In one, the "Emma Dean" is caught in a whirlpool, and set spinning about; and it is with great diffi-culty we are able to get out of it, with the loss of an oar. At noon, another is made; and on we go, running some of the rapids, letting down with lines past others, and making two short portages. We camp on the right bank, hungry and tired.

July 26.—We run a short distance this morning, and go into camp, to make oars and repair boats and barometers. The walls of the cañon have been steadily increasing in altitude to this point, and now they are more than two thousand feet high. In many places, they are vertical from the water's edge; in others, there is a talus between the river and the foot of the cliffs, and they are often broken down by side cañons. It is probable that the river is nearly as low now as it is ever found. High water mark can be observed forty, fifty, sixty, or a hundred feet above its present stage. Some-times logs and drift wood are seen wedged into the crevice overhead, where floods have carried them.

About ten o'clock, Powell, Bradley, Howland, Hall, and myself start up a side cañon to the east. We soon come to pools of water; then to a brook, which is lost in the sands below; and, passing up the brook, we find the cañon narrows, the walls close in, are often overhanging, and at last we find ourselves in a vast amphitheater, with a pool of deep, clear, cold water on the bottom. At first, our way seems cut off; but we soon discover a little shelf, along which we climb, and, passing beyond the pool, walk a hundred yards or more, turn to the right, and find ourselves in another dome shaped amphitheater. There is a winding cleft at the top, reaching out to the country above, nearly two thousand feet overhead. The rounded, basin shaped bottom is filled with water to the foot of the walls. There is no shelf by which we can pass around the foot. If we swim across, we meet with a face of rock hundreds of feet high, over which a little rill glides, and it will be impossible to climb. So we can go no farther up this cañon. Then we turn back, and examine the walls on either side carefully, to discover, if possible, some way of climbing out. In this search, every man takes his own course, and we are scattered. I almost abandon the idea of getting out, and am engaged in searching for fossils, when I discover, on the north, a broken place, up which it may be possible for me to climb. The way, for a distance, is up a slide of rocks; then up an irregular amphitheater, on points that form steps and give handhold, and then I reach a little shelf, along which I walk, and discover a vertical fissure, parallel to the face of the wall, and reaching to a higher shelf. This fissure is narrow, and I try to climb up to the bench, which is about forty feet overhead. I have a barometer on my back, which rather impedes my climbing. The walls of the fissure are of smooth limestone, offering neither foot nor hand hold. So I support myself by pressing my back against one wall and my knees against the other, and, in this way, lift my body, in a shuffling manner, a few inches at a time, until I have, perhaps, made twenty five feet of the distance, when the crevice widens a little, and I cannot press my knees against the rocks in front with sufficient power to give me support in lifting my body, and I try to go back. This I cannot do without falling. So I struggle along sidewise, farther into the crevice, where it narrows. But by this time my muscles are exhausted, and I cannot climb longer; so I move still a little farther into the crevice, where it is so narrow and wedging that I can lie in it, and there I rest. Five or ten minutes of this relief, and up once more I go, and reach the bench above. On this I can walk for a quarter of a mile, till I come to a place where the wall is again broken down, so that I can climb up still farther, and in an hour I reach the summit. I hang up my barometer, to give it a few minutes time to settle, and

Figure 21.—Water basin in Gypsum Cañon.

occupy myself in collecting resin from the piñon pines, which are found in great abundance. One of the principal objects in making this climb was to get this resin, for the purpose of smearing our boats; but I have with me no means of carrying it down. The day is very hot, and my coat was left in camp, so I have no linings to tear out. Then it occurs to me to cut off the sleeve of my shirt, tie it up at one end, and in this little sack I collect about a gallon of pitch. After taking observations for altitude, I wander back on the rock, for an hour or two, when suddenly I notice that a storm is coming from the south. I seek a shelter in the rocks; but when the storm bursts, it comes down as a flood from the heavens, not with gentle drops at first, slowly increasing in quantity, but as if suddenly poured out. I am thoroughly drenched, and almost washed away. It lasts not more than half an hour, when the clouds sweep by to the north, and I have sunshine again.

In the mean time, I have discovered a better way of getting down, and I start for camp, making the greatest haste possible. On reaching the bottom of the side cañon, I find a thousand streams rolling down the cliffs on every side, carrying with them red sand; and these all unite in the cañon below, in one great stream of red mud.

Traveling as fast as I can run, I soon reach the foot of the stream, for the rain did not reach the lower end of the cañon, and the water is running down a dry bed of sand; and, although it comes in waves, several feet high and fifteen or twenty feet in width, the sands soak it up, and it is lost. But wave follows wave, and rolls along, and is swallowed up; and still the floods come on from above. I find that I can travel faster than the stream; so I hasten to camp, and tell the men there is a river coming down the cañon. We carry our camp equipage hastily from the bank, to where we think it will be above the water. Then we stand by, and see the river roll on to join the Colorado. Great quantities of gypsum are found at the bottom of the gorge; so we name it Gypsum Cañon.

July 27.—We have more rapids and falls until noon; then we come to a narrow place in the cañon, with vertical walls for several hundred feet, above which are steep steps and sloping rocks back to the summits. The river is very narrow, and we make our way with great care and much

9 COL

anxiety, hugging the wall on the left, and carefully examining the way before us.

Late in the afternoon, we pass to the left, around a sharp point, which is somewhat broken down near the foot, and discover a flock of mountain sheep on the rocks, more than a hundred feet above us. We quickly land in a cove, out of sight, and away go all the hunters with their guns, for the sheep have not discovered us. Soon, we hear firing, and those of us who have remained in the boats climb up to see what success the hunters have had. One sheep has been killed, and two of the men are still pursuing them. In a few minutes, we hear firing again, and the next moment down come the flock, clattering over the rocks, within twenty yards of us. One of the hunters seizes his gun, and brings a second sheep down, and the next minute the remainder of the flock is lost behind the rocks. We all give chase; but it is impossible to follow their tracks over the naked rock, and we see them no more. Where they went out of this rock walled cañon is a mystery, for we can see no way of escape. Doubtless, if we could spare the time for the search, we could find some gulch up which they ran.

We lash our prizes to the deck of one of the boats, and go on for a short distance; but fresh meat is too tempting for us, and we stop early to have a feast. And a feast it is! Two fine, young sheep. We care not for bread, or beans, or dried apples to night; coffee and mutton is all we ask.

July 28.—We make two portages this morning, one of them very long. During the afternoon we run a chute, more than half a mile in length, narrow and rapid. This chute has a floor of marble; the rocks dip in the direction in which we are going, and the fall of the stream conforms to the inclination of the beds; so we float on water that is gliding down an inclined plane. At the foot of the chute, the river turns sharply to the right, and the water rolls up against a rock which, from above, seems to stand directly athwart its course. As we approach it, we pull with all our power to the right, but it seems impossible to avoid being carried headlong against the cliff, and we are carried up high on the waves—not against the rocks, for the rebounding water strikes us, and we are beaten back, and pass on with safety, except that we get a good drenching.

After this, the walls suddenly close in, so that the cañon is narrower than we have ever known it. The water fills it from wall to wall, giving us no landing place at the foot of the cliff; the river is very swift, the cañon is very tortuous, so that we can see but a few hundred yards ahead; the walls tower over us, often overhanging so as to almost shut out the light. I stand on deck, watching with intense anxiety, lest this may lead us into some danger; but we glide along, with no obstruction, no falls, no rocks, and, in a mile and a half, emerge from the narrow gorge into a more open and broken portion of the cañon. Now that it is past, it seems a very simple thing. indeed to run through such a place, but the fear of what might be ahead made a deep impression on us.

At three o'clock we arrive at the foot of Cataract Cañon. Here a long cañon valley comes down from the east, and the river turns sharply to the west in a continuation of the line of the lateral valley. In the bend on the right, vast numbers of crags, and pinnacles, and tower shaped rocks are seen. We call it Mille Crag Bend.

And now we wheel into another cañon, on swift water, unobstructed by rocks. This new cañon is very narrow and very straight, with walls vertical below and terraced above. The brink of the cliff is 1,300 feet above the water, where we enter it, but the rocks dip to the west, and, as the course of the cañon is in that direction, the walls are seen to slowly decrease in altitude. Floating down this narrow channel, and looking out through the cañon crevice away in the distance, the river is seen to turn again to the left, and beyond this point, away many miles, a great mountain is seen. Still floating down, we see other mountains, now to the right, now on the left, until a great mountain range is unfolded to view. We name this Narrow Cañon, and it terminates at the bend of the river below.

As we go down to this point, we discover the mouth of a stream, which enters from the right. Into this our little boat is turned. One of the men in the boat following, seeing what we have done, shouts to Dunn, asking if it is a trout-stream. Dunn replies, much disgusted, that it is "a dirty devil," and by this name the river is to be known hereafter. The water is exceedingly muddy, and has an unpleasant odor.

Some of us go out for half a mile, and climb a butte to the north. The course of the Dirty Devil River can be traced for many miles. It comes down through a very narrow cañon, and beyond it, to the southwest, there is a long line of cliffs, with a broad terrace, or bench, between it and the brink of the cañon, and beyond these cliffs is situated the range of mountains seen as we came down Narrow Cañon.

Looking up the Colorado, the chasm through which it runs can be seen, but we cannot look down on its waters. The whole country is a region of naked rock, of many colors, with cliffs and buttes about us, and towering mountains in the distance.

July 29.—We enter a cañon to-day, with low, red walls. A short distance below its head we discover the ruins of an old building, on the left wall. There is a narrow plain between the river and the wall just here, and on the brink of a rock two hundred feet high stands this old house. Its walls are of stone, laid in mortar, with much regularity. It was probably built three stories high; the lower story is yet almost intact; the second is much broken down, and scarcely anything is left of the third. Great quantities of flint chips are found on the rocks near by, and many arrow heads, some perfect, others broken; and fragments of pottery are strewn about in great profusion. On the face of the cliff, under the building, and along down the river, for two or three hundred yards, there are many etchings. Two hours are given to the examination of these interesting ruins, then we run down fifteen miles farther, and discover another group. The principal building was situated on the summit of the hill. A part of the walls are standing, to the height of eight or ten feet, and the mortar yet remains, in some places. The house was in the shape of an **L**, with five rooms on the ground floor, one in the angle, and two in each extension. In the space in the angle, there is a deep excavation. From what we know of the people in the province of Tusayan, who are, doubtless, of the same race as the former inhabitants of these ruins, we conclude that this was a "kiva," or underground chamber, in which their religious ceremonies were performed.

We leave these ruins, and run down two or three miles, and go into camp about mid-afternoon. And now I climb the wall and go out into the back country for a walk.

The sandstone, through which the cañon is cut, is red and homogeneous, being the same as that through which Labyrinth Cañon runs. The smooth, naked, rock stretches out on either side of the river for many miles, but curiously carved mounds and cones are scattered everywhere, and deep holes are worn out. Many of these pockets are filled with water. In one of these holes, or wells, twenty feet deep, I find a tree growing. The excavation is so narrow that I can step from its brink to a limb on the tree, and descend to the bottom of the well down a growing ladder. Many of these pockets are pot-holes, being found in the courses of little rills, or brooks, that run during the rains which occasionally fall in this region; and often a few harder rocks, which evidently assisted in their excavation, can be found in their bottoms. Others, which are shallower, are not so easily explained. Perhaps they are found where softer spots existed in the sandstone, places that yielded more readily to atmospheric degradation, and where the loose sands were carried away by the winds.

Just before sundown, I attempt to climb a rounded eminence, from which I hope to obtain a good outlook on the surrounding country. It is formed of smooth mounds, piled one above another. Up these I climb, winding here and there, to find a practicable way, until near the summit they become too steep for me to proceed. I search about, a few minutes, for a more easy way, when I am surprised at finding a stairway, evidently cut in the rock by hands. At one place, where there is a vertical wall of ten or twelve feet, I find an old, ricketty ladder. It may be that this was a watch-tower of that ancient people, whose homes we have found in ruins. On many of the tributaries of the Colorado I have heretofore examined their deserted dwellings. Those that show evidences of being built during the latter part of their occupation of the country, are, usually, placed on the most inaccessible cliffs. Sometimes, the mouths of caves have been walled across, and there are many other evidences to show their anxiety to secure defensible positions. Probably the nomadic tribes were sweeping down upon them, and they resorted to these cliffs and cañons for safety. It is not unreasonable to suppose that this orange mound was used as a watch-tower. Here I stand, where these now lost people stood centuries ago, and look over this strange country. I gaze off to great mountains, in the northwest, which are slowly covered by the night until they are lost, and then I return to camp. It is no easy task to find my way down the wall in the darkness, and I clamber about until it is nearly midnight, before I arrive.

July 30.—We make good progress to day, as the water, though smooth, is swift. Sometimes, the cañon walls are vertical to the top; sometimes, they are vertical below, and have a mound covered slope above; in other places, the slope, with its mounds, comes down to the water's edge.

Still proceeding on our way, we find the orange sandstone is cut in two by a group of firm, calcareous strata, and the lower bed is underlaid by soft gypsiferous shales. Sometimes, the upper homogeneous bed is a smooth, vertical wall, but usually it is carved with mounds, with gently meandering valley lines. The lower bed, yielding to gravity, as the softer shales below work out into the river, breaks into angular surfaces, often having a columnar appearance. One could almost imagine that the walls had been carved with a purpose, to represent giant architectural forms.

In the deep recesses of the walls, we find springs, with mosses and ferns on the moistened sandstone.

July 31.—We have a cool, pleasant ride to day, through this part of the cañon. The walls are steadily increasing in altitude, the curves are gentle, and often the river sweeps by an arc of vertical wall, smooth and unbroken, and then by a curve that is variegated by royal arches, mossy alcoves, deep, beautiful glens, and painted grottos.

Soon after dinner, we discover the mouth of the San Juan, where we camp. The remainder of the afternoon is given to hunting some way by which we can climb out of the cañon; but it ends in failure.

August 1.—We drop down two miles this morning, and go into camp again. There is a low, willow covered strip of land along the walls on the east. Across this we walk, to explore an alcove which we see from the river. On entering, we find a little grove of box-elder and cottonwood trees; and, turning to the right, we find ourselves in a vast chamber, carved out of the rock. At the upper end there is a clear, deep pool of water, bordered with verdure. Standing by the side of this, we can see the grove at the entrance. The chamber is more than two hundred feet high, five hundred feet long, and two hundred feet wide. Through the ceiling, and on through the rocks for a thousand feet above, there is a narrow, winding skylight; and

Figure 22.—Gleu Cañon.

this is all carved out by a little stream, which only runs during the few showers that fall now and then in this arid country. The waters from the bare rocks back of the cañon, gathering rapidly into a small channel, have eroded a deep side cañon, through which they run, until they fall into the farther end of this chamber. The rock at the ceiling is hard, the rock below, very soft and friable; and, having cut through the upper harder portion down into the lower and softer, the stream has washed out these friable sandstones; and thus the chamber has been excavated.

Here we bring our camp. When "Old Shady" sings us a song at night, we are pleased to find that this hollow in the rock is filled with sweet sounds. It was doubtless made for an academy of music by its storm born architect; so we name it Music Temple.

August 2.—We still keep our camp in Music Temple to-day.

I wish to obtain a view of the adjacent country, if possible; so, early in the morning, the men take me across the river, and I pass along by the foot of the cliff half a mile up stream, and then climb first up broken ledges, then two or three hundred yards up a smooth, sloping rock, and then pass out on a narrow ridge. Still, I find I have not attained an altitude from which I can overlook the region outside of the cañon; and so I descend into a little gulch, and climb again to a higher ridge, all the way along naked sandstone, and at last I reach a point of commanding view. I can look several miles up the San Juan, and a long distance up the Colorado; and away to the northwest I can see the Henry Mountains; to the northeast, the Sierra La Sal; to the southeast, unknown mountains; and to the southwest, the meandering of the cañon. Then I return to the bank of the river.

We sleep again in Music Temple.

August 3.—Start early this morning. The features of this cañon are greatly diversified. Still vertical walls at times. These are usually found to stand above great curves. The river, sweeping around these bends, undermines the cliffs in places. Sometimes, the rocks are overhanging; in other curves, curious, narrow glens are found. Through these we climb, by a rough stairway, perhaps several hundred feet, to where a spring bursts out from under an overhanging cliff, and where cottonwoods and willows stand, while, along the curves of the brooklet, oaks grow, and other rich vegetation is seen, in marked contrast to the general appearance of naked rock. We call these Oak Glens.

Other wonderful features are the many side cañons or gorges that we pass. Sometimes, we stop to explore these for a short distance. In some places, their walls are much nearer each other above than below, so that they look somewhat like caves or chambers in the rocks. Usually, in going up such a gorge, we find beautiful vegetation; but our way is often cut off by deep basins, or pot-holes, as they are called.

On the walls, and back many miles into the country, numbers of monument shaped buttes are observed. So we have a curious *ensemble* of wonderful features—carved walls, royal arches, glens, alcove gulches, mounds, and monuments. From which of these features shall we select a name? We decide to call it Glen Cañon.

Past these towering monuments, past these mounded billows of orange sandstone, past these oak set glens, past these fern decked alcoves, past these mural curves, we glide hour after hour, stopping now and then, as our attention is arrested by some new wonder, until we reach a point which is historic.

In the year 1776, Father Escalante, a Spanish priest, made an expedition from Santa Fé to the northwest, crossing the Grand and Green, and then passing down along the Wasatch Mountains and the southern plateaus, until he reached the Rio Virgen. His intention was to cross to the Mission of Monterey; but, from information received from the Indians, he decided that the route was impracticable. Not wishing to return to Santa Fé over the circuitous route by which he had just traveled, he attempted to go by one more direct, and which led him across the Colorado, at a point known as *El vado de los Padres*. From the description which we have read, we are enabled to determine the place. A little stream comes down through a very narrow side cañon from the west. It was down this that he came, and our boats are lying at the point where the ford crosses. A well beaten Indian trail is seen here yet. Between the cliff and the river there is a little meadow. The ashes of many camp fires are seen, and the bones of numbers of cattle are bleaching on the grass. For several years the Navajos have raided on the Mormons that dwell in the valleys to the west, and they doubtless cross frequently at this ford with their stolen cattle.

Figure 23.—Side Cañon.

Figure 24.—Island Monument in Glen Cañon.

August 4.—To day the walls grow higher, and the cañon much narrower.   Monuments are still seen on either side; beautiful glens, and alcoves,
and gorges, and side cañons are yet found.   After dinner, we find the river
making a sudden turn to the northwest, and the whole character of the
cañon changed.   The walls are many hundreds of feet higher, and the rocks
are chiefly variegated shales of beautiful colors—creamy orange above, then
bright vermilion, and below, purple and chocolate beds, with green and
yellow sands.   We run four miles through this, in a direction a little to the
west of north; wheel again to the west, and pass into a portion of the cañon
where the characteristics are more like those above the bend.   At night we
stop at the mouth of a creek coming in from the right, and suppose it to be
the Paria, which was described to me last year by a Mormon missionary.

Here the cañon terminates abruptly in a line of cliffs, which stretches
from either side across the river.

August 5.—With some feeling of anxiety, we enter a new cañon this
morning.   We have learned to closely observe the texture of the rock.   In
softer strata, we have a quiet river; in harder, we find rapids and falls.
Below us are the limestones and hard sandstones, which we found in Cataract Cañon.   This bodes toil and danger.   Besides the texture of the rocks,
there is another condition which affects the character of the channel, as we
have found by experience.   Where the strata are horizontal, the river is often
quiet; but, even though it may be very swift in places, no great obstacles
are found.   Where the rocks incline in the direction traveled, the river usually
sweeps with great velocity, but still we have few rapids and falls.   But
where the rocks dip up stream, and the river cuts obliquely across the
upturned formations, harder strata above, and softer below, we have rapids
and falls.   Into hard rocks, and into rocks dipping up stream, we pass this
morning, and start on a long, rocky, mad rapid.   On the left there is a
vertical rock, and down by this cliff and around to the left we glide, just
tossed enough by the waves to appreciate the rate at which we are traveling.

The cañon is narrow, with vertical walls, which gradually grow higher.
More rapids and falls are found.   We come to one with a drop of sixteen
feet, around which we make a portage, and then stop for dinner.

-Then a run of two miles, and another portage, long and difficult; then we camp for the night, on a bank of sand.

August 6.—Cañon walls, still higher and higher, as we go down through strata. There is a steep talus at the foot of the cliff, and, in some places, the upper parts of the walls are terraced.

About ten o'clock we come to a place where the river occupies the entire channel, and the walls are vertical from the water's edge. We see a fall below, and row up against the cliff. There is a little shelf, or rather a horizontal crevice, a few feet over our heads. One man stands on the deck of the boat, another climbs on his shoulders, and then into the crevice. Then we pass him a line, and two or three others, with myself, follow; then we pass along the crevice until it becomes a shelf, as the upper part, or roof, is broken off. On this we walk for a short distance, slowly climbing all the way, until we reach a point where the shelf is broken off, and we can pass no farther. Then we go back to the boat, cross the stream, and get some logs that have lodged in the rocks, bring them to our side, pass them along the crevice and shelf, and bridge over the broken place. Then we go on to a point over the falls, but do not obtain a satisfactory view. Then we climb out to the top of the wall, and walk along to find a point below the fall, from which it can be seen. From this point it seems possible to let down our boats, with lines, to the head of the rapids, and then make a portage; so we return, row down by the side of the cliff, as far as we dare, and fasten one of the boats to a rock. Then we let down another boat to the end of its line beyond the first, and the third boat to the end of its line below the second, which brings it to the head of the fall, and under an overhanging rock. Then the upper boat, in obedience to a signal, lets go; we pull in the line, and catch the nearest boat as it comes, and then the last. Then we make a portage, and go on.

We go into camp early this afternoon, at a place where it seems possible to climb out, and the evening is spent in "making observations for time."

August 7.—The almanac tells us that we are to have an eclipse of the sun to-day, so Captain Powell and myself start early, taking our instruments with us, for the purpose of making observations on the eclipse, to determine our longitude. Arriving at the summit, after four hours' hard climbing, to

Figure 25.—Noon-day rest in Marble Cañon.

attain 2,300 feet in height, we hurriedly build a platform of rocks, on which to place our instruments, and quietly wait for the eclipse; but clouds come on, and rain falls, and sun and moon are obscured.

Much disappointed, we start on our return to camp, but it is late, and the clouds make the night very dark. Still we feel our way down among the rocks with great care, for two or three hours, though making slow progress indeed. At last we lose our way, and dare proceed no farther. The rain comes down in torrents, and we can find no shelter. We can neither climb up nor go down, and in the darkness dare not move about, but sit and "weather out" the night.

August 8.—Daylight comes, after a long, oh! how long a night, and we soon reach camp.

After breakfast we start again, and make two portages during the forenoon.

The limestone of this cañon is often polished, and makes a beautiful marble. Sometimes the rocks are of many colors—white, gray, pink, and purple, with saffron tints. It is with very great labor that we make progress, meeting with many obstructions, running rapids, letting down our boats with lines, from rock to rock, and sometimes carrying boats and cargoes around bad places. We camp at night, just after a hard portage, under an overhanging wall, glad to find shelter from the rain. We have to search for some time to find a few sticks of driftwood, just sufficient to boil a cup of coffee.

The water sweeps rapidly in this elbow of river, and has cut its way under the rock, excavating a vast half circular chamber, which, if utilized for a theater, would give sitting to fifty thousand people. Objections might be raised against it, from the fact that, at high water, the floor is covered with a raging flood.

August 9.—And now, the scenery is on a grand scale. The walls of the cañon, 2,500 feet high, are of marble, of many beautiful colors, and often polished below by the waves, or far up the sides, where showers have washed the sands over the cliffs.

At one place I have a walk, for more than a mile, on a marble pavement, all polished and fretted with strange devices, and embossed in a thousand fantastic patterns. Through a cleft in the wall the sun shines on this pavement, which gleams in iridescent beauty.

I pass up into the cleft. It is very narrow, with a succession of pools standing at higher levels as I go back. The water in these pools is clear and cool, coming down from springs. Then I return to the pavement, which is but a terrace or bench, over which the river runs at its flood, but left bare at present. Along the pavement, in many places, are basins of clear water, in strange contrast to the red mud of the river. At length I come to the end of this marble terrace, and take again to the boat.

Riding down a short distance, a beautiful view is presented. The river turns sharply to the east, and seems inclosed by a wall, set with a million brilliant gems. What can it mean? Every eye is engaged, every one wonders. On coming nearer, we find fountains bursting from the rock, high overhead, and the spray in the sunshine forms the gems which bedeck the wall. The rocks below the fountain are covered with mosses, and ferns, and many beautiful flowering plants. We name it Vasey's Paradise, in honor of the botanist who traveled with us last year.

We pass many side cañons to day, that are dark, gloomy passages, back into the heart of the rocks that form the plateau through which this cañon is cut.

It rains again this afternoon. Scarcely do the first drops fall, when little rills run down the walls. As the storm comes on, the little rills increase in size, until great streams are formed. Although the walls of the cañon are chiefly limestone, the adjacent country is of red sandstone; and now the waters, loaded with these sands, come down in rivers of bright red mud, leaping over the walls in innumerable cascades. It is plain now how these walls are polished in many places.

At last, the storm ceases, and we go on. We have cut through the sandstones and limestones met in the upper part of the cañon, and through one great bed of marble a thousand feet in thickness. In this, great numbers of caves are hollowed out, and carvings are seen, which suggest architectural forms, though on a scale so grand that architectural terms belittle them. As this great bed forms a distinctive feature of the cañon, we call it Marble Cañon.

Figure 26.—Marble Cañon.

It is a peculiar feature of these walls, that many projections are set out into the river, as if the wall was buttressed for support. The walls themselves are half a mile high, and these buttresses are on a corresponding scale, jutting into the river scores of feet. In the recesses between these projections there are quiet bays, except at the foot of a rapid, when they are dancing eddies or whirlpools. Sometimes these alcoves have caves at the back, giving them the appearance of great depth. Then other caves are seen above, forming vast, dome shaped chambers. The walls, and buttresses, and chambers are all of marble.

The river is now quiet; the cañon wider. Above, when the river is at its flood, the waters gorge up, so that the difference between high and low water mark is often fifty or even seventy feet; but here, high-water mark is not more than twenty feet above the present stage of the river. Sometimes there is a narrow flood plain between the water and the wall.

Here we first discover *mesquite* shrubs, or small trees, with finely divided leaves and pods, somewhat like the locust

August 10.—Walls still higher; water, swift again. We pass several broad, ragged cañons on our right, and up through these we catch glimpses of a forest clad plateau, miles away to the west.

At two o'clock, we reach the mouth of the Colorado Chiquito. This stream enters through a cañon, on a scale quite as grand as that of the Colorado itself. It is a very small river, and exceedingly muddy and salt. I walk up the stream three or four miles, this afternoon, crossing and recrossing where I can easily wade it. Then I climb several hundred feet at one place, and can see up the chasm, through which the river runs, for several miles. On my way back, I kill two rattlesnakes, and find, on my arrival, that another has been killed just at camp.

August 11.—We remain at this point to day for the purpose of determining the latitude and longitude, measuring the height of the walls, drying our rations, and repairing our boats.

Captain Powell, early in the morning, takes a barometer, and goes out to climb a point between the two rivers.

I walk down the gorge to the left at the foot of the cliff, climb to a bench, and discover a trail, deeply worn in the rock. Where it crosses the side gulches, in some places, steps have been cut. I can see no evidence of its having been traveled for a long time. It was doubtless a path used by the people who inhabited this country anterior to the present Indian races—the people who built the communal houses, of which mention has been made.

I return to camp about three o'clock, and find that some of the men have discovered ruins, and many fragments of pottery; also, etchings and hieroglyphics on the rocks.

We find, to night, on comparing the readings of the barometers, that the walls are about three thousand feet high—more than half a mile—an altitude difficult to appreciate from a mere statement of feet. The ascent is made, not by a slope such as is usually found in climbing a mountain, but is much more abrupt—often vertical for many hundreds of feet—so that the impression is that we are at great depths; and we look up to see but a little patch of sky.

Between the two streams, above the Colorado Chiquito, in some places the rocks are broken and shelving for six or seven hundred feet; then there is a sloping terrace, which can only be climbed by finding some way up a gulch; then, another terrace, and back, still another cliff. The summit of the cliff is three thousand feet above the river, as our barometers attest.

Our camp is below the Colorado Chiquito, and on the eastern side of the cañon.

August 12.—The rocks above camp are rust colored sandstones and conglomerates. Some are very hard; others quite soft. These all lie nearly horizontal, and the beds of softer material have been washed out, and left the harder, thus forming a series of shelves. Long lines of these are seen, of varying thickness, from one or two to twenty or thirty feet, and the spaces between have the same variability. This morning, I spend two or three hours in climbing among these shelves, and then I pass above them, and go up a long slope, to the foot of the cliff, and try to discover some way by which I can reach the top of the wall; but I find my progress cut off by an amphitheater. Then, I wander away around to the left, up a little gulch, and along benches, and climb, from time to time, until I reach an altitude of nearly two thousand feet, and can get no higher. From this point, I can look off to the west, up side cañons of the Colorado, and see the edge of a great plateau, from which streams run down into the Colorado, and deep gulches, in the escarpment which faces us, continued by cañons, ragged and flaring, and set with cliffs and towering crags, down to the river. I can see far up Marble Cañon, to long lines of chocolate colored cliffs, and above these, the Vermilion Cliffs. I can see, also, up the Colorado Chiquito, through a very ragged and broken cañon, with sharp salients set out from the walls on either side, their points overlapping, so that a huge tooth of marble, on one side, seems to be set between two teeth on the opposite; and I can also get glimpses of walls, standing away back from the river, while over my head are mural escarpments, not possible to be scaled.

Cataract Cañon is forty one miles long. The walls are 1,300 feet high at its head, and they gradually increase in altitude to a point about halfway down, where they are 2,700 feet, and then decrease to 1,300 feet at the foot. Narrow Cañon is nine and a half miles long, with walls 1,300 feet in height at the head, and coming down to the water at the foot.

There is very little vegetation in this cañon, or in the adjacent country. Just at the junction of the Grand and Green, there are a number of hackberry trees; and along the entire length of Cataract Cañon, the high-water line is marked by scattered trees of the same species. A few nut-pines and cedars are found, and occasionally a red-bud or judas tree; but the general aspect of the cañons, and of the adjacent country, is that of naked rock.

The distance through Glen Cañon is 149 miles. Its walls vary from two or three hundred to sixteen hundred feet. Marble Cañon is 65½ miles long. At its head, it is 200 feet deep, and steadily increases in depth to its foot, where its walls are 3,500 feet high.

CHAPTER VIII.

August 13.—We are now ready to start on our way down the Great Unknown. Our boats, tied to a common stake, are chafing each other, as they are tossed by the fretful river. They ride high and buoyant, for their loads are lighter than we could desire. We have but a month's rations remaining. The flour has been resifted through the mosquito net sieve; the spoiled bacon has been dried, and the worst of it boiled; the few pounds of dried apples have been spread in the sun, and reshrunken to their normal bulk; the sugar has all melted, and gone on its way down the river; but we have a large sack of coffee. The lighting of the boats has this advantage: they will ride the waves better, and we shall have but little to carry when we make a portage.

We are three quarters of a mile in the depths of the earth, and the great river shrinks into insignificance, as it dashes its angry waves against the walls and cliffs, that rise to the world above; they are but puny ripples, and we but pigmies, running up and down the sands, or lost among the boulders.

We have an unknown distance yet to run; an unknown river yet to explore. What falls there are, we know not; what rocks beset the channel, we know not; what walls rise over the river, we know not. Ah, well! we may conjecture many things. The men talk as cheerfully as ever; jests are bandied about freely this morning; but to me the cheer is somber and the jests are ghastly.

With some eagerness, and some anxiety, and some misgiving, we enter the cañon below, and are carried along by the swift water through walls which rise from its very edge. They have the same structure as we noticed yesterday—tiers of irregular shelves below, and, above these, steep slopes to the foot of marble cliffs. We run six miles in a little more than half an

Figure 27.—View from camp at the mouth of the Little Colorado, looking west.

hour, and emerge into a more open portion of the cañon, where high hills and ledges of rock intervene between the river and the distant walls. Just at the head of this open place the river runs across a dike; that is, a fissure in the rocks, open to depths below, has been filled with eruptive matter, and this, on cooling, was harder than the rocks through which the crevice was made, and, when these were washed away, the harder volcanic matter remained as a wall, and the river has cut a gate-way through it several hundred feet high, and as many wide. As it crosses the wall, there is a fall below, and a bad rapid, filled with boulders of trap; so we stop to make a portage. Then on we go, gliding by hills and ledges, with distant walls in view; sweeping past sharp angles of rock; stopping at a few points to examine rapids, which we find can be run, until we have made another five miles, when we land for dinner.

Then we let down with lines, over a long rapid, and start again. Once more the walls close in, and we find ourselves in a narrow gorge, the water again filling the channel, and very swift. With great care, and constant watchfulness, we proceed, making about four miles this afternoon, and camp in a cave.

August 14.—At daybreak we walk down the bank of the river, on a little sandy beach, to take a view of a new feature in the cañon. Heretofore, hard rocks have given us bad river; soft rocks, smooth water; and a series of rocks harder than any we have experienced sets in. The river enters the granite !*

We can see but a little way into the granite gorge, but it looks threatening.

After breakfast we enter on the waves. At the very introduction, it inspires awe. The cañon is narrower than we have ever before seen it; the water is swifter; there are but few broken rocks in the channel; but the walls are set, on either side, with pinnacles and crags; and sharp, angular buttresses, bristling with wind and wave polished spires, extend far out into the river.

Ledges of rocks jut into the stream, their tops sometimes just below

* Geologists would call these rocks metamorphic crystalline schists, with dikes and beds of granite, but we will use the popular name for the whole series—granite.

the surface, sometimes rising few or many feet above; and island ledges, and island pinnacles, and island towers break the swift course of the stream into chutes, and eddies, and whirlpools. We soon reach a place where a creek comes in from the left, and just below, the channel is choked with boulders, which have washed down this lateral cañon and formed a dam, over which there is a fall of thirty or forty feet; but on the boulders we can get foot-hold, and we make a portage.

Three more such dams are found. Over one we make a portage; at the other two we find chutes, through which we can run.

As we proceed, the granite rises higher, until nearly a thousand feet of the lower part of the walls are composed of this rock.

About eleven o'clock we hear a great roar ahead, and approach it very cautiously. The sound grows louder and louder as we run, and at last we find ourselves above a long, broken fall, with ledges and pinnacles of rock obstructing the river. There is a descent of, perhaps, seventy five or eighty feet in a third of a mile, and the rushing waters break into great waves on the rocks, and lash themselves into a mad, white foam. We can land just above, but there is no foot-hold on either side by which we can make a portage. It is nearly a thousand feet to the top of the granite, so it will be impossible to carry our boats around, though we can climb to the summit up a side gulch, and, passing along a mile or two, can descend to the river. This we find on examination; but such a portage would be impracticable for us, and we must run the rapid, or abandon the river. There is no hesitation. We step into our boats, push off and away we go, first on smooth but swift water, then we strike a glassy wave, and ride to its top, down again into the trough, up again on a higher wave, and down and up on waves higher and still higher, until we strike one just as it curls back, and a breaker rolls over our little boat. Still, on we speed, shooting past projecting rocks, till the little boat is caught in a whirlpool, and spun around several times. At last we pull out again into the stream, and now the other boats have passed us. The open compartment of the "Emma Dean" is filled with water, and every breaker rolls over us. Hurled back from a rock, now on this side, now on that, we are carried into an eddy, in which we struggle for a few minutes, and are then out again, the breakers still rolling over us. Our boat

Figure 28.—Running a rapid.

is unmanageable, but she cannot sink, and we drift down another hundred yards, through breakers; how, we scarcely know. We find the other boats have turned into an eddy at the foot of the fall, and are waiting to catch us as we come, for the men have seen that our boat is swamped. They push out as we come near, and pull us in against the wall. We bail our boat, and on we go again.

The walls, now, are more than a mile in height—a vertical distance difficult to appreciate. Stand on the south steps of the Treasury building, in Washington, and look down Pennsylvania Avenue to the Capitol Park, and measure this distance overhead, and imagine cliffs to extend to that altitude, and you will understand what I mean; or, stand at Canal street, in New York, and look up Broadway to Grace Church, and you have about the distance; or, stand at Lake street bridge, in Chicago, and look down to the Central Depot, and you have it again.

A thousand feet of this is up through granite crags, then steep slopes and perpendicular cliffs rise, one above another, to the summit. The gorge is black and narrow below, red and gray and flaring above, with crags and angular projections on the walls, which, cut in many places by side cañons, seem to be a vast wilderness of rocks. Down in these grand, gloomy depths we glide, ever listening, for the mad waters keep up their roar; ever watching, ever peering ahead, for the narrow cañon is winding, and the river is closed in so that we can see but a few hundred yards, and what there may be below we know not; but we listen for falls, and watch for rocks, or stop now and then, in the bay of a recess, to admire the gigantic scenery. And ever, as we go, there is some new pinnacle or tower, some crag or peak, some distant view of the upper plateau, some strange shaped rock, or some deep, narrow side cañon. Then we come to another broken fall, which appears more difficult than the one we ran this morning.

A small creek comes in on the right, and the first fall of the water is over boulders, which have been carried down by this lateral stream. We land at its mouth, and stop for an hour or two to examine the fall. It seems possible to let down with lines, at least a part of the way, from point to point, along the right hand wall. So we make a portage over the first rocks, and find footing on some boulders below. Then we let down one of the boats to the end of her line, when she reaches a corner of the projecting rock, to which one of the men clings, and steadies her, while I examine an eddy below. I think we can pass the other boats down by us, and catch them in the eddy. This is soon done and the men in the boats in the eddy pull us to their side. On the shore of this little eddy there is about two feet of gravel beach above the water. Standing on this beach, some of the men take the line of the little boat and let it drift down against another projecting angle. Here is a little shelf, on which a man from my boat climbs, and a shorter line is passed to him, and he fastens the boat to the side of the cliff. Then the second one is let down, bringing the line of the third. When the second boat is tied up, the two men standing on the beach above spring into the last boat, which is pulled up alongside of ours. Then we let down the boats, for twenty five or thirty yards, by walking along the shelf, landing them again in the mouth of a side cañon. Just below this there is another pile of boulders, over which we make another portage. From the foot of these rocks we can climb to another shelf, forty or fifty feet above the water.

On this bench we camp for the night. We find a few sticks, which have lodged in the rocks. It is raining hard, and we have no shelter, but kindle a fire and have our supper. We sit on the rocks all night, wrapped in our ponchos, getting what sleep we can.

August 15.—This morning we find we can let down for three or four hundred yards, and it is managed in this way: We pass along the wall, by climbing from projecting point to point, sometimes near the water's edge, at other places fifty or sixty feet above, and hold the boat with a line, while two men remain aboard, and prevent her from being dashed against the rocks, and keep the line from getting caught on the wall. In two hours we have brought them all down, as far as it is possible, in this way. A few yards below, the river strikes with great violence against a projecting rock, and our boats are pulled up in a little bay above. We must now manage to pull out of this, and clear the point below. The little boat is held by the bow obliquely up the stream. We jump in, and pull out only a few strokes, and sweep clear of the dangerous rock. The other boats follow in the same manner, and the rapid is passed.

It is not easy to describe the labor of such navigation. We must prevent the waves from dashing the boats against the cliffs. Sometimes, where
the river is swift, we must put a bight of rope about a rock, to prevent her
being snatched from us by a wave; but where the plunge is too great, or
the chute too swift, we must let her leap, and catch her below, or the under-
tow will drag her under the falling water, and she sinks. Where we wish
to run her out a little way from shore, through a channel between rocks,
we first throw in little sticks of drift wood, and watch their course, to see
where we must steer, so that she will pass the channel in safety. And so we
hold, and let go, and pull, and lift, and ward, among rocks, around rocks,
and over rocks.

And now we go on through this solemn, mysterious way. The river
is very deep, the cañon very narrow, and still obstructed, so that there is no
steady flow of the stream; but the waters wheel, and roll, and boil, and we
are scarcely able to determine where we can go. Now, the boat is carried
to the right, perhaps close to the wall; again, she is shot into the stream,
and perhaps is dragged over to the other side, where, caught in a whirlpool,
she spins about. We can neither land nor run as we please. The boats are
entirely unmanageable; no order in their running can be preserved; now
one, now another, is ahead, each crew laboring for its own preservation. In
such a place we come to another rapid. Two of the boats run it perforce.
One succeeds in landing, but there is no foot-hold by which to make a portage, and she is pushed out again into the stream. The next minute a great
reflex wave fills the open compartment; she is water-logged, and drifts
unmanageable. Breaker after breaker rolls over her, and one capsizes her.
The men are thrown out; but they cling to the boat, and she drifts down
some distance, alongside of us, and we are able to catch her. She is soon
bailed out, and the men are aboard once more; but the oars are lost, so a
pair from the "Emma Dean" is spared. Then for two miles we find smooth
water.

Clouds are playing in the cañon to day. Sometimes they roll down
in great masses, filling the gorge with gloom; sometimes they hang above,
from wall to wall, and cover the cañon with a roof of impending storm;
and we can peer long distances up and down this cañon corridor, with its

cloud roof overhead, its walls of black granite, and its river bright with the sheen of broken waters. Then, a gust of wind sweeps down a side gulch, and, making a rift in the clouds, reveals the blue heavens, and a stream of sunlight pours in. Then, the clouds drift away into the distance, and hang around crags, and peaks, and pinnacles, and towers, and walls, and cover them with a mantle, that lifts from time to time, and sets them all in sharp relief. Then, baby clouds creep out of side cañons, glide around points, and creep back again, into more distant gorges. Then, clouds, set in strata, across the cañon, with intervening vista views, to cliffs and rocks beyond The clouds are children of the heavens, and when they play among the rocks, they lift them to the region above.

It rains! Rapidly little rills are formed above, and these soon grow into brooks, and the brooks grow into creeks, and tumble over the walls in innumerable cascades, adding their wild music to the roar of the river. When the rain ceases, the rills, brooks, and creeks run dry. The waters that fall, during a rain, on these steep rocks, are gathered at once into the river; they could scarcely be poured in more suddenly, if some vast spout ran from the clouds to the stream itself. When a storm bursts over the cañon, a side gulch is dangerous, for a sudden flood may come, and the impouring waters will raise the river, so as to hide the rocks before your eyes.

Early in the afternoon, we discover a stream, entering from the north, a clear, beautiful creek, coming down through a gorgeous red cañon. We land, and camp on a sand beach, above its mouth, under a great, overspreading tree, with willow shaped leaves.

August 16.—We must dry our rations again to day, and make oars

The Colorado is never a clear stream, but for the past three or four days it has been raining much of the time, and the floods, which are poured over the walls, have brought down great quantities of mud, making it exceedingly turbid now. The little affluent, which we have discovered here, is a clear, beautiful creek, or river, as it would be termed in this western country, where streams are not abundant. We have named one stream, away above, in honor of the great chief of the "Bad Angels," and, as this is in beautiful contrast to that, we conclude to name it "Bright Angel."

Early in the morning, the whole party starts up to explore the Bright

Figure 29.—Granite Walls.

Angel River, with the special purpose of seeking timber, from which to make oars. A couple of miles above, we find a large pine log, which has been floated down from the plateau, probably from an altitude of more than six thousand feet, but not many miles back. On its way, it must have passed over many cataracts and falls, for it bears scars in evidence of the rough usage which it has received. The men roll it on skids, and the work of sawing oars is commenced.

This stream heads away back, under a line of abrupt cliffs, that terminates the plateau, and tumbles down more than four thousand feet in the first mile or two of its course; then runs through a deep, narrow cañon, until it reaches the river.

Late in the afternoon I return, and go up a little gulch, just above this creek, about two hundred yards from camp, and discover the ruins of two or three old houses, which were originally of stone, laid in mortar. Only the foundations are left, but irregular blocks, of which the houses were constructed, lie scattered about. In one room I find an old mealing stone, deeply worn, as if it had been much used. A great deal of pottery is strewn around, and old trails, which in some places are deeply worn into the rocks, are seen.

It is ever a source of wonder to us why these ancient people sought such inaccessible places for their homes. They were, doubtless, an agricultural race, but there are no lands here, of any considerable extent, that they could have cultivated. To the west of Oraiby, one of the towns in the "Province of Tusayan," in Northern Arizona, the inhabitants have actually built little terraces along the face of the cliff, where a spring gushes out, and thus made their sites for gardens. It is possible that the ancient inhabitants of this place made their agricultural lands in the same way. But why should they seek such spots? Surely, the country was not so crowded with population as to demand the utilization of so barren a region. The only solution of the problem suggested is this: We know that, for a century or two after the settlement of Mexico, many expeditions were sent into the country, now comprised in Arizona and New Mexico, for the purpose of bringing the town building people under the dominion of the Spanish government. Many of their villages were destroyed, and the inhabitants fled to regions at that time unknown; and there are traditions, among the people who inhabit the *pueblos* that still remain, that the cañons were these unknown lands. Maybe these buildings were erected at that time; sure it is that they have a much more modern appearance than the ruins scattered over Nevada, Utah, Colorado, Arizona, and New Mexico. Those old Spanish conquerors had a monstrous greed for gold, and a wonderful lust for saving souls. Treasures they must have; if not on earth, why, then, in heaven; and when they failed to find heathen temples, bedecked with silver, they propitiated Heaven by seizing the heathen themselves. There is yet extant a copy of a record, made by a heathen artist, to express his conception of the demands of the conquerors. In one part of the picture we have a lake, and near by stands a priest pouring water on the head of a native. On the other side, a poor Indian has a cord about his throat. Lines run from these two groups, to a central figure, a man with beard, and full Spanish panoply. The interpretation of the picture writing is this: "Be baptized, as this saved heathen; or be hanged, as that damned heathen." Doubtless, some of these people preferred a third alternative, and, rather than be baptized or hanged, they chose to be imprisoned within these cañon walls.

August 17.—Our rations are still spoiling; the bacon is so badly injured that we are compelled to throw it away. By an accident, this morning, the saleratus is lost overboard. We have now only musty flour sufficient for ten days, a few dried apples, but plenty of coffee. We must make all haste possible. If we meet with difficulties, as we have done in the cañon above, we may be compelled to give up the expedition, and try to reach the Mormon settlements to the north. Our hopes are that the worst places are passed, but our barometers are all so much injured as to be useless, so we have lost our reckoning in altitude, and know not how much descent the river has yet to make.

The stream is still wild and rapid, and rolls through a narrow channel. We make but slow progress, often landing against a wall, and climbing around some point, where we can see the river below. Although very anxious to advance, we are determined to run with great caution, lest, by another accident, we lose all our supplies. How precious that little flour has become!

We divide it among the boats, and carefully store it away, so that it can be lost only by the loss of the boat itself.

We make ten miles and a half, and camp among the rocks, on the right. We have had rain, from time to time, all day, and have been thoroughly drenched and chilled; but between showers the sun shines with great power, and the mercury in our thermometers stands at 115°, so that we have rapid changes from great extremes, which are very disagreeable. It is especially cold in the rain to-night. The little canvas we have is rotten and useless; the rubber ponchos, with which we started from Green River City, have all been lost; more than half the party is without hats, and not one of us has an entire suit of clothes, and we have not a blanket apiece. So we gather drift wood, and build a fire; but after supper the rain, coming down in torrents, extinguishes it, and we sit up all night, on the rocks, shivering, and are more exhausted by the night's discomfort than by the day's toil.

August 18.—The day is employed in making portages, and we advance but two miles on our journey. Still it rains.

While the men are at work making portages, I climb up the granite to its summit, and go away back over the rust colored sandstones and greenish yellow shales, to the foot of the marble wall. I climb so high that the men and boats are lost in the black depths below, and the dashing river is a rippling brook; and still there is more cañon above than below. All about me are interesting geological records. The book is open, and I can read as I run. All about me are grand views, for the clouds are playing again in the gorges. But somehow I think of the nine days' rations, and the bad river, and the lesson of the rocks, and the glory of the scene is but half seen.

I push on to an angle, where I hope to get a view of the country beyond, to see, if possible, what the prospect may be of our soon running through this plateau, or, at least, of meeting with some geological change that will let us out of the granite; but, arriving at the point, I can see below only a labyrinth of deep gorges.

August 19.—Rain again this morning. Still we are in our granite prison, and the time is occupied until noon in making a long, bad portage.

After dinner, in running a rapid, the pioneer boat is upset by a wave

12 COL

We are some distance in advance of the larger boats, the river is rough and swift, and we are unable to land, but cling to the boat, and are carried down stream, over another rapid. The men in the boats above see our trouble, but they are caught in whirlpools, and are spinning about in eddies, and it seems a long time before they come to our relief. At last they do come; our boat is turned right side up, bailed out; the oars, which fortunately have floated along in company with us, are gathered up, and on we go, without even landing.

Soon after the accident the clouds break away, and we have sunshine again.

Soon we find a little beach, with just room enough to land. Here we camp, but there is no wood. Across the river, and a little way above, we see some drift wood lodged in the rocks. So we bring two boat loads over, build a huge fire, and spread everything to dry. It is the first cheerful night we have had for a week; a warm, drying fire in the midst of the camp, and a few bright stars in our patch of heavens overhead.

August 20.—The characteristics of the cañon change this morning. The river is broader, the walls more sloping, and composed of black slates, that stand on edge. These nearly vertical slates are washed out in places— that is, the softer beds are washed out between the harder, which are left standing. In this way, curious little alcoves are formed, in which are quiet bays of water, but on a much smaller scale than the great bays and buttresses of Marble Cañon.

The river is still rapid, and we stop to let down with lines several times, but make greater progress as we run ten miles. We camp on the right bank. Here, on a terrace of trap, we discover another group of ruins There was evidently quite a village on this rock. Again we find mealing stones, and much broken pottery, and up in a little natural shelf in the rock, back of the ruins, we find a globular basket, that would hold perhaps a third of a bushel. It is badly broken, and, as I attempt to take it up, it falls to pieces. There are many beautiful flint chips, as if this had been the home of an old arrow maker.

August 21.—We start early this morning, cheered by the prospect of a fine day, and encouraged, also, by the good run made yesterday. A quarter

Figure 30.—Mu'-av Cañon, a side gorge.

of a mile below camp the river turns abruptly to the left, and between camp and that point is very swift, running down in a long, broken chute, and piling up against the foot of the cliff, where it turns to the left. We try to pull across, so as to go down on the other side, but the waters are swift, and it seems impossible for us to escape the rock below; but, in pulling across, the bow of the boat is turned to the farther shore, so that we are swept broadside down, and are prevented, by the rebounding waters, from striking against the wall. There we toss about for a few seconds in these billows, and are carried past the danger. Below, the river turns again to the right, the cañon is very narrow, and we see in advance but a short distance. The water, too, is very swift, and there is no landing place. From around this curve there comes a mad roar, and down we are carried, with a dizzying velocity, to the head of another rapid. On either side, high over our heads, there are overhanging granite walls, and the sharp bends cut off our view, so that a few minutes will carry us into unknown waters. Away we go, on one long, winding chute. I stand on deck, supporting myself with a strap, fastened on either side to the gunwale, and the boat glides rapidly, where the water is smooth, or, striking a wave, she leaps and bounds like a thing of life, and we have a wild, exhilarating ride for ten miles, which we make in less than an hour. The excitement is so great that we forget the danger, until we hear the roar of a great fall below; then we back on our oars, and are carried slowly toward its head, and succeed in landing just above, and find that we have to make another portage. At this we are engaged until some time after dinner.

Just here we run out of the granite!

Ten miles in less than half a day, and limestone walls below. Good cheer returns; we forget the storms, and the gloom, and cloud covered cañons, and the black granite, and the raging river, and push our boats from shore in great glee.

Though we are out of the granite, the river is still swift, and we wheel about a point again to the right, and turn, so as to head back in the direction from which we come, and see the granite again, with its narrow gorge and black crags; but we meet with no more great falls, or rapids. Still, we run cautiously, and stop, from time to time, to examine some places which look bad. Yet, we make ten miles this afternoon; twenty miles, in all, to day.

August 22.—We come to rapids again, this morning, and are occupied several hours in passing them, letting the boats down, from rock to rock, with lines, for nearly half a mile, and then have to make a long portage. While the men are engaged in this, I climb the wall on the northeast, to a height of about two thousand five hundred feet, where I can obtain a good view of a long stretch of cañon below. Its course is to the southwest. The walls seem to rise very abruptly, for two thousand five hundred or three thousand feet, and then there is a gently sloping terrace, on each side, for two or three miles, and again we find cliffs, one thousand five hundred or two thousand feet high. From the brink of these the plateau stretches back to the north and south, for a long distance. Away down the cañon, on the right wall, I can see a group of mountains, some of which appear to stand on the brink of the cañon. The effect of the terrace is to give the appearance of a narrow winding valley, with high walls on either side, and a deep, dark, meandering gorge down its middle. It is impossible, from this point of view, to determine whether we have granite at the bottom, or not; but, from geological considerations, I conclude that we shall have marble walls below.

After my return to the boats, we run another mile, and camp for the night.

We have made but little over seven miles to day, and a part of our flour has been soaked in the river again.

August 23.—Our way to day is again through marble walls. Now and then we pass, for a short distance, through patches of granite, like hills thrust up into the limestone. At one of these places we have to make another portage, and, taking advantage of the delay, I go up a little stream, to the north, wading it all the way, sometimes having to plunge in to my neck; in other places being compelled to swim across little basins that have been excavated at the foot of the falls. Along its course are many cascades and springs gushing out from the rocks on either side. Sometimes a cotton-wood tree grows over the water. I come to one beautiful fall, of more than a hundred and fifty feet, and climb around it to the right, on the broken

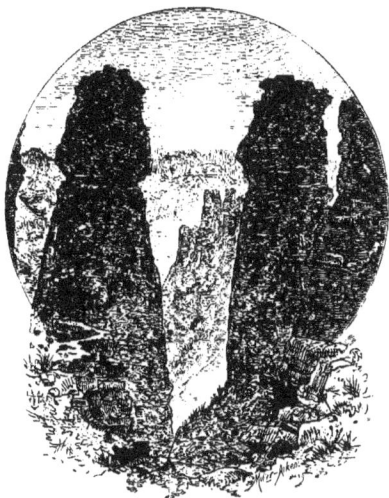

Figure 31.—Standing Rocks on the brink of Mu'-av Cañon.

rocks. Still going up, I find the cañon narrowing very much, being but fifteen or twenty feet wide; yet the walls rise on either side many hundreds of feet, perhaps thousands; I can hardly tell.

In some places the stream has not excavated its channel down vertically through the rocks, but has cut obliquely, so that one wall overhangs the other. In other places it is cut vertically above and obliquely below, or obliquely above and vertically below, so that it is impossible to see out overhead. But I can go no farther. The time which I estimated it would take to make the portage has almost expired, and I start back on a round trot, wading in the creek where I must, and plunging through basins, and find the men waiting for me, and away we go on the river.

Just after dinner we pass a stream on the right, which leaps into the Colorado by a direct fall of more than a hundred feet, forming a beautiful cascade. There is a bed of very hard rock above, thirty or forty feet in thickness, and much softer beds below. The hard beds above project many yards beyond the softer, which are washed out, forming a deep cave behind the fall, and the stream pours through a narrow crevice above into a deep pool below. Around on the rocks, in the cave like chamber, are set beautiful ferns, with delicate fronds and enameled stalks. The little frondlets have their points turned down, to form spore cases. It has very much the appearance of the Maiden's Hair fern, but is much larger. This delicate foliage covers the rocks all about the fountain, and gives the chamber great beauty. But we have little time to spend in admiration, so on we go.

We make fine progress this afternoon, carried along by a swift river, and shoot over the rapids, finding no serious obstructions.

The cañon walls, for two thousand five hundred or three thousand feet, are very regular, rising almost perpendicularly, but here and there set with narrow steps, and occasionally we can see away above the broad terrace, to distant cliffs.

We camp to night in a marble cave, and find, on looking at our reckoning, we have run twenty two miles.

August 24.—The cañon is wider to day. The walls rise to a vertical height of nearly three thousand feet. In many places the river runs under a cliff, in great curves, forming amphitheatres, half dome shaped.

Though the river is rapid, we meet with no serious obstructions, and run twenty miles. It is curious how anxious we are to make up our reckoning every time we stop, now that our diet is confined to plenty of coffee, very little spoiled flour, and very few dried apples. It has come to be a race for a dinner. Still, we make such fine progress, all hands are in good cheer, but not a moment of daylight is lost.

August 25.—We make twelve miles this morning, when we come to monuments of lava, standing in the river; low rocks, mostly, but some of them shafts more than a hundred feet high. Going on down, three or four miles, we find them increasing in number. Great quantities of cooled lava and many cinder cones are seen on either side; and then we come to an abrupt cataract. Just over the fall, on the right wall, a cinder cone, or extinct volcano, with a well defined crater, stands on the very brink of the cañon. This, doubtless, is the one we saw two or three days ago. From this volcano vast floods of lava have been poured down into the river, and a stream of the molten rock has run up the cañon, three or four miles, and down, we know not how far. Just where it poured over the cañon wall is the fall. The whole north side, as far as we can see, is lined with the black basalt, and high up on the opposite wall are patches of the same material, resting on the benches, and filling old alcoves and caves, giving to the wall a spotted appearance.

The rocks are broken in two, along a line which here crosses the river, and the beds, which we have seen coming down the cañon for the last thirty miles, have dropped 800 feet, on the lower side of the line, forming what geologists call a fault. The volcanic cone stands directly over the fissure thus formed. On the side of the river opposite, mammoth springs burst out of this crevice, one or two hundred feet above the river, pouring in a stream quite equal in volume to the Colorado Chiquito.

This stream seems to be loaded with carbonate of lime, and the water, evaporating, leaves an incrustation on the rocks; and this process has been continued for a long time, for extensive deposits are noticed, in which are basins, with bubbling springs. The water is salty.

We have to make a portage here, which is completed in about three hours, and on we go.

Figure 32.—The Grand Cañon, looking east from To ro -weap.

Figure 33.—The Grand Cañon, looking west from To-ro'-weap.

We have no difficulty as we float along, and I am able to observe the wonderful phenomena connected with this flood of lava. The cañon was doubtless filled to a height of twelve or fifteen hundred feet, perhaps by more than one flood. This would dam the water back; and in cutting through this great lava bed, a new channel has been formed, sometimes on one side, sometimes on the other. The cooled lava, being of firmer texture than the rocks of which the walls are composed, remains in some places; in others a narrow channel has been cut, leaving a line of basalt on either side. It is possible that the lava cooled faster on the sides against the walls, and that the centre ran out; but of this we can only conjecture. There are other places, where almost the whole of the lava is gone, patches of it only being seen where it has caught on the walls. As we float down, we can see that it ran out into side cañons. In some places this basalt has a fine, columnar structure, often in concentric prisms, and masses of these concentric columns have coalesced. In some places, when the flow occurred, the cañon was probably at about the same depth as it is now, for we can see where the basalt has rolled out on the sands, and, what seems curious to me, the sands are not melted or metamorphosed to any appreciable extent. In places the bed of the river is of sandstone or limestone, in other places of lava, showing that it has all been cut out again where the sandstones and limestones appear; but there is a little yet left where the bed is of lava.

What a conflict of water and fire there must have been here! Just imagine a river of molten rock, running down into a river of melted snow. What a seething and boiling of the waters; what clouds of steam rolled into the heavens!

Thirty five miles to day. Hurrah!

August 26.—The cañon walls are steadily becoming higher as we advance. They are still bold, and nearly vertical up to the terrace. We still see evidence of the eruption discovered yesterday, but the thickness of the basalt is decreasing, as we go down the stream; yet it has been reinforced at points by streams that have come down from volcanoes standing on the terrace above. but which we cannot see from the river below.

Since we left the Colorado Chiquito, we have seen no evidences that the tribe of Indians inhabiting the plateaus on either side ever come down to the river; but about eleven o'clock to day we discover an Indian garden, at the foot of the wall on the right, just where a little stream, with a narrow flood plain, comes down through a side cañon. Along the valley, the Indians have planted corn, using the water which burst out in springs at the foot of the cliff, for irrigation. The corn is looking quite well, but is not sufficiently advanced to give us roasting ears; but there are some nice, green squashes. We carry ten or a dozen of these on board our boats, and hurriedly leave, not willing to be be caught in the robbery, yet excusing ourselves by pleading our great want. We run down a short distance, to where we feel certain no Indians can follow; and what a kettle of squash sauce we make! True, we have no salt with which to season it, but it makes a fine addition to our unleavened bread and coffee. Never was fruit so sweet as these stolen squashes.

After dinner we push on again, making fine time, finding many rapids, but none so bad that we cannot run them with safety, and when we stop, just at dusk, and foot up our reckoning, we find we have run thirty five miles again.

What a supper we make; unleavened bread, green squash sauce, and strong coffee. We have been for a few days on half rations, but we have no stint of roast squash.

A few days like this, and we are out of prison.

August 27.—This morning the river takes a more southerly direction. The dip of the rocks is to the north, and we are rapidly running into lower formations. Unless our course changes, we shall very soon run again into the granite. This gives us some anxiety. Now and then the river turns to the west, and excites hopes that are soon destroyed by another turn to the south. About nine o'clock we come to the dreaded rock. It is with no little misgiving that we see the river enter these black, hard walls. At its very entrance we have to make a portage; then we have to let down with lines past some ugly rocks. Then we run a mile or two farther, and then the rapids below can be seen.

About eleven o'clock we come to a place in the river where it seems much worse than any we have yet met in all its course. A little creek comes down from the left. We land first on the right, and clamber up over the granite pinnacles for a mile or two, but can see no way by which we can let down, and to run it would be sure destruction. After dinner we cross to examine it on the left. High above the river we can walk along on the top of the granite, which is broken off at the edge, and set with crags and pinnacles, so that it is very difficult to get a view of the river at all. In my eagerness to reach a point where I can see the roaring fall below, I go too far on the wall, and can neither advance nor retreat. I stand with one foot on a little projecting rock, and cling with my hand fixed in a little crevice. Finding I am caught here, suspended 400 feet above the river, into which I should fall if my footing fails, I call for help. The men come, and pass me a line, but I cannot let go of the rock long enough to take hold of it. Then they bring two or three of the largest oars. All this takes time which seems very precious to me; but at last they arrive. The blade of one of the oars is pushed into a little crevice in the rock beyond me, in such a manner that they can hold me pressed against the wall. Then another is fixed in such a way that I can step on it, and thus I am extricated.

Still another hour is spent in examining the river from this side, but no good view of it is obtained, so now we return to the side that was first examined, and the afternoon is spent in clambering among the crags and pinnacles, and carefully scanning the river again. We find that the lateral streams have washed boulders into the river, so as to form a dam, over which the water makes a broken fall of eighteen or twenty feet; then there is a rapid, beset with rocks, for two or three hundred yards, while, on the other side, points of the wall project into the river. Then there is a second fall below; how great, we cannot tell. Then there is a rapid, filled with huge rocks, for one or two hundred yards. At the bottom of it, from the right wall, a great rock projects quite half way across the river. It has a sloping surface extending up stream, and the water, coming down with all the momentum gained in the falls and rapids above, rolls up this inclined plane many feet, and tumbles over to the left. I decide that it is possible to let down over the first fall, then run near the right cliff to a point just above the second, where we can pull out into a little chute, and, having run over that in safety, we must pull with all our power across the stream, to avoid the great rock below. On my return to the boat, I announce to the men that we are to

13 COL.

run it in the morning. Then we cross the river, and go into camp for the night on some rocks, in the mouth of the little side cañon

After supper Captain Howland asks to have a talk with me. We walk up the little creek a short distance, and I soon find that his object is to remonstrate against my determination to proceed. He thinks that we had better abandon the river here. Talking with him, I learn that his brother, William Dunn, and himself have determined to go no farther in the boats. So we return to camp. Nothing is said to the other men.

For the last two days, our course has not been plotted. I sit down and do this now, for the purpose of finding where we are by dead reckoning. It is a clear night, and I take out the sextant to make observation for latitude, and find that the astronomic determination agrees very nearly with that of the plot—quite as closely as might be expected, from a meridian observation on a planet. In a direct line, we must be about forty five miles from the mouth of the Rio Virgen. If we can reach that point, we know that there are settlements up that river about twenty miles. This forty five miles, in a direct line, will probably be eighty or ninety in the meandering line of the river. But then we know that there is comparatively open country for many miles above the mouth of the Virgen, which is our point of destination.

As soon as I determine all this, I spread my plot on the sand, and wake Howland, who is sleeping down by the river, and show him where I suppose we are, and where several Mormon settlements are situated.

We have another short talk about the morrow, and he lies down again; but for me there is no sleep. All night long, I pace up and down a little path, on a few yards of sand beach, along by the river. Is it wise to go on? I go to the boats again, to look at our rations. I feel satisfied that we can get over the danger immediately before us; what there may be below I know not. From our outlook yesterday, on the cliffs, the cañon seemed to make another great bend to the south, and this, from our experience heretofore, means more and higher granite walls. I am not sure that we can climb out of the cañon here, and, when at the top of the wall, I know enough of the country to be certain that it is a desert of rock and sand, between this and the nearest Mormon town, which, on the most direct line, must be sev-

Fig. 34.—Climbing the Grand Cañon.

enty five miles away. True, the late rains have been favorable to us, should we go out, for the probabilities are that we shall find water still standing in holes, and, at one time, I almost conclude to leave the river. But for years I have been contemplating this trip. To leave the exploration unfinished, to say that there is a part of the cañon which I cannot explore, having already almost accomplished it, is more than I am willing to acknowledge, and I determine to go on.

I wake my brother, and tell him of Howland's determination, and he promises to stay with me; then I call up Hawkins, the cook, and he makes a like promise; then Sumner, and Bradley, and Hall, and they all agree to go on.

August 28.—At last daylight comes, and we have breakfast, without a word being said about the future. The meal is as solemn as a funeral. After breakfast, I ask the three men if they still think it best to leave us. The elder Howland thinks it is, and Dunn agrees with him. The younger Howland tries to persuade them to go on with the party, failing in which, he decides to go with his brother.

Then we cross the river. The small boat is very much disabled, and unseaworthy. With the loss of hands, consequent on the departure of the three men, we shall not be able to run all of the boats, so I decide to leave my "Emma Dean."

Two rifles and a shot gun are given to the men who are going out. I ask them to help themselves to the rations, and take what they think to be a fair share. This they refuse to do, saying they have no fear but that they can get something to eat; but Billy, the cook, has a pan of biscuits prepared for dinner, and these he leaves on a rock.

Before starting, we take our barometers, fossils, the minerals, and some ammunition from the boat, and leave them on the rocks. We are going over this place as light as possible. The three men help us lift our boats over a rock twenty five or thirty feet high, and let them down again over the first fall, and now we are all ready to start. The last thing before leaving, I write a letter to my wife, and give it to Howland. Sumner gives him his watch, directing that it be sent to his sister, should he not be heard from again. The records of the expedition have been kept in duplicate. One set of these is given to Howland, and now we are ready. For the last time, they entreat us not to go on, and tell us that it is madness to set out in this place; that we can never get safely through it; and, further, that the river turns again to the south into the granite, and a few miles of such rapids and falls will exhaust our entire stock of rations, and then it will be too late to climb out. Some tears are shed; it is rather a solemn parting; each party thinks the other is taking the dangerous course.

My old boat left, I go on board of the "Maid of the Cañon." The three men climb a crag, that overhangs the river, to watch us off. The "Maid of the Cañon" pushes out. We glide rapidly along the foot of the wall, just grazing one great rock, then pull out a little into the chute of the second fall, and plunge over it. The open compartment is filled when we strike the first wave below, but we cut through it, and then the men pull with all their power toward the left wall, and swing clear of the dangerous rock below all right. We are scarcely a minute in running it, and find that, although it looked bad from above, we have passed many places that were worse.

The other boat follows without more difficulty. We land at the first practicable point below and fire our guns, as a signal to the men above that we have come over in safety. Here we remain a couple of hours, hoping that they will take the smaller boat and follow us. We are behind a curve in the cañon, and cannot see up to where we left them, and so we wait until their coming seems hopeless, and push on.

And now we have a succession of rapids and falls until noon, all of which we run in safety. Just after dinner we come to another bad place. A little stream comes in from the left, and below there is a fall, and still below another fall. Above, the river tumbles down, over and among the rocks, in whirlpools and great waves, and the waters are lashed into mad, white foam. We run along the left, above this, and soon see that we cannot get down on this side, but it seems possible to let down on the other. We pull up stream again, for two or three hundred yards, and cross. Now there is a bed of basalt on this northern side of the cañon, with a bold escarpment, that seems to be a hundred feet high. We can climb it, and walk along its summit to a point where we are just at the head of the fall.

Here the basalt is broken down again, so it seems to us, and I direct the men to take a line to the top of the cliff, and let the boats down along the wall. One man remains in the boat, to keep her clear of the rocks, and prevent her line from being caught on the projecting angles. I climb the cliff, and pass along to a point just over the fall, and descend by broken rocks, and find that the break of the fall is above the break of the wall, so that we cannot land; and that still below the river is very bad, and that there is no possibility of a portage. Without waiting further to examine and determine what shall be done, I hasten back to the top of the cliff, to stop the boats from coming down. When I arrive, I find the men have let one of them down to the head of the fall. She is in swift water, and they are not able to pull her back; nor are they able to go on with the line, as it is not long enough to reach the higher part of the cliff, which is just before them; so they take a bight around a crag. I send two men back for the other line. The boat is in very swift water, and Bradley is standing in the open compartment, holding out his oar to prevent her from striking against the foot of the cliff. Now she shoots out into the stream, and up as far as the line will permit, and then, wheeling, drives headlong against the rock, then out and back again, now straining on the line, now striking against the rock. As soon as the second line is brought, we pass it down to him; but his attention is all taken up with his own situation, and he does not see that we are passing the line to him. I stand on a projecting rock, waving my hat to gain his attention, for my voice is drowned by the roaring of the falls. Just at this moment, I see him take his knife from its sheath, and step forward to cut the line. He has evidently decided that it is better to go over with the boat as it is, than to wait for her to be broken to pieces. As he leans over, the boat sheers again into the stream, the stem-post breaks away, and she is loose. With perfect composure Bradley seizes the great scull oar, places it in the stern rowlock, and pulls with all his power (and he is an athlete) to turn the bow of the boat down stream, for he wishes to go bow down, rather than to drift broadside on. One, two strokes he makes, and a third just as she goes over, and the boat is fairly turned, and she goes down almost beyond our sight, though we are more than a hundred feet above the river. Then she comes up again, on a great wave, and down and up, then around behind some great rocks, and is lost in the mad, white foam below. We stand frozen with fear, for we see no boat. Bradley is gone, so it seems. But now, away below, we see something coming out of the waves. It is evidently a boat. A moment more, and we see Bradley standing on deck, swinging his hat to show that he is all right. But he is in a whirlpool. We have the stem-post of his boat attached to the line. How badly she may be disabled we know not. I direct Sumner and Powell to pass along the cliff, and see if they can reach him from below. Rhodes, Hall, and myself run to the other boat, jump aboard, push out, and away we go over the falls. A wave rolls over us, and our boat is unmanageable. Another great wave strikes us, the boat rolls over, and tumbles and tosses, I know not how. All I know is that Bradley is picking us up. We soon have all right again, and row to the cliff, and wait until Sumner and Powell can come. After a difficult climb they reach us. We run two or three miles farther, and turn again to the northwest, continuing until night, when we have run out of the granite once more.

August 29.—We start very early this morning. The river still continues swift, but we have no serious difficulty, and at twelve o'clock emerge from the Grand Cañon of the Colorado.

We are in a valley now, and low mountains are seen in the distance, coming to the river below. We recognize this as the Grand Wash.

A few years ago, a party of Mormons set out from St. George, Utah, taking with them a boat, and came down to the mouth of the Grand Wash, where they divided, a portion of the party crossing the river to explore the San Francisco Mountains. Three men—Hamblin, Miller, and Crosby—taking the boat, went on down the river to Callville, landing a few miles below the mouth of the Rio Virgen. We have their manuscript journal with us, and so the stream is comparatively well known.

To night we camp on the left bank, in a *mesquite* thicket.

The relief from danger, and the joy of success, are great. When he who has been chained by wounds to a hospital cot, until his canvas tent seems like a dungeon cell, until the groans of those who lie about, tortured with probe and knife, are piled up, a weight of horror on his ears that he cannot throw off, cannot forget, and until the stench of festering wounds and anæsthetic drugs has filled the air with its loathsome burthen, at last goes out into the open field, what a world he sees!   How beautiful the sky; how bright the sunshine; what "floods of delirious music" pour from the throats of birds; how sweet the fragrance of earth, and tree, and blossom! The first hour of convalescent freedom seems rich recompense for all— pain, gloom, terror.

Something like this are the feelings· we experience to night.   Ever before us has been an unknown danger, heavier than immediate peril. Every waking hour passed in the Grand Cañon has been one of toil.   We have watched with deep solicitude the steady disappearance of our scant supply of rations, and from time to time have seen the river snatch a portion of the little left, while we were ahungered.   And danger and toil were endured in those gloomy depths, where ofttimes the clouds hid the sky by day, and but a narrow zone of stars could be seen at night.   Only during the few hours of deep sleep, consequent on hard labor, has the roar of the waters been hushed.   Now the danger is over; now the toil has ceased; now the gloom has disappeared; now the firmament is bounded only by the horizon; and what a vast expanse of constellations can be seen!

The river rolls by us in silent majesty; the quiet of the camp is sweet; our joy is almost ecstacy.   We sit till long after midnight, talking of the Grand Cañon, talking of home, but chiefly talking of the three men who left us.   Are they wandering in those depths, unable to find a way out? are they searching over the desert lands above for water? or are they nearing the settlements?

August 30.—We run through two or three short, low cañons to day, and on emerging from one, we discover a band of Indians in the valley below. They see us, and scamper away in most eager haste, to hide among the rocks.   Although we land, and call for them to return, not an Indian can be seen.

Two or three miles farther down, in turning a short bend in the river, we come upon another camp.   So near are we before they can see us that I can shout to them, and, being able to speak a little of their language, I tell them we are friends; but they all flee to the rocks, except a man, a woman, and two children.   We land, and talk with them.   They are without lodges, but have built little shelters of boughs, under which they wallow in the sand. The man is dressed in a hat; the woman in a string of beads only. At first they are evidently much terrified; but when I talk to them in their own language, and tell them we are friends, and inquire after people in the Mormon towns, they are soon reassured, and beg for tobacco. Of this precious article we have none to spare. Sumner looks around in the boat for something to give them, and finds a little piece of colored soap, which they receive as a valuable present, rather as a thing of beauty than as a useful commodity, however. They are either unwilling or unable to tell us anything about the Indians or white people, and so we push off, for we must lose no time.

We camp at noon under the right bank. And now, as we push out, we are in great expectancy, for we hope every minute to discover the mouth of the Rio Virgen.

Soon one of the men exclaims: "Yonder's an Indian in the river." Looking for a few minutes, we certainly do see two or three persons. The men bend to their oars, and pull toward them. Approaching, we see that there are three white men and an Indian hauling a seine, and then we discover that it is just at the mouth of the long sought river.

As we come near, the men seem far less surprised to see us than we do to see them. They evidently know who we are, and, on talking with them, they tell us that we have been reported lost long ago, and that some weeks before, a messenger had been sent from Salt Lake City, with instructions for them to watch for any fragments or relics of our party that might drift down the stream.

Our new found friends, Mr. Asa and his two sons, tell us that they are pioneers of a town that is to be built on the bank.

Eighteen or twenty miles up the valley of the Rio Virgen there are two Mormon towns, St. Joseph and St. Thomas. To night we dispatch an Indian to the last mentioned place, to bring any letters that may be there for us.

Our arrival here is very opportune. When we look over our store of supplies, we find about ten pounds of flour, fifteen pounds of dried apples, but seventy or eighty pounds of coffee.

Figure 35.—Our Indian messenger.

August 31.—This afternoon the Indian returns with a letter, informing us that Bishop Leithhead, of St. Thomas, and two or three other Mormons are coming down with a wagon, bringing us supplies. They arrive about sundown. Mr. Asa treats us with great kindness, to the extent of his ability; but Bishop Leithhead brings in his wagon two or three dozen melons, and many other little luxuries, and we are comfortable once more.

September 1.—This morning Sumner, Bradley, Hawkins, and Hall. taking on a small supply of rations, start down the Colorado with the boats. It is their intention to go to Fort Mojave, and perhaps from there overland to Los Angeles.

Captain Powell and myself return with Bishop Leithhead to St. Thomas. From St. Thomas we go to Salt Lake City.

14 COL

CHAPTER IX.

THE RIO VIRGEN AND THE U-IN-KA-RET MOUNTAINS.

We have determined to continue the exploration of the cañons of the Colorado. Our last trip was so hurried, owing to the loss of rations, and the scientific instruments were so badly injured, that we are not satisfied with the results obtained, so we shall once more attempt to pass through the cañons in boats, devoting two or three years to the trip.

It will not be possible to carry in the boats sufficient supplies for the party for that length of time, so it is thought best to establish dépôts of supplies, at intervals of one or two hundred miles along the river.

Between Gunnison's Crossing and the foot of the Grand Cañon, we know of only two points where the river can be reached—one at the Crossing of the Fathers, and another a few miles below, at the mouth of the Paria, on a route which has been explored by Jacob Hamblin, a Mormon missionary. These two points are so near each other that only one of them can be selected for the purpose above mentioned, and others must be found. We have been unable, up to this time, to obtain, either from Indians or white men, any information which will give us a clue to any other trail to the river.

At the head waters of the Sevier, we are on the summit of a great water-shed. The Sevier itself flows north, and then westward, into the lake of the same name. The Rio Virgen, heading near by, flows to the southwest, into the Colorado, sixty or seventy miles below the Grand Cañon. The Kanab, also heading near by, runs directly south, into the very heart of the Grand Cañon. The Paria, also heading near by, runs a little south of east, and enters the river at the head of Marble Cañon. To the northeast from this point, other streams, which run into the Colorado, have their sources, until, forty or fifty miles away, we reach the southern branches of the

Figure 36.—Mary's Veil, the upper fall on Pine Creek, a small tributary of the Sevier.

Figure 37.—Pilling's Cascade, the lower fall on Pine Creek.

Dirty Devil River, the mouth of which stream is but a short distance below the junction of the Grand and Green.

The Pouns-a'-gunt Plateau terminates in a point, which is bounded by a line of beautiful pink cliffs. At the foot of this plateau, on the west, the Rio Virgen and Sevier Rivers are dovetailed together, as their minute upper branches interlock. The upper surface of the plateau inclines to the northeast, so that its waters roll off into the Sevier; but from the foot of the cliffs, quite around the sharp angle of the plateau, for a dozen miles, we find numerous springs, whose waters unite to form the Kanab. But a little farther to the northeast the springs gather into streams that feed the Paria.

Here, by the upper springs of the Kanab, we make a camp, and from this point we are to radiate on a series of trips, southwest, south, and east.

Jacob Hamblin, who has been a missionary among the Indians for more than twenty years, has collected a number of *Kai'-vav-its*, with *Chu-ar'-ru-um-peak*, their chief, and they are all camped with us. They assure us that we cannot reach the river; that we cannot make our way into the depths of the cañon, but promise to show us the springs and water pockets, which are very scarce in all this region, and to give us all the information in their power.

Here we fit up a pack train, for our bedding and instruments, and supplies are to be carried on the backs of mules and ponies.

September 5, 1870.—The several members of the party are engaged in general preparation for our trip down to the Grand Cañon.

Taking with me a white man and an Indian, I start on a climb to the summit of the Pouns-a'-gunt Plateau, which rises above us on the east. Our way, for a mile or more, is over a great peat bog, that trembles under our feet, and now and then a mule sinks through the broken turf, and we are compelled to pull it out with ropes.

Passing the bog, our way is up a gulch, at the foot of the Pink Cliffs, which form the escarpment, or wall, of the great plateau. Soon we leave the gulch, and climb a long ridge, which winds around to the right toward the summit of the great table.

Two hours' riding, climbing, and clambering brings us near the top. We look below, and see clouds drifting up from the south, and rolling tumultuously toward the foot of the cliffs, beneath us. Soon, all the country below is covered with a sea of vapor—a billowy, raging, noiseless sea—and as the vapory flood still rolls up from the south, great waves dash against the foot of the cliffs and roll back; another tide comes in, is hurled back, and another and another, lashing the cliffs until the fog rises to the summit, and covers us all.

There is a heavy pine and fir forest above, beset with dead and fallen timber, and we make our way through the undergrowth to the east.

It rains! The clouds discharge their moisture in torrents, and we make for ourselves shelters of boughs, which are soon abandoned, and we stand shivering by a great fire of pine logs and boughs, which we have kindled, but which the pelting storm half extinguishes.

One, two, three, four hours' of the storm, and at last it partially abates.

During this time our animals, which we have turned loose, have sought for themselves shelter under the trees, and two of them have wandered away beyond our sight. I go out to follow their tracks, and come near to the brink of a ledge of rocks, which, in the fog and mist, I suppose to be a little ridge, and I look for a way by which I can go down. Standing just here, there is a rift made in the fog below, by some current or blast of wind, which reveals an almost bottomless abyss. I look from the brink of a great precipice of more than two thousand feet; but, through the mist, the forms below are half obscured, and all reckoning of distance is lost, and it seems ten thousand feet, ten miles—any distance the imagination desires to make it.

Catching our animals, we return to the camp. We find that the little streams which come down from the plateau are greatly swollen, but at camp they have had no rain. The clouds which drifted up from the south, striking against the plateau, were lifted up into colder regions, and discharged their moisture on the summit, and against the sides of the plateau, but there was no rain in the valley below.

September 9.—We make a fair start this morning, from the beautiful meadow at the head of the Kanab, and cross the line of little hills at the headwaters of the Rio Virgen, and pass, to the south, a pretty valley, and at ten o'clock come to the brink of a great geographic bench—a line of cliffs. Behind us are cool springs, green meadows, and forest clad slopes; below us, stretching to the south, until the world is lost in blue haze, is a painted

Figure 38.—Entrance to Pa-ru′-nu-weap.

desert; not a desert plain, but a desert of rocks, cut by deep gorges, and relieved by towering cliffs and pinnacled rocks—naked rocks, brilliant in the sunlight.

By a difficult trail, we make our way down the basaltic ledge, through which innumerable streams here gather into a little river, running in a deep cañon. The river runs close to the foot of the cliffs, on the right hand side, and the trail passes along to the right. At noon we rest, and our animals feed on luxuriant grass.

Again we start, and make slow progress along a stony way. At night we camp under an overarching cliff.

September 10.—Here the river turns to the west, and our way, properly, is to the south; but we wish to explore the Rio Virgen as far as possible. The Indians tell us that the cañon narrows gradually, a few miles below, and that it will be impossible to take our animals much farther down the river. Early in the morning, I go down to examine the head of this narrow part. After breakfast, having concluded to explore the cañon for a few miles on foot, we arrange that the main party shall climb the cliff, and go around to a point eighteen or twenty miles below, where, the Indians say, the animals can be taken down by the river, and three of us set out on foot.

The Indian name of the cañon is *Pa-ru'-nu-weap*, or Roaring Water Cañon. Between the little river and the foot of the walls, is a dense growth of willows, vines, and wild rose bushes, and, with great difficulty, we make our way through this tangled mass. It is not a wide stream—only twenty or thirty feet across in most places; shallow, but very swift. After spending some hours in breaking our way through the mass of vegetation, and climbing rocks here and there, it is determined to wade along the stream. In some places this is an easy task, but here and there we come to deep holes, where we have to wade to our arm pits. Soon we come to places so narrow that the river fills the entire channel, and we wade perforce. In many places the bottom is a quicksand, into which we sink, and it is with great difficulty that we make progress. In some places the holes are so deep that we have to swim, and our little bundles of blankets and rations are fixed to a raft made of driftwood, and pushed before us. Now and then there is a little flood-plain, on which we can walk, and we cross and recross the stream, and wade along the channel where the water is so swift as to almost carry us off our feet, and we are in danger every moment of being swept down, until night comes on. We estimate we have traveled eight miles to day. We find a little patch of flood-plain, on which there is a huge pile of driftwood and a clump of box-elders, and near by a great stream, which bursts from the rocks—a mammoth spring.

We soon have a huge fire, our clothes are spread to dry, we make a cup of coffee, take out our bread and cheese and dried beef, and enjoy a hearty supper.

The cañon here is about twelve hundred feet deep. It has been very narrow and winding all the way down to this point.

September 11.—Wading again this morning; sinking in the quicksand, swimming the deep waters, and making slow and painful progress where the waters are swift, and the bed of the stream rocky.

The cañon is steadily becoming deeper, and, in many places, very narrow—only twenty or thirty feet wide below, and in some places no wider, and even narrower, for hundreds of feet overhead. There are places where the river, in sweeping by curves, has cut far under the rocks, but still preserving its narrow channel, so that there is an overhanging wall on one side and an inclined wall on the other. In places a few hundred feet above, it becomes vertical again, and thus the view to the sky is entirely closed. Everywhere this deep passage is dark and gloomy, and resounds with the noise of rapid waters. At noon we are in a cañon 2,500 feet deep, and we come to a fall where the walls are broken down, and huge rocks beset the channel, on which we obtain a foothold to reach a level two hundred feet below. Here the cañon is again wider, and we find a flood-plain, along which we can walk, now on this, and now on that side of the stream. Gradually the cañon widens; steep rapids, cascades, and cataracts are found along the river, but we wade only when it is necessary to cross. We make progress with very great labor, having to climb over piles of broken rocks.

Late in the afternoon, we come to a little clearing in the valley, and see other signs of civilization, and by sundown arrive at the Mormon town of Schnnesburg; and here we meet the train, and feast on melons and grapes.

Figure 39.—Mu-koon'-tu-weap Cañon.

September 12.—Our course, for the last two days, through *Pa-ru'-nu-weap*
Cañon, was directly to the west. Another stream comes down from the
north, and unites just here at Schunesburg with the main branch of the Rio
Virgen. We determine to spend a day in the exploration of this stream.
The Indians call the cañon, through which it runs, *Mu-koon'-tu-weap*, or
Straight Cañon. Entering this, we have to wade up stream; often the water
fills the entire channel, and, although we travel many miles, we find no flood-
plain, talus, or broken piles of rock at the foot of the cliff. The walls have
smooth, plain faces, and are everywhere very regular and vertical for a
thousand feet or more, where they seem to break back in shelving slopes to
higher altitudes; and everywhere, as we go along, we find springs bursting
out at the foot of the walls, and, passing these, the river above becomes
steadily smaller; the great body of water, which runs below, bursts out
from beneath this great bed of red sandstone; as we go up the cañon, it
comes to be but a creek, and then a brook. On the western wall of the
cañon stand some buttes, towers, and high pinnacled rocks. Going up the
cañon, we gain glimpses of them, here and there. Last summer, after our
trip through the cañons of the Colorado, on our way from the mouth of the
Virgen to Salt Lake City, these were seen as conspicuous landmarks, from
a distance, away to the southwest, of sixty or seventy miles. These tower
rocks are known as the Temples of the Virgen.

Having explored this cañon nearly to its head, we return to Schunesburg, arriving quite late at night.

Sitting in camp this evening, *Chu-ar'-ru-um-peak*, the chief of the *Kai'-
vav-its*, who is one of our party, tells us there is a tradition among the tribes
of this country, that many years ago a great light was seen somewhere in
this region by the *Pa-ru'-sha-pats*, who lived to the southwest, and that
they supposed it to be a signal, kindled to warn them of the approach of
the *Navajos*, who live beyond the Colorado River to the east. Then other
signal fires were kindled on the Pine Valley Mountain, Santa Clara Mountains, and *U-in-ka-ret* Mountains, so that all the tribes of Northern Arizona,
Southern Utah, Southern Nevada, and Southern California were warned of
the approaching danger; but when the *Pa-ru'-sha-pats* came nearer, they
discovered that it was a fire on one of the great Temples; and then they

knew that the fire was not kindled by men, for no human being could scale the rocks. The *Tŭ'-mu-ur-ru-gwait'-si-gaip*, or Rock Rovers, had kindled a fire to deceive the people. In the Indian language this is called *Tŭ'-mu-ur-ru-gwait'-si-gaip Tŭ-weap'*, or Rock Rovers' Land.

September 13.—We start very early this morning, for we have a long day's travel before us. Our way is across the Rio Virgen to the south. Coming to the bank of the stream here, we find a strange metamorphosis. The streams we have seen above, running in narrow channels, leaping and plunging over the rocks, raging and roaring in their course, are here united, and spread in a thin sheet several hundred yards wide, and only a few inches deep, but running over a bed of quicksand. Crossing the stream, our trail leads up a narrow cañon, not very deep, and then among the hills of golden, red, and purple shales and marls. Climbing out of the valley of the Rio Virgen, we pass through a forest of dwarf cedars, and come out at the foot of the Vermilion Cliffs. All day we follow this Indian trail toward the east, and at night camp at a great spring, known to the Indians as Yellow Rock Spring, but to the Mormons as Pipe Spring; and near by there is a cabin in which some Mormon herders find shelter. Pipe Spring is a point just across the Utah line in Arizona, and we suppose it to be about sixty miles from the river. Here the Mormons design to build a fort another year, as an outpost for protection against the Indians.

Here we discharge a number of the Indians, but take two with us for the purpose of showing us the springs, for they are very scarce, very small, and not easily found. Half a dozen are not known in a district of country large enough to make as many good sized counties in Illinois. There are no running streams, and these springs and water-pockets—that is, holes in the rocks, which hold water from shower to shower—are our only dependence for this element.

Starting, we leave behind a long line of cliffs, many hundred feet high, composed of orange and vermilion sandstones. I have named them "Vermilion Cliffs." When we are out a few miles, I look back, and see the morning sun shining in splendor on their painted faces; the salient angles are on fire, and the retreating angles are buried in shade, and I gaze on them until my vision dreams, and the cliffs appear a long bank of purple clouds,

Figure 40.—Temples of Rock-Rovers' Land.

piled from the horizon high into the heavens. At noon we pass along a ledge of chocolate cliffs, and, taking out our sandwiches, we make a dinner as we ride along.

Yesterday, our Indians discussed for hours the route which we should take. There is one way, farther by ten or twelve miles, with sure water; another shorter, where water is found sometimes; their conclusion was that water would be found now; and this is the way we go, yet all day long we are anxious about it. To be out two days, with only the water that can be carried in two small kegs, is to have our animals suffer greatly. At five o'clock we come to the spot, and there is a huge water-pocket, containing several barrels. What a relief! Here we camp for the night.

September 15.—Up at day-break, for it is a long day's march to the next water. They say we must "run very hard" to reach it by dark.

Our course is to the south. From Pipe Spring we can see a mountain, and I recognize it as the one seen last summer from a cliff overlooking the Grand Cañon; and I wish to reach the river just behind the mountain. There are Indians living in the group, of which it is the highest, whom I wish to visit on the way. These mountains are of volcanic origin, and we soon come to ground that is covered with fragments of lava. The way becomes very difficult. We have to cross deep ravines, the heads of cañons that run into the Grand Cañon. It is curious now to observe the knowledge of our Indians. There is not a trail but what they know; every gulch and every rock seems familiar. I have prided myself on being able to grasp and retain in my mind the topography of a country; but these Indians put me to shame. My knowledge is only general, embracing the more important features of a region that remains as a map engraved on my mind; but theirs is particular. They know every rock and every ledge, every gulch and cañon, and just where to wind among these to find a pass; and their knowledge is unerring. They cannot describe a country to you, but they can tell you all the particulars of a route.

I have but one pony for the two, and they were to ride "turn about"; but *Chu-ar'-ru-um-peak*, the chief, rides, and *Shuts*, the one-eyed, bare-legged, merry-faced pigmy, walks, and points the way with a slender cane; then leaps and bounds by the shortest way, and sits down on a rock and waits demurely until we come, always meeting us with a jest, his face a rich mine of sunny smiles.

At dusk we reach the water-pocket. It is in a deep gorge, on the flank of this great mountain. During the rainy season the water rolls down the mountain side, plunging over precipices, and excavates a deep basin in the solid rock below. This basin, hidden from the sun, holds water the year round.

September 16.—This morning, while the men are packing the animals, I climb a little mountain near camp, to obtain a view of the country. It is a huge pile of volcanic scoria, loose and light as cinders from a forge, which give way under my feet, and I climb with great labor; but reaching the summit, and looking to the southeast, I see once more the labyrinth of deep gorges that flank the Grand Cañon; in the multitude, I cannot determine whether it be in view or not. The memories of grand and awful months spent in their deep, gloomy solitudes come up, and I live that life over again for a time.

I supposed, before starting, that I could get a good view of the great mountain from this point; but it is like climbing a chair to look at a castle. I wish to discover some way by which it can be ascended, as it is my intention to go to the summit before I return to the settlements. There is a cliff near the summit, and I do not see the way yet. Now down I go, sliding on the cinders, making them rattle and clang.

The Indians say we are to have a short ride to day, and that we will reach an Indian village, situated by a good spring. Our way is across the spurs that put out from the great mountain, as we pass it to the left.

Up and down we go, across deep ravines, and the fragments of lava clank under our horses' feet; now among cedars, now among pines, and now across mountain side glades. At one o'clock we descend into a lovely valley, with a carpet of waving grass; sometimes there is a little water in the upper end of it, and, during some seasons, the Indians we wish to find are encamped here. *Chu-ar'-ru-um-peak* rides on to find them, and to say we are friends, otherwise they would run away, or propose to fight us, should we come without notice. Soon we see *Chu-ar'-ru-um-peak* riding at full speed, and hear him shouting at the top of his voice, and away in the dis-

Figure 41.—U-nu'-pin Pi-ka'-vu, or Elfin Water Pocket.

Figure 42.—Wu-nav'-ai gathering seeds.

tance are two Indians, scampering up the mountain side. One stops; the other still goes on, and is soon lost to view. We ride up, and find *Chu-ar'-ru-um-peak* talking with the one who had stopped. It is one of the ladies resident in these mountain glades; she is evidently paying taxes, Godiva like. She tells us that her people are at the spring; that it is only two hours' ride; that her good master has gone on to tell them we are coming, and that she is harvesting seeds.

We sit down and eat our luncheon, and share our biscuit with the woman of the mountains; then on we go, over a divide between two rounded peaks. I send the party on to the village, and climb the peak on the left, riding my horse to the upper limit of trees, and then tugging up afoot. From this point I can see the Grand Cañon, and know where I am. I can see the Indian village, too, in a grassy valley, embosomed in the mountains, the smoke curling up from their fires; my men are turning out their horses, and a group of natives stand around. Down the mountain I go, and reach camp at sunset.

After supper we put some cedar boughs on the fire, the dusky villagers sit around, and we have a smoke and a talk. I explain the object of my visit, and assure them of my friendly intentions. Then I ask them about a way down into the cañon. They tell me that years ago, a way was discovered by which parties could go down, but that no one has attempted it for a long time; that it is a very difficult and very dangerous undertaking to reach the "Big Water." Then I inquire about the *Shi'-vwits*, a tribe that lives about the springs on the mountain sides and cañon cliffs to the southwest. They say that their village is now about thirty miles away, and promise to send a messenger for them to-morrow morning.

Having finished our business for the evening, I ask if there is a *tu-gwi'-na-gunt* in camp: that is, if there is any one present who is skilled in relating their mythology. *Chu-ar'-ru-um-peak* says *To-mor'-ro-un-ti-kai*, the chief of these Indians, is a very noted man for his skill in this matter; but they both object, by saying that the season for *tu-gwi'-nai* has not yet arrived. But I had anticipated this, and soon some members of the party come with pipes and tobacco, a large kettle of coffee, and a tray of biscuits, and, after sundry ceremonies of pipe lighting and smoking, we all feast, and, warmed up by this, to them, unusual good living, it is decided that the night shall be spent in relating mythology. I ask *To-mor'-ro-un-ti-kai* to tell us about the *So'-kus Wai'-un-ats*, or One Two Boys, and to this he agrees.

The long winter evenings of an Indian camp are usually devoted to the relation of mythological stories, which purport to give a history of an ancient race of animal gods. The stories are usually told by some old man, assisted by others of the party, who take secondary parts, while the members of the tribe gather about, and make comments, or receive impressions from the morals which are enforced by the story teller, or, more properly, story tellers; for the exercise partakes somewhat of the nature of a theatrical performance.

THE SO'-KUS WAI'-UN-ATS.

Tum-pwi-nai'-ro-gwi-nump, he who had a stone shirt, killed *Si-kor'*, the Crane, and stole his wife, and seeing that she had a child, and thinking it would be an incumbrance to them on their travels, he ordered her to kill it. But the mother, loving the babe, hid it under her dress, and carried it away to its grandmother. And Stone Shirt carried his captured bride to his own land.

In a few years the child grew to be a fine lad, under the care of his grandmother, and was her companion wherever she went.

One day they were digging flag roots, on the margin of the river, and putting them in a heap on the bank. When they had been at work a little while, the boy perceived that the roots came up with greater ease than was customary, and he asked the old woman the cause of this, but she did not know; and, as they continued their work, still the reeds came up with less effort, at which their wonder increased, until the grandmother said, "Surely, some strange thing is about to transpire." Then the boy went to the heap, where they had been placing the roots, and found that some one had taken them away, and he ran back, exclaiming, "Grandmother, did you take the roots away?" And she answered, "No, my child; perhaps some ghost has taken them off; let us dig no more; come away." But the boy was not satisfied, as he greatly desired to know what all this meant; so he searched about for a time, and at length found a man sitting under a tree, whom he taunted with being a thief, and threw mud and stones at him, until he broke the stranger's leg, who answered not the boy, nor resented the injuries he received, but remained silent and sorrowful; and, when his leg was broken, he tied it up in sticks, and bathed it in the river, and sat down again under the tree, and beckoned the boy to approach. When the lad came near, the stranger told him he had something of great importance to reveal. "My son," said he, "did that old woman ever tell you about your father and mother?" "No," answered the boy; "I have never heard of them." "My son, do you see these bones scattered on the ground? Whose bones are these?" "How should I know?" answered the boy. "It may be that some elk or deer has been killed here." "No," said the old man. "Perhaps they are the bones of a bear;" but the old man shook his head. So the boy mentioned many other animals, but the stranger still shook his head, and finally said, "These are the bones of your father; Stone Shirt killed him, and left him to rot here on the ground, like a wolf." And the boy was filled with indignation against the slayer of his father. Then the stranger asked, "Is your mother in yonder lodge?" and the boy replied, "No." "Does your mother live on the banks of this river?" and the boy answered, "I don't know my mother; I have never seen her; she is dead." "My son," replied the stranger, "Stone Shirt, who killed your father, stole your mother, and took her away to the shore of a distant lake, and there she is his wife to day." And the boy wept bitterly, and while the tears filled his eyes so that he could not see, the stranger disappeared. Then the boy was filled with wonder at what he had seen and heard, and malice grew in his heart against his father's enemy. He returned to the old woman, and said, "Grandmother, why have you lied to me about my father and mother?" and she answered not, for she knew that a ghost had told all to the boy. And the boy fell upon the ground weeping and sobbing, until he fell into a deep sleep, when strange things were told him.

His slumber continued three days and three nights, and when he awoke, he said to his grandmother: "I am going away to enlist all nations in my fight;" and straightway he departed.

(Here the boy's travels are related with many circumstances concerning the way he was received by the people, all given in a series of conversations, very lengthy, so they will be omitted.)

Finally he returned in advance of the people whom he had enlisted, bringing with him *Shin-au'-av*, the wolf, and *To-go'-av*, the rattlesnake. When the three had eaten food, the boy said to the old woman: "Grand-mother, cut me in two!" But she demurred, saying she did not wish to kill one whom she loved so dearly. "Cut me in two!" demanded the boy; and he gave her a stone ax, which he had brought from a distant country, and with a manner of great authority he again commanded her to cut him in two. So she stood before him, and severed him in twain, and fled in terror. And lo! each part took the form of an entire man, and the one beautiful boy appeared as two, and they were so much alike no one could tell them apart.

When the people or natives, whom the boy had enlisted, came pouring into the camp, *Shin-au'-av* and *To-go'-av* were engaged in telling them of the wonderful thing that had happened to the boy, and that now there were two; and they all held it to be an augury of a successful expedition to the land of Stone Shirt. And they started on their journey.

Now the boy had been told in the dream of his three days' slumber, of a magical cup, and he had brought it home with him from his journey among the nations, and the *So'-kus Wai'-un-ats* carried it between them, filled with water. *Shin-au'-av* walked on their right, and *To-go'-av* on their left, and the nations followed in the order in which they had been enlisted There was a vast number of them, so that when they were stretched out in line it was one day's journey from the front to the rear of the column.

When they had journeyed two days, and were far out on the desert, all the people thirsted, for they found no water, and they fell down upon the sand, groaning, and murmuring that they had been deceived, and they cursed the One-Two.

But the *So'-kus Wai'-un-ats* had been told in the wonderful dream of the suffering which would be endured, and that the water which they carried in the cup was only to be used in dire necessity; and the brothers said to each other: "Now the time has come for us to drink the water." And when one had quaffed of the magical bowl, he found it still full; and he gave it to the other to drink, and still it was full; and the One-Two gave it to the

and would make a rich feast for the people, his anger was appeased. "What matters it," said he, "who kills the game, when we can all eat it?"

So all the people were fed in abundance, and they proceeded on their journey.

The next day the people again suffered for water, and the magical cup was empty; but the *So'-kus Wai'-un-ats*, having been told in their dream what to do, transformed themselves into doves, and flew away to a lake, on the margin of which was the home of Stone Shirt.

Coming near to the shore, they saw two maidens bathing in the water; and the birds stood and looked, for the maidens were very beautiful. Then they flew into some bushes, near by, to have a nearer view, and were caught in a snare which the girls had placed for intrusive birds. The beautiful maidens came up, and, taking the birds out of the snare, admired them very much, for they had never seen such birds before. They carried them to their father, Stone Shirt, who said: "My daughters, I very much fear these are spies from my enemies, for such birds do not live in our land;" and he was about to throw them into the fire, when the maidens besought him, with tears, that he would not destroy their beautiful birds; but he yielded to their entreaties with much misgiving. Then they took the birds to the shore of the lake, and set them free.

When the birds were at liberty once more, they flew around among the bushes, until they found the magical cup which they had lost, and taking it up, they carried it out into the middle of the lake and settled down upon the water, and the maidens supposed they were drowned.

The birds, when they had filled their cup, rose again, and went back to the people in the desert, where they arrived just at the right time to save them with the cup of water, from which each drank; and yet it was full until the last was satisfied, and then not a drop remained.

The brothers reported that they had seen Stone Shirt and his daughters.

The next day they came near to the home of the enemy, and the brothers, in proper person, went out to reconnoitre. Seeing a woman gleaning seeds, they drew near, and knew it was their mother, whom Stone Shirt had stolen from *Si-kor'*, the crane. They told her they were her sons, but she denied it, and said she had never had but one son; but the boys related

to her their history, with the origin of the two from one, and she was con-
vinced. She tried to dissuade them from making war upon Stone Shirt, and
told them that no arrow could possibly penetrate his armor, and that he
was a great warrior, and had no other delight than in killing his enemies,
and that his daughters also were furnished with magical bows and arrows,
which they could shoot so fast that the arrows would fill the air like a cloud,
and that it was not necessary for them to take aim, for their missiles went
where they willed; they *thought* the arrows to the hearts of their enemies;
and thus the maidens could kill the whole of the people before a common
arrow could be shot by a common person. But the boys told her what the
spirit had said in the long dream, and had promised that Stone Shirt should
be killed. They told her to go down to the lake at dawn, so as not to be
endangered by the battle.

During the night, the *So'-kus Wai'-un-ats* transformed themselves into
mice, and proceeded to the home of Stone Shirt, and found the magical bows
and arrows that belonged to the maidens, and with their sharp teeth they cut
the sinew on the backs of the bows, and nibbled the bow strings, so that
they were worthless; while *To-go'-av* hid himself under a rock near by.

When dawn came into the sky, *Tum-pwi-nai'-ro-gwi-nump*, the Stone
Shirt man, arose and walked out of his tent, exulting in his strength and
security, and sat down upon the rock under which *To-go'-av* was hiding; and
he, seeing his opportunity, sunk his fangs into the flesh of the hero. Stone
Shirt sprang high into the air, and called to his daughters that they were
betrayed, and that the enemy was near; and they seized their magical bows,
and their quivers filled with magical arrows, and hurried to his defense.
At the same time, all the nations who were surrounding the camp rushed
down to battle. But the beautiful maidens, finding their weapons were
destroyed, waved back their enemies, as if they would parley; and, standing for a few moments over the body of their slain father, sang the death
song, and danced the death dance, whirling in giddy circles about the dead
hero, and wailing with despair, until they sank down and expired.

The conquerors buried the maidens by the shores of the lake; but
Tum-pwi-nai'-ro-gwi-nump was left to rot, and his bones to bleach on the
sands, as he had left *Si-kor'*.

16 COL

There is this proverb among the Utes: "Do not murmur when you suffer in doing what the spirits have commanded, for a cup of water is provided." And another: "What matters it who kills the game, when we can all eat of it."

It is long after midnight when the performance is ended. The story itself was interesting, though I had heard it many times before; but never, perhaps, under circumstances more effective. Stretched beneath tall, sombre pines; a great camp fire, and by the fire, men, old, wrinkled, and ugly; deformed, blear eyed, wry faced women; lithe, stately young men; pretty but simpering maidens, naked children, all intently listening, or laughing and talking by times, their strange faces and dusky forms lit up with the glare of the pine-knot fire. All the circumstances conspired to make it a scene strange and weird. One old man, the sorcerer or medicine-man of the tribe, peculiarly impressed me. Now and then he would interrupt the play for the purpose of correcting the speakers, or impressing the moral of the story with a strange dignity and impressiveness that seemed to pass to the very border of the ludicrous; yet at no time did it make me smile.

The story is finished, but there is yet time for an hour or two's sleep. I take *Chu-ar'-ru-um-peak* to one side for a talk. The three men who left us in the cañon last year found their way up the lateral gorge, by which they went into the *Shi'-vwits* Mountains, lying west of us, where they met with the Indians, and camped with them one or two nights, and were finally killed. I am anxious to learn the circumstances, and as the people of the tribe who committed the deed live but a little way from and are intimate with these people, I ask *Chu-ar'-ru-um-peak* to make inquiry for me. Then we go to bed.

September 17.—Early this morning the Indians come up to our camp. They have concluded to send out a young man after the *Shi'-vwits*. The runner fixes his moccasins, puts some food in a sack and water in a little wicker work jug, straps them on his back, and starts at a good round pace.

We have concluded to go down the cañon, hoping to meet the *Shi'-vwits* on our return. Soon we are ready to start, leaving the camp and pack animals in charge of the two Indians who came with us. As we move out, our new guide comes up, a blear eyed, weazen faced, quiet old man, with

Figure 44.—An'-ti-naints, Pu-tu'-siv, and Wi'-chuts.

.

Figure 45.—The Human Pickle.

his bow and arrows in one hand, and a small cane in the other. These Indians all carry canes with a crooked handle, they say to kill rattlesnakes, and to pull rabbits from their holes. The valley is high up in the mountain, and we descend from it, by a rocky, precipitous trail, down, down, down for two long, weary hours, leading our ponies and stumbling over the rocks. At last we are at the foot of the mountain, standing on a little knoll, from which we can look into a cañon below. Into this we descend, and then we follow it for miles, clambering down and still down. Often we cross beds of lava, that have been poured into the cañon by lateral channels, and these angular fragments of basalt make the way very rough for the animals. About two o'clock the guide halts us with his wand, and springing over the rocks he is lost in a gulch. In a few minutes he returns, and tells us there is a little water below in a pocket. It is vile and stinking, and our ponies refuse to drink it. We pass on, still ever descending. A mile or two from the water basin we come to a precipice, more than a thousand feet to the bottom. There is a cañon running at a greater depth, and at right angles to this, into which this enters by the precipice; and this second cañon is a lateral one to the greater one, in the bottom of which we are to find the river. Searching about, we find a way by which we can descend along the shelves, and steps, and piles of broken rocks.

We start leading our ponies; a wall upon our left; unknown depths on our right. At places our way is along shelves so narrow, or so sloping, that I ache with fear lest a pony should make a misstep, and knock a man over the cliffs with him. Now and then we start the loose rocks under our feet, and over the cliffs they go, thundering down, down, as the echoes roll through distant cañons. At last we pass along a level shelf for some distance, then we turn to the right, and zigzag down a steep slope to the bottom. Now we pass along this lower cañon, for two or three miles, to where it terminates in the Grand Cañon, as the other ended in this, only the river is 1,800 feet below us, and it seems, at this distance, to be but a creek. Our withered guide, the human pickle, seats himself on a rock, and seems wonderfully amused at our discomfiture, for we can see no way by which to descend to the river. After some minutes, he quietly rises, and, beckoning us to follow, he points out a narrow sloping shelf on the right, and this is to be our way. It leads along the cliff, for half a mile, to a wider bench beyond, which, he says, is broken down on the other side in a great slide, and there we can get to the river. So we start out on the she'f; it is so steep we can hardly stand on it, and to fall, or slip, is to go—don't look and see!

It is soon manifest that we cannot get the ponies along the ledge. The storms have washed it down, since our guide was here last, years ago. One of the ponies has gone so far that we cannot turn him back until we find a wider place, but at last we get him off. With part of the men, I take the horses back to the place where there are a few bushes growing, and turn them loose; in the mean time the other men are looking for some way by which we can get down to the river. When I return, one, Captain Bishop, has found a way, and gone down. We pack bread, coffee, sugar, and two or three blankets among us, and set out. It is now nearly dark, and we cannot find the way by which the captain went, and an hour is spent in fruitless search. Two of the men go away around an amphitheater, more than a fourth of a mile, and start down a broken chasm that faces us, who are behind. These walls, that are vertical, or nearly so, are often cut by chasms, where the showers run down, and the top of these chasms will be back a distance from the face of the wall, and the bed of the chasm will slope down, with here and there a fall. At other places, huge rocks have fallen, and block the way. Down such a one the two men start. There is a curious plant growing out from the crevices of the rock. A dozen stems will start from one root, and grow to the length of eight or ten feet, and not throw out a branch or twig, but these stems are thickly covered with leaves. Now and then the two men come to a bunch of dead stems, and make a fire to mark for us their way and progress.

In the mean time we find such a gulch, and start down, but soon come to the "jumping off place," where we can throw a stone, and hear it faintly striking, away below. We fear that we shall have to stay here, clinging to the rocks until daylight. Our little Indian gathers a few dry stems, ties them into a bundle, lights one end, and holds it up. The others do the same, and with these torches we find a way out of trouble. Helping each other, holding torches for each other, one clinging to another's hand until we can get footing, then supporting the other on his shoulders, so we make our passage into the depths of the cañon. And now Captain Bishop has kindled a huge fire of driftwood, on the bank of the river. This, and the fires in the gulch opposite, and our own flaming torches, light up little patches, that make more manifest the awful darkness below. Still, on we go, for an hour or two, and at last we see Captain Bishop coming up the gulch, with a huge torch-light on his shoulders. He looks like a fiend, waving brands and lighting the fires of hell, and the men in the opposite gulch are imps, lighting delusive fires in inaccessible crevices, over yawning chasms; our own little Indian is surely the king of wizards, so I think, as I stop for a few moments on a rock to rest. At last we meet Captain Bishop, with his flaming torch, and, as he has learned the way, he soon pilots us to the side of the great Colorado. We are hungry and athirst, almost to starvation. Here we lie down on the rocks and drink, just a mouthful or so, as we dare; then we make a cup of coffee, and, spreading our blankets on a sand beach, the roaring Colorado lulls us to sleep.

September 18.—We are in the Grand Cañon, by the side of the Colorado, more than six thousand feet below our camp on the mountain side, which is eighteen miles away; but the miles of horizontal distance represent but a small part of the days' labor before us. It is the mile of altitude we must gain that makes it a herculean task. We are up early; a little bread and coffee, and we look about us. Our conclusion is, that we can make this a dépôt of supplies, should it be necessary; that we can pack our rations to the point where we left our animals last night, and that we can employ Indians to bring them down to the water's edge.

On a broad shelf, we find the ruins of an old stone house, the walls of which are broken down, and we can see where the ancient people who lived here—a race more highly civilized than the present—had made a garden, and used a great spring, that comes out of the rocks, for irrigation. On some rocks near by we discover some curious etchings. Still, searching about, we find an obscure trail up the cañon wall, marked, here and there, by steps which have been built in the loose rock, elsewhere hewn stairways, and we find a much easier way to go up than that by which we came down in the darkness last night. Coming to the top of the wall, we catch our horses, and start. Up the cañon our jaded ponies toil, and we reach the second cliff; up this we go, by easy stages, leading the animals. Now we reach the stinking water pocket; our ponies have had no water for thirty hours, and are eager even for this foul fluid. We carefully strain a kettleful for ourselves, then divide what is left between them—two or three gallons for each; but this does not satisfy them, and they rage around, refusing to eat the scanty grass. We boil our kettle of water, and skim it; straining, boiling, and skimming makes it a little better, for it was full of loathsome, wriggling larvæ, with huge black heads. But plenty of coffee takes away the bad smell, and so modifies the taste that most of us can drink, though our little Indian seems to prefer the original mixture. We reach camp about sunset, and are glad to rest.

September 19.—We are tired and sore, and must rest a day with our Indian neighbors. During the inclement season they live in shelters, made of boughs, or bark of the cedar, which they strip off in long shreds. In this climate, most of the year is dry and warm, and during such time they do not care for shelter. Clearing a small, circular space of ground, they bank it around with brush and sand, and wallow in it during the day, and huddle together in a heap at night, men, women, and children; buckskin, rags, and sand. They wear very little clothing, not needing much in this lovely climate.

Altogether, these Indians are more nearly in their primitive condition than any others on the continent with whom I am acquainted. They have never received anything from the Government, and are too poor to tempt the trader, and their country is so nearly inaccessible that the white man never visits them. The sunny mountain side is covered with wild fruits, nuts, and native grains, upon which they subsist. The *oose*, the fruit of the yucca, or Spanish bayonet, is rich, and not unlike the paw-paw of the valley of the Ohio. They eat it raw, and also roast it in the ashes. They gather the fruits of a cactus plant, which is rich and luscious, and eat them as grapes, or from them express the juice, making the dry pulp into cakes, and saving them for winter; the wine they drink about their camp fires, until the midnight is merry with their revelries.

They gather the seeds of many plants, as sunflowers, golden rods, and grasses. For this purpose, they have large conical baskets, which hold two or more bushels. The women carry them on their backs, suspended from their foreheads by broad straps, and with a smaller one in the left hand, and a willow woven fan in the right, they walk among the grasses, and sweep the seed into the smaller basket, which is emptied, now and then, into the larger, until it is full of seeds and chaff; then they winnow out the chaff and roast the seeds. They roast these curiously; they put the seeds, with a quantity of red hot coals, into a willow tray, and, by rapidly and dexterously shaking and tossing them, keep the coals aglow, and the seeds and tray from burning. As if by magic, so skilled are the crones in this work, they roll the seeds to one side of the tray, as they are roasted, and the coals to the other. Then they grind the seeds into a fine flour, and make it into cakes and mush. It is a merry sight, sometimes, to see the women grinding at the mill. For a mill, they use a large flat rock, lying on the ground, and another small cylindrical one in their hands. They sit prone on the ground, hold the large flat rock between the feet and legs, then fill their laps with seeds, making a hopper to the mill with their dusky legs, and grind by pushing the seeds across the larger rock, where it drops into a tray. I have seen a group of women grinding together, keeping time to a chant, or gossiping and chatting, while the younger lassies would jest and chatter, and make the pine woods merry with their laughter. Mothers carry their babes curiously in baskets. They make a wicker board, by plaiting willows, and sew a buckskin cloth to either edge, and this is fulled in the middle, so as to form a sack, closed at the bottom. At the top, they make a wicker shade, like "my grandmother's sun bonnet," and, wrapping the little one in a wild cat robe, place it in the basket, and this they carry on their backs, strapped over the forehead, and the little brown midgets are ever peering over their mother's shoulders. In camp, they stand the basket against the trunk of a tree, or hang it to a limb.

There is little game in the country, yet they get a mountain sheep now and then, or a deer, with their arrows, for they are not yet supplied with guns. They get many rabbits, sometimes with arrows, sometimes with nets. They make a net of twine, made of the fibers of a native flax. Sometimes this is made a hundred yards in length, and is placed in a half circular position, with wings of sage brush. They have a circle hunt, and drive great numbers of rabbits into the snare, where they are shot with arrows. Most of their bows are made of cedar, but the best are made of the horns of mountain sheep. These are taken, soaked in water, until quite soft, cut into long thin strips, and glued together, and are then quite elastic. During the autumn, grasshoppers are very abundant. When cold weather sets in, these insects are numbed, and can be gathered by the bushel. At such a time, they dig a hole in the sand, heat stones in a fire near by, put some in the bottom of the hole, put on a layer of grasshoppers, then a layer of hot stones, and continue this, until they put bushels on to roast. There they are left until cool, when they are taken out, thoroughly dried, and ground into meal. Grasshopper gruel, or grasshopper cake, is a great treat.

Their lore consists in a mass of traditions, or mythology. It is very difficult to induce them to tell it to white men; but the old Spanish priests, in the days of the conquest of New Mexico, have spread among the Indians of this country many Bible stories, which the Indians are usually willing to tell. It is not always easy to recognize them, the Indian mind being a strange receptacle for such stories, and they are apt to sprout new limbs. May be much of their added quaintness is due to the way in which they were told by the "fathers." But in a confidential way, while you are alone, or when you are admitted to their camp fire on a winter night, you will hear the stories of their mythology. I believe that the greatest mark of friendship, or confidence, that an Indian can give, is to tell you his religion. After one has so talked with me, I should ever trust him; and I feel on very good terms with these Indians, since our experience of the other night.

A knowledge of the watering places, and of the trails and passes, is considered of great importance, and is necessary, to give standing to a chief.

This evening, the *Shi'-rwits*, for whom we have sent, come in, and, after supper, we hold a long council. A blazing fire is built, and around this we sit—the Indians living here, the *Shi'-rwits*, Jacob Hamblin, and myself. This man, Hamblin, speaks their language well, and has a great influence over all the Indians in the region round about. He is a silent, reserved man, and when he speaks, it is in a slow, quiet way, that inspires great awe. His talk is so low that they must listen attentively to hear, and they sit around him in deathlike silence. When he finishes a measured sentence, the chief

Figure 46.—Indians gambling.

repeats it, and they all give a solemn grunt. But, first, I fill my pipe, light it, and take a few whiffs, then pass it to Hamblin; he smokes, and gives it to the man next, and so it goes around. When it has passed the chief, he takes out his own pipe, fills, and lights it, and passes it around after mine. I can smoke my own pipe in turn, but, when the Indian pipe comes around, I am nonplussed. It has a large stem, which has, at some time, been broken, and now there is a buckskin rag wound around it, and tied with sinew, so that the end of the stem is a huge mouthful, and looks like the burying ground of old dead spittle, venerable for a century. To gain time, I refill it, then engage in very earnest conversation, and, all unawares, I pass it to my neighbor unlighted.

I tell the Indians that I wish to spend some months in their country during the coming year, and that I would like them to treat me as a friend. I do not wish to trade; do not want their lands. Heretofore I have found it very difficult to make the natives understand my object, but the gravity of the Mormon missionary helps me much. I tell them that all the great and good white men are anxious to know very many things; that they spend much time in learning, and that the greatest man is he who knows the most. They want to know all about the mountains and the valleys, the rivers and the cañons, the beasts, and birds, and snakes. Then I tell them of many Indian tribes, and where they live; of the European nations; of the Chinese, of Africans, and all the strange things about them that come to my mind. I tell them of the ocean, of great rivers and high mountains, of strange beasts and birds. At last I tell them I wish to learn about their cañons and mountains, and about themselves, to tell other men at home; and that I want to take pictures of everything, and show them to my friends All this occupied much time, and the matter and manner made a deep impression.

Then their chief replies: "Your talk is good, and we believe what you say. We believe in Jacob, and look upon you as a father. When you are hungry, you may have our game. You may gather our sweet fruits. We will give you food when you come to our land. We will show you the springs, and you may drink; the water is good. We will be friends, and when you come we will be glad. We will tell the Indians who live on the

17 COL

other side of the great river that we have seen *Ka'-pu-rats*, and he is the Indians' friend. We will tell them he is Jacob's friend. We are very poor. Look at our women and children; they are naked. We have no horses; we climb the rocks, and our feet are sore. We live among rocks, and they yield little food and many thorns. When the cold moons come, our children are hungry. We have not much to give; you must not think us mean. You are wise; we have heard you tell strange things. We are ignorant. Last year we killed three white men. Bad men said they were our enemies. They told great lies. We thought them true. We were mad; it made us big fools. We are very sorry. Do not think of them, it is done; let us be friends. We are ignorant—like little children in understanding compared with you. When we do wrong, do not get mad, and be like children too.

"When white men kill our people, we kill them. Then they kill more of us. It is not good. We hear that the white men are a great number. When they stop killing us, there will be no Indian left to bury the dead. We love our country; we know not other lands. We hear that other lands are better; we do not know. The pines sing, and we are glad. Our children play in the warm sand; we hear them sing, and are glad. The seeds ripen, and we have to eat, and we are glad. We do not want their good lands; we want our rocks, and the great mountains where our fathers lived. We are very poor; we are very ignorant; but we are very honest. You have horses, and many things. You are very wise; you have a good heart. We will be friends. Nothing more have I to say."

Ka'-pu-rats is the name by which I am known among the Utes and Shoshones, meaning "arm off." There was much more repetition than I have given, and much emphasis. After this a few presents were given, we shook hands, and the council broke up.

Mr. Hamblin fell into conversation with one of the men, and held him until the others had left, and then learned more of the particulars of the death of the three men. They came upon the Indian village almost starved and exhausted with fatigue. They were supplied with food, and put on their way to the settlements. Shortly after they had left, an Indian from the east side of the Colorado arrived at their village, and told them about a number of miners having killed a squaw in drunken brawl, and no doubt these were the men. No person had ever come down the cañon; that was impossible; they were trying to hide their guilt. In this way he worked them into a great rage. They followed, surrounded the men in ambush, and filled them full of arrows.

That night I slept in peace, although these murderers of my men, and their friends, the *U-in-ka-rets*, were sleeping not five hundred yards away. While we were gone to the cañon, the pack-train and supplies, enough to make an Indian rich beyond his wildest dreams, were all left in their charge, and were all safe; not even a lump of sugar was pilfered by the children.

September 20.—For several days we have been discussing the relative merits of several names for these mountains. The Indians call them *U-in-ka-rets*, the region of pines, and we adopt the name. The great mountain we call Mount Trumbull, in honor of the Senator. To day the train starts back to the cañon water pocket, while Captain Bishop and I climb Mount Trumbull. On our way we pass the point that was the last opening to the volcano.

It seems but a few years since the last flood of fire swept the valley. Between two rough, conical hills it poured, and run down the valley to the foot of a mountain standing almost at the lower end, then parted, and ran on either side of the mountain. This last overflow is very plainly marked; there is soil, with trees and grass, to the very edge of it, on a more ancient bed. The flood was everywhere on its border from ten to twenty feet in height, terminating abruptly, and looking like a wall from below. On cooling, it shattered into fragments, but these are still in place, and you can see the outlines of streams and waves. So little time has elapsed since it ran down, that the elements have not weathered a soil, and there is scarcely any vegetation on it, but here and there a lichen is found. And yet, so long ago was it poured from the depths, that where ashes and cinders have collected in a few places, some huge cedars have grown. Near the crater the frozen waves of black basalt are rent with deep fissures, transverse to the direction of the flow. Then we ride through a cedar forest, up a long ascent, until we come to cliffs of columnar basalt. Here we tie our horses, and prepare for a climb among the columns. Through crevices we work, till at last we are on the mountain, a thousand acres of pine land spread out before us, gently rising to the other edge. There are two peaks on the mountain. We walked two miles to the foot of the one looking to be the highest, then a long, hard climb to its summit. And here, oh, what a view is before us! A vision of glory! Peaks of lava all around below us. The Vermilion Cliffs to the north, with their splendor of colors; the Pine Valley Mountain to the northwest, clothed in mellow, perspective haze; unnamed mountains to the southwest, towering over cañons, bottomless to my peering gaze, like chasms to the nadir hell; and away beyond, the San Francisco Mountains, lifting their black heads into the heavens. We find our way down the mountain, reaching the trail made by the pack-train just at dusk, and follow it through the dark until we see the camp-fire—a welcome sight.

Two days more, and we are at Pipe Spring; one day, and we are at Kanab. Eight miles above the town is a cañon, on either side of which is a group of lakes. Four of these are in caves, where the sun never shines. By the side of one of these I sit, the crystal waters at my feet, at which I may drink at will.

Figure 47.—Cave Lake in Kanab Cañon.

CHAPTER X.

By A. H. THOMPSON.

KANAB, UTAH TER., *July* 30, 1872.

SIR: In accordance with your instructions, I proceeded, in the latter part of May, 1872, with the party under my charge, to Kanab, Utah Territory, and immediately refitted for a trip to the junction of the Colorado and Dirty Devil Rivers, having in view the double object of exploring the country, and bringing the boat left, in October, 1871, at that point, to the mouth of the Paria River.

In the summer of 1871, a small party, belonging to this expedition, attempted to reach the junction of the Colorado and Dirty Devil Rivers, by proceeding east from Glencove, Utah Territory; but, after traveling forty or fifty miles, they found it impossible to induce their Indian guides to go farther, and impracticable to proceed without them, so the attempt was abandoned.

Soon after, another party, under charge of Jacob Hamblin, attempted to reach the same point, by proceeding in a northeast direction from Kanab. They discovered the head waters of a stream flowing in an easterly direction to the Colorado River, and followed its course a hundred miles, and until within an estimated distance of ten miles from its mouth. From the volume of water which Mr. Hamblin represented it as carrying, its length, and general course, I had but little doubt it was the Dirty Devil; the more especially as, on our voyage down the Colorado, we had discovered the mouth of no other considerable stream between the junction of the Grand and Green and the Paria. From the report of the same party, I supposed no serious difficulties would be encountered, and that the time necessary for the round trip would be about six weeks, including that occupied by the river party in descending the Colorado through Glen Cañon to the mouth of the Paria River. As re-organized, my party consisted of S. V. Jones and F. S. Dellenbaugh, topographers; J. Fennemore, photographic artist, with W. C. Powell and J. K. Hillers, assistants; P. Dodds, W. D. Johnson, A. Hattan, and G. Adair, packers and general assistants.

Our preparations being completed, we left Kanab on May 27, 1872, traveling that day thirteen miles, in a northeast direction. At first our way was over low, sandy ridges, running out from the base of the Vermilion Cliffs.

At the end of ten miles, we entered a cañon, half a mile wide, cut through the Vermilion Cliffs, and known as Johnson Cañon. At the entrance the walls rose 1,000 feet, but rapidly decreased in height, so that at our camp, three miles above its mouth, we had low, rocky hills on either side.

Our course from Camp No. 2 to Camp No. 3 was nearly north. For six miles we were in a broad, sandy valley, bounded by vertical walls of sandstone on the east, and on the west by low, rocky hills, that, gradually rising, form the northeast slope of the plateau above the Vermilion Cliffs.

Six miles from Camp No. 2 we entered a narrow cañon, cut through the White Cliffs. At the entrance it is half a mile wide, with vertical walls one thousand to one thousand two hundred feet high, often beautifully arched in bas relief. As we ascended, the cañon narrowed to fifty feet, its floor rose rapidly, the walls grew lower, and at the end of three miles we came out into the open country, near the Mormon settlement of Skoompa, having risen 1,098 feet above Kanab settlement. Here we made a camp, and established a topographic station on the summit of a near hill.

Toward the south, between Kanab and Skoompa, the country is traversed by two lines of cliffs—the Vermilion and White—having a general trend north 55° east, and presenting bold, vertical faces from one thousand two hundred to one thousand five hundred feet high. Through these cliffs but three passes were known between the Virgen and the Paria Rivers, a distance of one hundred and ten miles. The first, that known as the Long Valley Pass; the second, up the Kanab Creek; the third, the route which we followed. From the very brink, or crest, of these cliffs, the surface of the country slopes back at an angle of about 2°, so that the general appearance is that of terraces, with escarpments fronting southward and summits sloping toward the north. Scattered over these declivities are fields of loose sand, with continually changing boundaries, in some places burying trees and rocks; in others heaped in huge drifts.

North of our camp, and eight miles distant, the south end of the table land known as the Pauns-a'-gunt Plateau rose to an altitude which we determined to be 3,295 feet above our camp, or about nine thousand two hundred feet above sea level. The eastern boundary of this plateau is a line of cliffs, having a general trend north 45° east. These cliffs show in the distance a beautiful pink color, and, for the upper 2,000 feet, present bold, perpendicular faces, with here and there steep, rocky slopes. From the foot of these slopes and vertical faces long, narrow ridges run out on the plain below. Between these ridges are many beautiful valleys, but probably the whole country is too much elevated for permanent settlement.

From Camp No. 3 to Camp No. 4 our course was northeast. Camp No. 4 was in a beautiful, grassy valley, half a mile wide and six miles long, lying between two cedar covered ridges. At its foot, a small lake stands at the entrance of a narrow cañon, that drains the valley, and cuts its way through both the White and Vermilion Cliffs, furnishing, as we determined by exploration, another practicable route through these escarpments to the valley connecting the Kanab and Paria settlements.

From Camp No. 4 to Camp No. 5 our course was nearly northeast. For four miles we passed over low, grass covered ridges, when we came to the brink of a basin like region, drained by the head waters of the Paria River. The extension of the White Cliffs to the east forms the southern boundary of this basin, and the Pink Cliffs (forming the eastern face of the Pauns-a'-gunt Plateau, and here swinging in a great curve to the north) the northern.

From underneath the cliffs standing around the northern rim of this basin many springs burst forth. These gather at first into five considerable streams, which, uniting near the southern limit of the basin, form the Paria River, and cut through the White and Vermilion Cliffs in deep cañons. In the soft, easily eroded rock within this basin each of these five streams has cut a deep, narrow cañon. Literally, hundreds of side cañons are tributary to these. Between the side cañons stand long, narrow *mesas*. Sometimes the cañon is cut two or three hundred feet, and then, in its floor, a still narrower cañon, often as deep as the first, will be found. One such that we followed is ten miles long, from fifty to three hundred feet deep, and frequently not more than ten feet wide at the top.

As peculiar as the cañons, are the *mesas*, sometimes miles in length, and only a few hundred yards in width, presenting in the distance the appearance of huge knife blades. These *mesas* are usually covered by a loose, sandy soil, though occasionally wide surfaces of bare rock are seen.

Occasionally the cañons widen into little, alcovelike valleys, a few acres in extent, rock walled, and covered by dense growths of grass, canes, or willows. Travel through this country was exceedingly slow and difficult. Our progress was often barred by a cañon, along whose brink we were compelled to follow, till some broken down slope afforded a way to descend, then up or down the cañon, till another broken slope permitted us to ascend, then across a *mesa* to another cañon, repeating the same maneuver a dozen times in half that number of miles.

After a laborious day's work we made fifteen miles, and camped on the right bank of the Paria River, 800 feet below Camp No. 4, and at an altitude of about five thousand seven hundred feet above the level of the sea.

From Camp No. 5 we followed up the Paria River to its junction with Table Cliff Creek; then up the latter to its source. Here we climbed a thousand feet up a steep, clay ridge, having an average slope of 20°, and often not more than five feet in thickness at the top, to the head of a narrow valley called Potato Valley. Down this we traveled three miles, and made Camp No. 6 at a cool spring, in the middle of a beautiful meadow, 1,500 feet above our camp on the Paria River, and about seven thousand two hundred feet above the sea. To the north, and three miles distant, Table Cliff Plateau rose 3,000 feet above us, its face a succession of inaccessible precipices, and steep, broken, tree-clad slopes. From the base of the cliffs, long ridges run out to the edge of the valley. To the east, low, rounded hills gradually rise higher and higher, till, at an elevation of 1,800 feet above camp, they roll off into a long, narrow plateau, bounded on the west by a well marked line of cliffs, beginning near the foot of Table Cliff Plateau, and continuing southeast sixty miles, to a point on the Colorado River opposite the Navajo Mountain. At the western terminus this line is somewhat broken, but

Figure 48.—Cañon in Escalante Basin.

toward the east it increases in height, till at last it stands for thirty miles an inaccessible, vertical wall, 2,500 feet high. Its eastern boundary is a line of cliffs, commencing at the foot of Potato Valley, and presenting an almost unbroken front to the Colorado River, at a point but four miles above the terminus of the western line, thus giving to the plateau a trapezoidal outline, having a length of fifty five miles, a breadth at the base of fifteen, at the apex of four, and standing at an altitude of 9,000 feet above sea level. For fifteen or twenty miles the western end is cut by a perfect net work of cañons and short lines of cliffs, making travel across it almost impossible. The middle and eastern portions are quite level, and when once on the summit progress in any direction is easy. So far as I have been able to ascertain, we were the first white men to visit the plateau. The Indian name for a small elevation near the north end is *Kai-par'-o-wits*, so we called the whole plateau by that name.

Our course from Camp No. 6 was northeast, down Potato Valley. At first we had low, rolling hills on either side, but these soon changed into vertical walls, and the valley became a wide cañon, with a floor descending seventy five feet to the mile. Three miles from camp we came to the head of a small creek, which, receiving accessions from the north side, soon became a considerable stream, with such steep banks and swift current that great difficulty was experienced in fording. We called the creek by the same name as the valley, Potato Creek.

At the end of twenty miles this cañon valley was abruptly ended by a line of cliffs, that stood directly across its course, and into which the stream we followed entered by a narrow cañon, 1,200 feet deep at the very outset, and filled from wall to wall by a torrent. It was down this gorge Mr. Hamblin and party traveled in 1871; but as such a route was manifestly impracticable in the present stage of water, we went into camp, and climbed the cliff to get a view of the country.

On reaching the summit we found we were on the western rim of a basinlike region, seventy miles in length by fifty in breadth, and extending from the eastern slope of the Aquarius Plateau, on the north, to the Colorado River, on the south, and from the Henry Mountains, on the east, to our point of observation, on the west. A large portion of this area is naked,

18 COL

sandstone rock, traversed in all directions by a perfect labyrinth of narrow gorges, sometimes seeming to cross each other, but finally uniting in a principal one, whose black line could be traced, cutting its way to the Colorado, a few miles above the mouth of the San Juan River.

The perilous character of the journey of Mr. Hamblin and party was apparent. For eighty miles they traveled in a cañon, finding, in all that distance, but two places where the walls could be scaled. They crossed, recrossed, waded, and sometimes swam a rapid stream, that often filled the gorge from wall to wall. A single shower, on the rock land above, would have changed the stream to a raging torrent, that would have swept them into the Colorado, or imprisoned them in some rock walled alcove, with no possible way of escape.

Away to the east, and fifty miles distant, rose the Henry Mountains, their gray slopes streaked with long lines of white by the snow which yet remained in the gulches near their summits. On our voyage down the Colorado River, in 1871, we had determined the mouth of the Dirty Devil River to be about thirty miles northeast from these mountains, making it at least eighty miles from our present camp, and directly across the net work of cañons before us. To proceed farther in the direction we had been pursuing was impossible. No animal without wings could cross the deep gulches in the sandstone basin at our feet. The stream which we had followed, and whose course soon became lost in the multitude of chasms before us, was not the one we were in search of, but an unknown, unnamed river, draining the eastern slope of the Aquarius Plateau, and flowing, through a deep, narrow cañon, to the Colorado River. Believing our party to be the discoverers, we decided to call this stream, in honor of Father Escalante, the old Spanish explorer, Escalante River, and the country which it drains, Escalante Basin.

The western boundary of the basin is the vertical wall forming the eastern edge of the Kai-par'-o-wits Plateau. From the very base of this cliff, the drainage is to the Escalante River, by narrow, deep cañons, presenting apparently impassable barriers to travel toward the south. To the north, and twenty miles away, rose the eastern slope of the Aquarius Plateau. Its general trend is north and south, but away to the northwest, and about forty miles from our point of observation, a great, salient angle projects eastward toward the Henry Mountains, the slopes at its base seeming to continue out a long distance, and form a low, broken ridge between cañons running southward, to the Escalante River, and others running northward. Here, if anywhere, this cañon region could be crossed, and I decided to go eastward along the slope of the great plateau, to the salient spoken of, and then attempt the passage along the ridge.

To carry out this plan would require more supplies and time than were allotted, so I decided to divide my party, sending three men to bring rations from Kanab to the foot of Potato Valley, while I prosecuted the exploration with the remainder.

Leaving the foot of Potato Valley, we traveled a little west of north, up a creek called, from the many fine pine trees in its valley, Pine Creek. This stream rises in a semicircular alcove in the eastern wall of the Aquarius Plateau, and flows at the foot of the sandstone cliff which forms the western wall of the Escalante Basin, till near Potato Creek, when it turns abruptly to the eastward, cuts a deep, narrow cañon in the cliff, and unites with the main stream in the heart of the basin.

After pursuing this course for twelve miles, and rising about five hundred feet, we turned to the right, climbed 900 feet of steep slope to the crest of a long, narrow, ridge running out from the Aquarius Plateau. On this we traveled toward the north till night, when we camped on the bank of a beautiful birch fringed brook, 2,000 feet above the foot of Potato Valley.

The table land, which we called Aquarius Plateau, is about forty miles long, by twenty broad. Its general surface is a level, rocky plain, dotted by numerous lakes. Its eastern side, near the summit, is a steep, and often vertical wall, over which little streams plunge in most beautiful cascades and falls. From the foot of this wall, a long, gentle slope reaches to the level of the Escalante Basin. Lakes dot the upper portion, and, at intervals, cascade brooks make the air musical with running waters.

For two days we traveled along this slope, having, all the time, the snow covered crest of the Aquarius Plateau on our left, and the Escalante Basin with its wilderness of dark cañons, white capped buttes, and orange cliffs, ·with intervening miles of naked rock, and loose, drifting sands on our right, till we reached the salient spoken of. Here we found that the eastern line of the plateau swung in another great curve to the north, and thus again projected in a salient, like the one we had reached.

In the angle between these salients lies a beautiful valley, drained by a stream flowing northward, being, in fact, as we afterward ascertained, one of the southern branches of the Dirty Devil River. We went into camp at this point, and spent a day in exploration.

The stream draining the valley between the salients soon enters a narrow cañon, and the whole country becomes so cut by transverse gorges that travel in that direction was manifestly impracticable. During the day an old Indian trail was discovered, leading along the low, broken ridge noticed from the foot of Potato Valley. This we followed the next morning, and after many wanderings around the heads of cañons, running both northward and southward, came to the edge of the cliff forming the eastern rim of the Escalante Basin, and overlooking a valley 2,000 feet below. After some trouble we found a practicable way to descend, though most of the time we were on bare rock, often sloping at an angle of twenty five degrees. Reaching the foot, we found ourselves on the bank of a clear stream, flowing through groves of cottonwood, and well entitled to the name which we gave it—Pleasant Creek. During the day we had observed many fresh signs of Indians, and early the next morning we found a small party gathering seeds. From their questions, and the surprise they evinced at our appearance, it was evident that we were the first white men who had been known to visit this portion of their country. We traveled but three miles this day, spending the most of the time in endeavoring to induce the Indians to accompany us, but with no success.

On leaving this camp our course was south fifteen degrees east, for eight miles, when we turned to the left, and entered a narrow cañon, with vertical walls 800 feet high. We followed this for ten miles, and to its head, finding no place where its walls could be scaled, and reluctantly returned, and camped for the night near its mouth. The next day, after much searching and considerable labor, we made a trail up a rocky point, and camped that night at a water pocket, in the head of a cañon, on the *mesa* above. The next day we crossed the *mesa*, to the flank of the Henry Mountains, and

Figure 19.—Tower at the mouth of the Dirty Devil River.

camped on the side of the second peak of the range, at an elevation of about eight thousand feet above the sea. Our camp was on a small stream, evidently formed by the melting snows in the gulches above us.

The Henry Mountains consist of five peaks, having a northerly and southerly axis, standing on the back of the plateau lying between the Dirty Devil and Colorado Rivers. They are completely isolated, being fifty miles from the Wasatch Plateau and Thousand Lake Mountain, on the west; about the same distance from the Sierra Abajo, on the east, and sixty miles from a huge, lone peak, which we have called the Navajo Mountain, on the south. The three northern peaks have an elevation of about eleven thousand feet above the sea; the others, less. The crest of the most northern is a long, irregular ridge; but the others rise to sharp points.

From the summits of these mountains we could see the junction of the cañons of the Dirty Devil and Colorado Rivers. So, after such an examination of the range as our limited time would permit, we pursued a course a little north of east, and camped, the night after leaving the mountains, by a small stream, which, from the boulders in its bed, we called Trachyte Creek. The next day we followed its course, with considerable difficulty, until we found it would take us to the Colorado, at a point south of our point of destination. We then camped, and, after much search, found a way up and across the sand covered *mesa* lying north of the creek, and came to the head of a deep cañon, that joined the Colorado two miles south of the mouth of the Dirty Devil River. I recognized it as one explored by members of our party when camped near its mouth last year, and felt confident that if we could once get down its precipitous side to the bottom, we could easily make our way to the river. After many efforts, we succeeded in descending, and camped that night near a spring in the cañon. The next day we followed down its course without difficulty, and came to the river about two miles below the point where our boat was *cached*.

Here we went into camp, and made our way on foot along the west bank of the Colorado to our boat, finding it undisturbed, although the high water had washed the sand from underneath her keel. The next day was spent in repairing the boat. With the aid of the materials brought from Kanab we were able to make her perfectly seaworthy.

I again divided my small party, detaching Messrs. Hillers, Fenni-more, Dellenbaugh, and Johnson as a boat party, to proceed through the cañon, to the mouth of the Paria, while, with the remainder, I returned, by the same route we had explored, to the foot of Potato Valley, passing over in six days the distance we were fifteen days in making on our journey out.

Here we found the party sent to Kanab awaiting us with supplies. After spending two days at this point making astronomic observations, we returned to Kanab, establishing several geodetic and topographic stations on our way, and arriving July 8, having been absent forty-one days.

The boat party arrived at the mouth of the Paria, after a successful trip, on July 11.

FORESTS.

The low ridges running out from the base of the Vermilion Cliffs are usually covered by a scanty growth of cedars, fit only for fencing and fire wood. About one-fourth of the area of the plateaus above—the Vermilion and the White Cliffs—is covered by a scattered growth of pine and cedar; but neither the quantity, quality, nor accessibility renders it of much value.

The ridges spoken of as running out from the foot of the eastern face of the Pauns-a′-gunt Plateau, are usually covered by a scanty growth of low, scrubby cedars; but in the intervening valleys are groves of pine, from which considerable quantities of lumber might be cut; while on the plateau itself is the finest forest of pine and spruce in Southern Utah. It is easily accessible from the valley of the Sevier River, on the west, and when the country is settled must become quite valuable.

The *mesas* in the basin of the Paria River are mostly covered by cedars and piñon pines. Where the cañons of the streams widen into valleys, small groves of cottonwoods are often found, and near the sources of these streams are scattered pitch pines, thickets of birch, and a low, scrubby oak of no value.

The eastern end of the Kai-par′-o-wits Plateau, the ridges running down from Table Cliff Plateau, as well as its summit, and the broken country around the foot of Potato Valley, are covered by a forest of pine and cedar.

No timber of any value is found in the Escalante Basin. The summit of the Aquarius Plateau is crowned by a forest of spruce, that also extends in dark masses along the foot of the nearly vertical wall that forms the eastern crest of the eastern slope, while aspens and birches fringe its lakes and streams. Farther down, pines stand in open groves, and give to the whole country a park like appearance. These continue till near the level of Escalante Basin, where they give way to cedars.

Upon the foot-hills of the Henry Mountains is a dense growth of low, scrubby cedars, and in the gulches near their summits are a few groves of aspen, pine, and spruce; but generally the timber upon these mountains is in almost inaccessible places.

In the cañon of the Dirty Devil River, and in other cañons draining into the Colorado, are considerable quantities of cottonwood. From the data collected, I estimate that ten per cent. of the country explored is covered by forests, valuable for lumber, thirty per cent. by forests valuable only for fuel and fencing, and the remainder by grass, sage, greasewood, loose sands, or naked rock.

WATER, ARABLE LAND, GRASS, ETC.

Irrigation is a necessary adjunct to successful cultivation in all the region explored, so the amount of arable land depends solely upon the amount of water that can be used for that purpose. In Johnson's Cañon springs burst out from the foot of the cliffs, and form a small stream, that flows a mile or two before sinking in the sand, furnishing enough water, during the dry season, to irrigate one hundred acres of land.

At Skoompa, a small stream, coming down from the Pink Cliffs, furnishes sufficient water to irrigate one hundred and fifty acres, but the altitude is so great that only the more hardy cereals can be grown.

Over all the country between the Pauns-a'-gunt Plateau and the White Cliffs grass grows abundantly, and the many fine springs in the valleys lying between the ridges furnish sufficient water for grazing.

In the Paria Basin the streams are from fifty to three hundred feet below the general level of the country, so no land can be cultivated except where the cañons widen into narrow valleys. At Camp No. 5 the cañon of the Paria expands into a valley, half a mile wide and about three miles long The river carries here about the same volume of water as at its mouth, fifty miles distant. In fact, no permanent stream joins it below this point. Freshets often occur, and, as every shower washes down great quantities of the soft, clayey soil of the basin, the stream frequently presents the appearance of a river of mud. So great is the quantity of the clay held in solution that considerable difficulty is experienced in using its waters for irrigation at the Paria settlement. When turned into the fields it soon covers the whole surface with an impervious coat, that effectually prevents the water from sinking into the soil.

The cañon of Table Cliff Creek is wider than that of the Paria, and contains some hundreds of acres of land that might be cultivated, except for the limited quantity of water the creek affords.

On the *mesas*, in the Paria Basin, is a considerable extent of grazing land. The lower end of Potato Valley is elevated about five thousand feet above the sea level, and contains two thousand acres of arable land. Potato Creek would easily furnish sufficient water to irrigate it. In the upper portion of this valley are many acres of fine, natural meadows, while on the *mesas* and in the broken country is a fine range for cattle.

We found no arable land within the limits of Escalante Basin.

The eastern slope of the Aquarius Plateau has an average elevation of 7,000 feet, and, though too high for cultivation, it furnishes the finest natural facilities for grazing. Grass grows abundantly everywhere, and streams of pure, cool water are met at intervals of every two or three miles. Indeed, from the depth, rapidity, and number of the streams we crossed flowing into the Escalante Basin, we supposed the river of that name carried twice the amount of water as the Paria, but when the boat party arrived at its junction with the Colorado, they found only a small stream, that a man could leap across; the greater portion had been absorbed, or evaporated in the sandstone basin.

Along Pleasant Creek are about a thousand acres of land, which the water of the creek might be used to irrigate. We saw no arable land, and but one spring that we thought permanent, in the Henry Mountains. There is a small stream, which we called Trachyte Creek, east of the range, and flowing into the Colorado. There are some good grazing lands along its course, but none fit for cultivation.

I estimate that not more than one per cent. of the land adjacent to our route of travel can be cultivated, but sixty per cent. is of greater or less value for grazing.

DISTANCE, ETC.

The distance traveled by the main party, to the mouth of the Dirty Devil River, was two hundred and eighty miles, through a country, for the most part, completely unknown. I have not been able to find any evidence that white men ever before visited any considerable portion of the country explored.

With the data collected, we shall be able to make a valuable reconnaissance map, showing the general features of the region, and quite full in detail, along the route traveled.

I am, with great respect, your obedient servant,

A. H. THOMPSON.

J. W. POWELL,
In charge Exploration of the Colorado River, and its Tributaries.

19 COL

PART SECOND.

ON THE PHYSICAL FEATURES OF THE VALLEY OF THE COLORADO.

CHAPTER XI.

ON THE PHYSICAL FEATURES OF THE VALLEY OF THE COLORADO.

The topographic features of the valley of the Colorado, or the area drained by the Colorado River and its tributaries, are, in many respects, unique, as some of these features, perhaps, are not reproduced, except to a very limited extent, on any other portion of the surface of the globe. Mountains, hills, plateaus, plains, and valleys are here found, as elsewhere throughout the earth; but, in addition to these topographic elements in the scenic features of the region, we find buttes, outlying masses of stratified rocks, often of great altitude, not as dome shaped or conical mounds, but usually having angular outlines; their sides are vertical walls, terraced or buttressed, and broken by deep, re-entering angles, and often naked of soil and vegetation.

Then we find lines of cliffs, abrupt escarpments of rock, of great length and great height, revealing the cut edges of strata swept away from the lower side. Thirdly, we find cañons, narrow gorges, scores or hundreds of miles in length, and hundreds or thousands of feet in depth, with walls of precipitous rocks.

In the arid region of the western portion of the United States, there are certain tracts of country which have received the name of *mauvaises terres*, or bad-lands. These are dreary wastes—naked hills, with rounded or conical forms, composed of sand, sandy clays, or fine fragments of shaly rocks, with steep slopes, and, yielding to the pressure of the foot, they are climbed only by the greatest toil, and it is a labor of no inconsiderable magnitude to penetrate or cross such a district of country. The steep hills are crowded together, and the water-ways separating them are deep *arroyas*. Where the mud rocks or sandy clays and shales, of which the hills are composed, are interstratified with occasional harder beds, the slopes are terraced; and when these thinly bedded, though harder, rocks prevail, the outlines of the topography are changed, and present angular surfaces, and give rise to another type of topographic features, which I have denominated Alcove Lands.

The agencies and conditions under which all of these features have been formed deserve mention, and in this and following chapters I shall briefly discuss this subject, in a manner as free from technical terms as will be consistent with accurate description.

The discussion will by no means be exhaustive, and I hope hereafter to treat this subject in a more thorough manner. In view of these facts, I shall not attempt any logical classification of the elements of the topography, nor of the agencies and conditions under which they were produced; but, commencing at the north, at the initial point of the exploration, I shall take them up in geographic order, as we proceed down the river.

BAD-LANDS AND ALCOVE LANDS NORTH OF THE UINTA MOUNTAINS.

The area north of the Uinta Mountains embraced in the survey is but small. Through the middle of it runs Green River, in a deep, narrow valley, the sides or walls of which sometimes approach so near to each other, and are so precipitous, as to form a cañon.

The general surface of the country, on the north of this district, is about a thousand feet above the river, with peaks, here and there, rising a few hundred feet higher; but south, toward the Uinta Mountains, this general surface, within a few miles of the river, gradually descends, and at the foot of the mountains we find a valley on either side, with a direction transverse to that of the course of Green River, and parallel to the mountain range.

To the north, the water-ways are all deeply eroded; the permanent streams have flood-plains of greater or lesser extent, but the channels of the wet weather streams, i. e., those which are dry during the greater part of the year, are narrow, and much broken by abrupt falls.

The rocks are the sediments of a dead lake, and are quite variable in lithologic characteristics. We find thinly laminated shales, hard limestones, breaking with an angular fracture, crumbling bad-land rocks, and homogeneous, heavily bedded sandstones.

Figure 50.—Bad-land mountains near Black's Fork.

The scenic features of the country are alike variable. On the cliffs about Green River City, towers and buttes are seen as you look from below, always regarded by the passing traveler as strange freaks of nature. The limestones, interstratified with shales, give terraced and buttressed characteristics to the escarpments of the cañons and narrow valleys.

Immediately south of Bitter Creek, on the east side of Green River, there is a small district of country which we have called the Alcove Land. On the east, it is drained by Little Bitter Creek, a dry gulch much of the year. This run north into Bitter Creek, a permanent stream, which empties into the Green. The crest of this water-shed is an irregular line, only two to four miles back from the river, but usually more than a thousand feet above it, so that the waters have a rapid descent, and every shower born rill has excavated a deep, narrow channel, and these narrow cañons are so close to each other as to be separated by walls of rock so steep, in most places, that they cannot be scaled, and many of these little cañons are so broken by falls as to be impassable in either direction.

The whole country is cut, in this way, into irregular, angular blocks, standing as buttresses, benches, and towers, about deep water-ways and gloomy alcoves.

The conditions under which the cañons have been carved will be more elaborately discussed hereafter.

To the west of Green River, and back some miles, between Black's Fork and Henry's Fork, we have a region of buff, chocolate, and lead colored bad-lands. This bad-land country differs from the Alcove Land, above mentioned, in that its outlines are everywhere beautifully rounded, as the rocks of which it is composed crumble quickly under atmospheric agencies, so that an exposure of solid rock is rarely seen; but we have the same abrupt descent of the streams, and the same elaborate system of water channels. Here we have loose, incoherent sandstones, shales, and clays, carved, by a net-work of running waters, into domes and cones, with flowing outlines. But still there is no vegetation, and the loose earth is naked. Occasionally, a thin stratum of harder rock will be found. Such strata will here and there form shelves or steps upon the sides of the mountains.

Traces of iron, and rarer minerals, are found in these beds, and on exposure to the air, the chemical agencies give a greater variety of colors, so that the mountains and cones, and the strange forms of the bad-lands, are elaborately and beautifully painted; not with the delicate tints of verdure, but with brilliant colors, that are gorgeous when first seen, but which soon pall on the senses.

THE UINTA MOUNTAINS.

To the west of Green River stand the Wasatch Mountains, a system of peaks, tables, and elevated valleys, having a northerly and southerly direction, nearly parallel to the river. The range known as the Uinta Mountains stands at right angles to the Wasatch, extending toward the east, and no definite line of division can be noticed. The Wasatch is a great trunk, with a branch called the Uinta. Near the junction, the two ranges have about the same altitude, and the gulches of their summits are filled with perpetual snow; but toward the east, the Uinta peaks are lower, gradually diminishing in altitude, until they are lost in low ridges and hills.

Through this range Green River runs, and a series of cañons forms its channel.

To a person studying the physical geography of this country, without a knowledge of its geology, it would seem very strange that the river should cut through the mountains, when, apparently, it might have passed around them to the east, through valleys, for there are such along the north side of the Uintas, extending to the east, where the mountains are degraded to hills, and, passing around these, there are other valleys, extending to the Green, on the south side of the range. Then, why did the river run through the mountains?

The first explanation suggested is that it followed a previously formed fissure through the range; but very little examination will show that this explanation is unsatisfactory. The proof is abundant that the river cut its own channel; that the cañons are gorges of corrasion. Again, the question returns to us, why did not the stream turn around this great obstruction, rather than pass through it? The answer is that the river had the right of way; in other words, it was running ere the mountains were formed: not before the rocks of which the mountains are composed, were deposited, but before the formations were folded, so as to make a mountain range.

The contracting or shriveling of the earth causes the rocks near the surface to wrinkle or fold, and such a fold was started athwart the course of the river. Had it been suddenly formed, it would have been an obstruction sufficient to turn the water in a new course to the east, beyond the extension of the wrinkle; but the emergence of the fold above the general surface of the country was little or no faster than the progress of the corrasion of the channel. We may say, then, that the river did not cut its way *down* through the mountains, from a height of many thousand feet above its present site, but, having an elevation differing but little, perhaps, from what it now has, as the fold was lifted, it cleared away the obstruction by cutting a cañon, and the walls were thus elevated on either side. The river preserved its level, but mountains were lifted up; as the saw revolves on a fixed pivot, while the log through which it cuts is moved along. The river was the saw which cut the mountains in two.

Recurring to the time before this wrinkle was formed, there were beds of sandstone, shale, and limestone, more than twenty four thousand feet in thickness, spread horizontally over a broad stretch of this country. Then the summit of the fold slowly emerged, until the lower beds of sandstone were lifted to the altitude at first occupied by the upper beds, and if these upper beds had not been carried away, they would now be found more than twenty four thousand feet above the river, and we should have a billow of sandstone, with its axis lying in an easterly and westerly direction, more than a hundred miles in length, fifty miles in breadth, and over twenty four thousand feet higher than the present altitude of the river, gently rounded from its central line above to the foot of the slope on either side. But as the rocks were lifted, rains fell upon them and gathered into streams, and the wash of the rains and the corrasion of the rivers cut the billow down almost as fast as it rose, so that the present altitude of these mountains marks only the difference between the elevation and the denudation.

It has been said that the elevation of the wrinkle was twenty-four thousand feet, but it is probable that this is not the entire amount, for the present altitude of the river, above the sea, is nearly six thousand feet, and when this

20 COL

folding began we have reason to believe that the general surface of this country was but slightly above that general standard of comparison.

Then there were down-turned as well as up-turned wrinkles, or, as the geologist would say, there were synclinal as well as anticlinal folds. Had there been no degradation of the fold, there would have been a bed of rock turned over its summit twenty-four thousand feet above the present level of the river. Now that bed is gone from the mountains, yet it can be seen turned up on edge against the flanks of the mountains, dipping under the beds of rocks found still farther out from the range. Follow it down, and doubtless we could trace it to a depth much below the level of the sea. While the folds were forming, the upturned flexures were cut down, and the troughs in the down-turned flexures were filled up, and we have more than eight thousand feet of these later sediments to the north of the Uinta Mountains.

It will thus be seen that the upheaval was not marked by a great convulsion, for the lifting of the rocks was so slow that the rains removed the sandstones almost as fast as they came up. The mountains were not thrust up as peaks, but a great block was slowly lifted, and from this the mountains were carved by the clouds—patient artists, who take what time may be necessary for their work.

We speak of mountains forming clouds about their tops; the clouds have formed the mountains. Lift a district of granite, or marble, into their region, and they gather about it, and hurl their storms against it, beating the rocks into sands, and then they carry them out into the sea, carving out cañons, gulches, and valleys, and leaving plateaus and mountains embossed on the surface.

Instead of having a rounded billow, we have an irregular table, with beds dipping to the north, on the north side of the axis, and to the south, on the south side, and in passing over the truncated fold we pass over their upturned edges.

Go out on the flank of the fold, and find the bed of rock which would form the summit of the great wrinkle, had there been no erosion, and there sink a shaft 24,000 feet, and you will be able to study a certain succession of beds of sandstones, shales, and limestones. Go two or three miles farther from the mountains, and sink a shaft; the first eight thousand feet or more

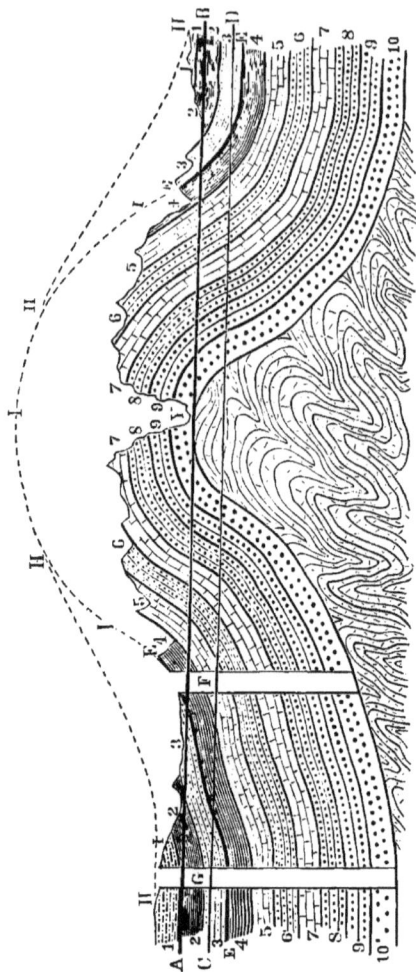

Figure 51.—Generalized section through the Uinta Mountains from north to south.

will be through sandstones and shales, unlike those seen in the first section; then you will strike the summit of the first section. Continuing down for 24,000 feet. the first will be reproduced, stratum for stratum. Now start on either side of the fold, and cross to its center, and you will pass over the same series of strata in the same order as you would in descending the first mentioned shaft, and in the second also, below the upper 8,000 feet. Now pass again from the center to the flank of the fold, in either direction, and you can study the same rocks in the same order as you would in ascending these shafts. It will thus be seen that in these truncated wrinkles we are enabled to study geological formations without descending into the depths of the earth.

Figure 51 has been constructed for the purpose of graphically express-ing some of the important facts observed in the great Uinta Fold. In this, the beds are seen to turn up in a great flexure, and to be cut away above, the higher beds more than the lower; thus 4, 4–1, 4, has been cut away much more than 5, 5–5, 5; and 10, 10–10, 10 has suffered much less erosion than the beds above it. The only place where the water has carried it away is at Y, the bottom of the cañon.

In this diagram, the line A–B represents the lowest line of observation, as exhibited in the bed of the river. All below this line is theoretical. The line C–D represents the level of the sea. The stratum E, E–E, E was the last deposited antecedent to the commencement of the emergence of the summit of the fold. Had there been no erosion of the fold, the beds inter-vening between the broken line I, I, I, (which is a continuation of the lines E, E–E, E,) and the irregular line which represents the surface of the country, cutting the edges of the eroded beds, and passing through the lowest, No. 10, at Y, would still be found, but they have been carried away.

The diagram does not properly represent the entire amount of erosion, from the fact that the vertical scale is exaggerated, and the beds have been extended beyond their proper limits, for the purpose of representing more clearly other facts of interest.

It will be seen that in passing along the line A–B, (the bottom of the river channel,) from the shaft F, to the bottom of the cañon Y, we are able to observe the beds 4, 5, 6, 7, 8, 9, 10, in the same order that we would in descending the shaft F. The beds 1–1, 2–2 have been deposited since the emergence of the summit of the fold, and hence never extended quite across it; yet the lower members of these beds, doubtless, at one time extended much farther up on the flanks of the fold. They have been cut away, however, as represented in the diagram. Let the lines II, II–II, II, represent the limit of the continuation of these beds. In the shaft G these beds also are exposed above those seen in shaft F.

The altitude of the rocks above the line of observation, (A, B,) is exaggerated about five times. If they were reduced to one-fifth, the proportion between the rocks seen in the various escarpments of these mountains, and those carried away below the broken lines, would be properly represented.

By sinking a shaft, only a little surface along the edge of the strata could be seen; but on the sides of the fold they are exposed for many miles, and often the top or bottom is cleared off for a great space, revealing even the ripple marks of the ancient sea, or rounded impressions of rain drops which fell in that elder time; or the sands have buried shells and bones of ancient animals, and they are still encased in the rock; and even impressions of leaves that were buried in the mud can yet be seen in such a fine state of preservation that you can trace their delicate veins.

In speaking of the great upheaval of rocks from which the Uinta Mountains are carved, I have spoken of wrinkling and folding, as if the rocks were always flexed; but these displacements are sometimes attended with fractures, on one side of which the rocks are upheaved, or thrown down on the other. Such displacements are called faults. Faults like these are seen in many places in the Uinta Mountains; one great one, on the north side, the throw of which is nearly twenty thousand feet, and many others are found of lesser magnitude.

In speaking of elevation and depression by faulting or folding, it must be understood that reference is made to a change of altitude in relation to the surface of the sea, so that upheaval or throw is only relative to this general standard of comparison. But during the geological ages represented in the folding and carving of the Uinta Mountains, it is possible the level of the sea itself has been changed by the shrinking of the earth, and a part, at least, of the apparent upheaval above mentioned may be accounted for by a depression of the formations in synclinal folds, and the letting down of broad areas of the earth's surface by lateral contraction exhibited in corrugation.

When we arrive at a point a few miles north of Flaming Gorge, we strike the flank of this great fold, and find the rocks dipping to the north, and, as we run south, the course of the stream is against the inclination of the beds; and this is true, in the main, until we reach Bee Hive Point, where the river turns to the east, almost at right angles to its former course, and to the dip; then it runs nearly in the direction of the strike, but the axis is not crossed until after passing through Red Cañon. The rocks on both sides of this cañon dip to the north; that is, they incline to the river on the south, and from it on the north. Under these conditions, the two walls of Red Cañon present very different characteristics; that on the south exhibits steep slopes, covered, to a greater or lesser extent, with forests; the north wall is a bold escarpment, often vertical, and almost treeless; high cliffs, set with pinnacles and towers, and narrow side cañons, are its salient features.

From the foot of Red Cañon to the Gate of Lodore, a distance of more than thirty miles, the river runs through a valley known as Brown's Park, five or six miles wide, and enclosed by mountains. It is a curious fact that the central line of this valley corresponds to the axis of the fold; that is, had the fold been made, and left without erosion, the very summit would have been directly above the deepest part of the park.

When we enter the Gate of Lodore, we are in rocks dipping to the south, having crossed the axis of the fold. From here to Split Mountain Cañon the general course is southwest, hence not directly across the dip, but passing obliquely through the formations. The great billow or wave has a rippled surface, or wavelets are formed across it, some of which have their axis nearly at right angles to that of the great fold, others more or less oblique.

Split Mountain Cañon is cut lengthwise through one of the rock wavelets, a southward spur of the Uintas. The course of the river does not chance to be in the direction of the billow for its whole length, but, running down the wavelet for a few miles, it runs out of it to the right, where it passes through Island Park, then into it again at the head of Split Mountain Cañon, and then it divides the fold by a gorge to its foot.

Leaving Split Mountain Cañon, and entering the valley below, we run into a down-turned wrinkle, or, in the language of the geologist, into a synclinal fold. The axis of the fold is parallel to the Uinta Mountains. The valley of the Uinta, on the west, and the valley of White River, on the east, mark, in a general way, the bed of this down-turned wrinkle; and still continuing to the south, we pass into another up-turned fold.

It has already been said that the cutting off of the fold has left the upturned edges of the formations exposed to view. Some of these beds are quite hard, others are composed of very soft material, so there are alternating beds of harder and softer rocks running in an easterly and westerly direction, both on the north and south side of the range. The soft rocks, yielding much more readily to atmospheric degradation, have been washed out in irregular valleys, between intervening ridges of harder rock, so that we have a series of nearly parallel valleys, and also a series of intervening parallel ridges, and both valleys and ridges are approximately parallel to the range. But as the great fold of the Uinta Mountains is greatly complicated by minor oblique and transverse flexures, while the general direction of these ridges is as described, they are turned back and forth from these lines in gentle or abrupt curves. These ridges are sometimes low mountain ranges.

So, if we approach these mountains from either direction, north or south, we first meet with ridges, or, as they are usually called in the western country, hog-backs. In many places these are so steep as to form a complete barrier to progress.

Figure 52.—Northern slope of the Uinta Mountains, showing Red Cañon and hog-backs, with intervening valleys.

Usually the slope away from the side of the mountain corresponds above with the dip of the rock, and is gentle or steep, as the dip is lesser or greater. The side of the hog-back, next to the mountain, is composed of the cut edges of the strata, and varies greatly with the texture of the rock, but usually it is steep or broken, sometimes buttressed, sometimes terraced, sometimes columned and fluted.

On the south side of the Yampa Plateau, near the head of Cliff Creek Valley, there is an abrupt, oblique flexure, on the side of the great fold, by which the rocks are turned up, so as to stand vertically. In the rocks at this place there are two very hard conglomerates; the intervening strata are soft sandstones and marls, and have been carried away, and the conglomerates stand as vertical walls, thirty or forty feet in thickness, fifty to three hundred feet in height, and several miles in length, and between these is a broad avenue, or narrow valley, beset with ragged boulders of conglomerate.

The drainage of these narrow valleys between the hog-backs is not always along their lengths, but the water is sometimes carried by channels crossing them and cutting through intervening ridges; hence there are numbers of transverse streams and wet weather channels running across valleys and through ridges.

Now, if the great axis of the Uinta Fold was everywhere the summit of a water-shed, we should find the streams heading along that irregular line running off to the flank of the fold on either side; but, as the fold is bisected by Green River, some of the minor water courses, especially those near the river, and those near the center of the fold, follow the strike of the rocks directly into that stream. On the north side, some head back near the summit of the fold, and run to the north, crossing the hog-backs in a direction with the dip, and then turn, at the foot of the mountains, and run into the Green, where the waters take a general southerly direction. Others, again, head back on the hog-backs, or even beyond them, on the plains and the bad-lands to the north, and cut quite through the hog-backs and mountains in a direction against the dip of the rocks, and empty into the Green. This is especially true where the river has its easterly and westerly direction through Brown's Park. On the other side of the range, streams head high up in the mountains, and cut directly or obliquely against the upturned edges of the strata, and run in a general direction with the dip of the strata until they reach the long valleys between hog-backs, then down these valleys they turn, sometimes cutting through intervening ridges, until they find their way into the Green, where they are turned to the south, away from the mountain.

It will thus be seen that the relation of the direction of the streams to the dip of the rocks is very complex, and, for convenience of description, I have elsewhere classified these valleys, on the basis of these relations, in the following manner:

Order first. *Transverse* valleys, having a direction at right angles to the strike.

Order second. *Longitudinal* valleys, having a direction the same as the strike.

Of the first order, three varieties are noticed:

a, diaclinal, those which pass through a fold. (Fig. 53.)

b, cataclinal, valleys that run in the direction of the dip. (Fig. 54.)

c, anaclinal, valleys that run against the dip of the beds. (Fig. 57.)

Of the second order, we have, also, three varieties:

A, anticlinal valleys, which follow anticlinal axes. (Fig. 55.)

B, synclinal valleys, which follow synclinal axes. (Fig. 56.)

C, monoclinal valleys, which run in the direction of the strike between the axes of the fold—one side of the valley formed of the summits of the beds, the other composed of the cut edges of the formation. (Fig. 58.)

Many of the valleys are thus simple in their relations to the folds; but, as we may have two systems of displacements, a valley may belong to one class, in relation to one fold, and to another in its relation to a second. Such we designate as *complex* valleys.

Again, a valley may belong to one class in one part of its course and to another elsewhere in its course. Such we designate as *compound* valleys. It will be further noticed that valleys may have many branches, but, in relegating a valley to its class, we consider only the stem of the valley proper, and not its branches.

A great diversity in the features of all these valleys is observed. Most of these modifications are due to three principal causes: First, a greater or

Figure 53.—A Diaclinal Valley.

Figure 54.—A Cataclinal Valley.

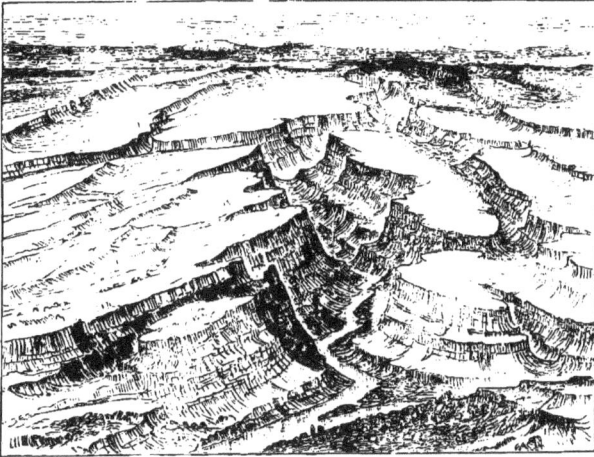

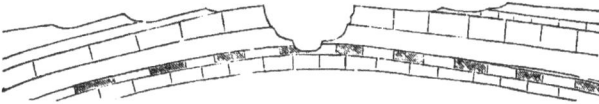

Figure 55.—An Anticlinal Valley, with section.

Figure 56.—A Synclinal Valley.

Figure 57.—An Anaclinal Valley.

Figure 58.—A Monoclinal Valley.

lesser inclination of the rocks. Second, the texture of the beds—that is, their greater or lesser degree of heterogeneity. The third class of modifying influences is found in the eruptive beds.

The last mentioned agencies are not found in the region under immediate discussion.

No sharp line of division can be drawn between cañons and valleys. For convenience, we designate intervening depressions, caused by erosion, cañon valleys, but all these excavated basins, troughs, and channels will be included under the general head of valleys, and the above terms will be used in describing them.

I should remark, farther, that species are not found in structural geology, if we use that term as it has heretofore been used in the description of organic nature; that is, there are no definite "hard and fast" lines of demarkation between valleys of one class and those of another, and the classification rests solely on typical examples.

With these terms before us, let us again describe the valleys of the Uinta Mountains.

The cañons through which the river passes from Flaming Gorge to Bee Hive Point are anaclinal. Red Cañon is obliquely anaclinal; Brown's Park is anticlinal; the Cañon of Lodore is cataclinal; Whirlpool Cañon above is anaclinal where it runs into a fold, and then obliquely cataclinal in cutting through the other side of the fold.

Split Mountain Cañon is at first anaclinal, then along its central course anticlinal, and at its foot, where it runs out on the opposite side of the fold, is cataclinal; hence it is structurally compound. This is the relation it bears to the minor fold of Split Mountain; but it bears another relation to the great fold of the Uinta Mountains, and is complex. Hence it is a compound, complex valley.

The cañons and valleys heading near the summit of the range running with the strike of the rocks into Green River, as above mentioned, are monoclinal. A good example of this is Summit Valley. Those on the north, which head near the summit of the range, and, running down the flank, turn into Green River, are, in their upper courses, cataclinal, and when they turn to follow the strike of the rocks into Green River, are monoclinal. Those

21 COL

which head back in the plains and bad-lands, and cut across ridges and through mountains, are anaclinal, while those on the south side, which head near the summits of the mountains, and roll down to the foot of the range, and then turn off into the Green, are also cataclinal above, and monoclinal below.

Taking the general course of Green River through the Uinta Mountains, without regard to the several portions, as above mentioned, it would be described as diaclinal.

The explanation of the cañons of Green River will assist us in understanding the origin of the lateral valleys and cañons. The streams were there before the mountains were made—that is, the streams carved out the valleys, and left the mountains. The direction of the streams is indubitable evidence that the elevation of the fold was so slow as not to divert the streams, although the total amount of elevation was many thousands of feet. Had the fold been lifted more rapidly than the principal streams could have cut their channels, Green River would have been turned about it, and all the smaller streams and water-ways would have been cataclinal.

Thus it is that the study of the structural characteristics of the valleys and cañons teaches us, in no obscure way, the relation between the progress of upheaval and that of erosion and corrasion, showing that these latter were *pari passu* with the former, and that the agencies of nature produce great results—results no less than the carving of a mountain range out of a much larger block lifted from beneath the sea; not by an extravagant and violent use of power, but by the slow agencies which may be observed general'y throughout the world, still acting in the same slow, patient manner.

There are yet some interesting facts to be observed concerning these inter-hog-back valleys. Their floors are usually lower than the general surface farther away from the mountains. There seem to be two causes for this. The great fold having been lifted and truncated prior to the exposure of the rocks farther away from the mountains, its strata present their edges, instead of their upper surfaces, to the down falling rain, and the softer beds are not so well shielded by the harder. Erosion hence progresses more rapidly than where the beds are approximately horizontal.

Again, the mountains, with peaks among the clouds, condense their

Figure 59.—Horse-Shoe Cañon.

moisture, and a greater quantity of rain falls on them, or in their vicinity. The region of country adjacent to the mountains receives a portion of this extra rain-fall, so that this dynamic agency increases from the plains to the summits of the mountains, probably in some direct ratio. This increase of the eroding agency, and the greater exposure of the soft beds, probably accounts for the fact that the lowest country is at the foot of the mountains.

There is a limit to the effect of these conditions, for it should be observed no valley can be eroded below the level of the principal stream, which carries away the products of its surface degradation; and where the floor of such a valley has been cut down nearly to the level of such a stream, it receives the *débris* of the adjacent cliffs and mountains, and in this way the rocks composing the floor are usually masked, to a greater or lesser extent. The same topographic facts, under like conditions, are found on the eastern slope of the Rocky Mountains, in Colorado Territory, and the valleys which run into the South Platte from the south, between the hog-backs, are lower than the *mesas* and plateaus farther away from the mountains, but not lower than the flood plain of the river.

I have endeavored above to explain the relation of the valleys of the Uinta Mountains to the stratigraphy, or structural geology, of the region, and, further, to state the conclusion reached, that the drainage was established antecedent to the corrugation or displacement of the beds by faulting and folding. I propose to call such valleys, including the orders and varieties before mentioned, *antecedent valleys*.

In other parts of the mountain region of the west, valleys are found having directions dependent on corrugation. I propose to call these *consequent valleys*. Such valleys have been observed only in limited areas, and have not been thoroughly studied, and I omit further discussion of them.

In the great metamorphic belt extending through the Territory of Colorado, comprising the Rocky Mountain chain of this Territory, the structural geology is exceedingly complex, while the drainage is comparatively simple, and only to a limited extent does it seem to be governed by geological structure. The conclusions to which I arrived were that the present drainage was established in rocks now carried away from the higher regions, but still seen to be turned up against the flanks of most of the ranges.

A part of the district in which my observations were made has since been much more thoroughly studied by Mr. Archibald R. Marvine, one of the geologists of the First Division of the "Geological and Geographical Survey of the Territories." In his report of June 19, 1874, he says:

"Three causes combine to render the rapid study of the stratigraphy of the archæan rocks difficult and its results uncertain: First, their structure is not only often complex, but obscure, the evidence of it being at times nearly or wholly obliterated by the metamorphism, and often over large areas very difficult to find; second, this metamorphism renders lithological characters inconstant, so that a stratum that at one point may be characteristic among its neighbors, may, at another, become like them, or all may change so as to retain none of their geological features, becoming again like other series, so that lithological resemblances cannot often be taken as a guide to follow, and may even become misleading; third, the erosion producing the present surface features of the mountain region had the direction of its action determined by movements of the surface which were not closely connected with the extended plications of its rocks; and, moreover, since this erosion has not long been acting among these rocks, there appears no well defined connection between the topography and the structural geology. The ancient erosion gradually wore down the mass to the surface of the sea, and while previously to this it was no doubt directed by the structure, yet the mass was finally leveled off irrespective of structure or relative hardness of its beds by the encroaching ocean, which worked over its ruins and laid them down upon the smoothed surface in the form of the Triassic and other beds. The recent great uplift, while it probably added new plications to the accumulated plications of the past in the ancient rocks, was quite simple with respect to their total plication, and left the upper Triassic and other sedimentary beds comparatively simply structured, they having been affected alone by the later movements.

"As the mass appeared above the sea and surface erosion once more commenced, but which now acts upon the recent rocks covering probably in greater part the complex underlying rocks, it was directed off from the line of greater uplift down the long slopes of the rising continent to the retiring sea. The channels of drainage started were directed solely by the structure and characters of the upper rocks, and when they gradually cut down through these and commenced sinking their cañons into the under-lying complicated rocks, these cañons bore no relation whatever to their complications. It is but recently that the upper rocks have been completely removed from the summits of the mountain-spurs, the ancient level of sub-aqueous erosion being still indicated by the often uniform level of the spurs and hill-tops over considerable areas, and large plateau-like regions which became very marked from certain points of view. Two or three such levels are indicated at a few places, showing not only that the sedimentaries have once extended up over what are now the mountain rocks, but that the uplift-ing has been mainly confined along certain partly well-defined lines, the intermediate belts, though uplifted bodily, remaining comparatively level, a type of folding, probably, not uncommon farther west, and which will be referred to again in the following chapter.

  *   *   *   *   *   *   *

"It is true that the structure of the lower rocks has begun to affect the courses of the streams, and in places to a considerable extent. Meeting a softer bed a cañon will often have its course directed by it, and follow it for some distance, leaving the adjacent harder beds plainly indicated by the ridges, and sometimes the sinuosities of structure are very curiously fol-lowed by a stream in all its windings, but it soon breaks away and runs independently of the bedding. Many of the smaller ravines have had their positions determined by the structure; but in a broad sense the drainage is from the main mountain crest eastward, independent of structure. Thus, while in places geological features may find expression in surface form, yet, as often, there may be no conceivable relation between topography and geology. The subaqueous erosion, in smoothing all to a common level, destroys all former surface expression of geological character, and the present erosion has not yet been in progress sufficiently long to recreate the lost features."

I fully concur with Mr. Marvine in the above explanation of the valleys in the main Rocky Mountains of Colorado, as my own observations in that country had led me to the same conclusion. There can be no doubt that the present courses of the streams were determined by conditions not found

in the rocks through which the channels are now carved, but that the beds
in which the streams had their origin when the district last appeared above
the level of the sea, have been swept away. I propose to call such *superimposed valleys*. Thus the valleys under consideration, if classified·on the
basis of their relation to the rocks in which they originated, would be called
consequent valleys, but if classified on the basis of their relation to the rocks
in which they are now found, would be called *superimposed valleys*.

Recurring again to the valleys of the Uinta Mountains, it may be well
to remark here that, coming from the Rocky Mountains to the study of the
Uinta Mountains, I at first supposed that the valleys of this region also were
superimposed upon the rocks now seen, but gradually, on a more thorough
study, the hypothesis was found to be not only inadequate to the explanation of the facts, but to be entirely inconsistent with them; and again and
again I visited the region, and re-examined the facts, and at last reached the
conclusion which I have heretofore stated.

A brief reference to the character of this evidence may not be out of
place here, though I reserve the subject for a more full discussion in my
report on the geology of the Uinta Mountains. If the valleys were superimposed on the present rocks, they must be consequent to rocks which have
been carried away; but the valleys consequent upon the corrugation, which
was one of the conditions of the origin of the Uinta Mountains, could not
have taken the direction observed in this system; they would have all been
cataclinal, as they ran down from the mountains, and turned into synclinal
valleys at the foot, forming a very different system from that which now
obtains. Again, the later sedimentary beds, both to the north and south,
were found not to have been continuous over the mountain system, but to
have been deposited in waters whose shores were limited by the lower
reaches of the range; that is, they all gave evidence of littoral origin, and,
further, that the principal cañons through the mountains had been carved
nearly to their present depth before the last of these sediments were
deposited.

BAD-LANDS AND ALCOVE LANDS SOUTH OF THE UINTA MOUNTAINS.

South of the Uinta Mountains, and beyond the hog-backs on either
side of the river, is a district known to the Indians as *Wa-ka-ri'-chits*, or the

Figure 60.—Alcove-Lands and Bad-Lands south of the Uinta Mountains.

Yellow Hills. This country is elaborately embossed with low, rounded, naked hills. The rocks from which they are carved are yellow clays and shales. Some few of the shales are slate colored, others pink; none so glaring and brilliant as the bad-lands of Black's Fork, but the tints are soft and delicate. The whole country is carved by a net-work of water-ways, which descend rapidly toward Green River, and the intervening hills are entirely destitute of vegetation. Looking at it from an eminence, and in the light of the mid-day sun, it appears like a billowy sea of molten gold.

To the south of these yellow hills, and separated from them by a gently curved, but well defined ridge of upturned sandstone, there is a broad stretch of red and buff colored bad-lands. Some of the beds are highly bituminous, and a fresh fracture reveals a black surface, but usually they weather gray. Where these bituminous rocks are found, hills and *mesas* are seen, covered, more or less, with vegetation, and the bad-land forms disappear. Still farther to the south, across White River, we find a continuation of these beds, but here more shaly, and interstratified with harder beds, and the alcove structure appears, somewhat like that in the Alcove Land near Green River Station. These White River alcove lands were, by General Hughes, named "Goblin City."

THE TERRACE CAÑONS AND CLIFFS.

A few miles south of the mouth of the Uinta, Green River enters the Cañon of Desolation. The walls of this gorge steadily increase in altitude to its foot, where it terminates abruptly at the Brown Cliffs; then the river immediately enters Gray Cañon, with low walls, steadily increasing in altitude until the foot is reached, where it terminates abruptly at the Book Cliffs. In like manner the walls of Labyrinth Cañon are low above, and increase in altitude as we descend the river, until the cañon terminates as those above, in a line of cliffs. To these last we have given the name Orange Cliffs.

We sometimes call these the Terrace Cañons. They are cut through three great inclined plateaus.

Conceive of three geographic terraces, many hundred feet high, and many miles in width, forming a great stairway, from the *Toom'-pin Wu-near' Tu-weap'*, below, to the valley of the Uinta, above. The lower step of this stairway, the Orange Cliffs, is more than one thousand two hundred feet high, and the step itself is two or three score miles in width. The second step, the Book Cliffs, is two thousand feet high, or more, and a score of miles in width. The third, or upper step, is more than two thousand feet high. Passing along this step, for two or three score miles, we reach the valley of the Uinta; but this valley is not five or six thousand feet higher than the *Toom'-pin Wu-near' Tu-weap'*, for the stairway is tipped backward.

Climb the Orange Cliffs, 1,200 feet high, and go north to the foot of the Book Cliffs, and you have gradually descended, so that at the foot of the Book Cliffs you are not more than a hundred feet above the foot of the Orange Cliffs. In like manner the foot of the Brown Cliffs is but 200 feet higher than the foot of the Book Cliffs, and the valley of the Uinta is not quite three hundred feet higher than the foot of the Brown Cliffs.

To go by land from the valley of White River to the *Toom'-pin Wu-near' Tu-weap'*, you must gradually, almost imperceptibly climb as you pass to the south, for a distance of forty or fifty miles, until you attain an altitude of two thousand five hundred or three thousand feet above the starting point. Then you descend from the first terrace, by an abrupt step, to a lower. Still continuing to the south, you gradually climb again, until you attain an altitude of more than a thousand feet, when you arrive at the brink of another cliff, and descend abruptly to the top of the lowest terrace. Still extending your travels in the same direction, you climb gradually for a third time, until you reach the brink of the third line of cliffs, or the edge of the escarpment of the lower terrace, and here you descend by another sudden step to the plane of the river, at the foot of Labyrinth Cañon. In coming down by the river, of course you do not ascend, but you pass these terraces along the plane of the river, the upper terrace, through the Cañon of Desolation, the middle terrace through Gray Cañon, and the third through Labyrinth Cañon.

The beds, or series of rocks, through which Labyrinth Cañon is cut, extend under the beds of Gray Cañon, and these run under the beds of the Cañon of Desolation. At one time the Desolation series and the Gray Cañon series extended over the Labyrinth Cañon series, but they have been washed away.

It will be remembered that in the description of the country lying to the north of Red Cañon and Brown's Park, it was explained that ridges were formed by the unequal progress of erosion through the upturned edges of the formations lying on the flank of the fold.

Thus ridges are seen where the dip of the rocks is at a high angle—often twenty to forty five degrees; but where the dip is at a low angle—from one to five degrees—such ridges are not found; the cut edges of the formations stand in steep escarpments, or lines of cliffs, while the slope of the summit of the formation is very gentle, so that when you climb one cliff the descent is almost imperceptible to the foot of another. (Compare lines of cliffs, seen in Figure 61, with hog-back cliffs, seen in Figure 52.)

In passing through the last three cañons, we have observed that the rocks have thus gently dipped to the north, and so, in following the river to the south, we are constantly running into rocks of lower geological position and greater age. In this way we are able to study successive beds from higher to lower, as we would should we descend a shaft many thousands of feet in depth, as previously explained.

Expand a fold like that of the Uinta Mountains, where the rocks dip from ten to ninety degrees, to a more gentle curve, where the rocks dip at a much smaller angle, so that the inclination is scarcely perceptible to the eye, and can only be determined by an extended leveling and tracing of the strata, and the hog-backs are thrown farther apart. The escarpments of these hog-backs, facing the axis of the fold, are still lines of cliffs; but the slopes on the opposite sides are so gently inclined as not, at once, to be apparent, and the streams heading near the brink of the cliffs, and running down the gentle slope away from this line, excavate their own valleys and cañons, and so break up the plane of this slope that its inclination is not at once observed; in fact, it can only be discovered as a generalization from a careful study, and such an inclined plateau, when seen from the side away from the axis of plication, would usually be considered a range of mountains. Yet it has some features which readily distinguish it. The peaks are low mountains and hills, bordering the foot of the slope, and the table lands are beyond and above them, near the crest of the cliffs which face the axis.

22 COL

The bird's-eye view (Figure 61) is intended to show these topographic features. The escarpment below, and in the foreground, represents the Orange Cliffs, at the foot of Labyrinth Cañon; the second escarpment, the Book Cliffs, at the foot of Gray Cañon; the third, away in the distance, the Brown Cliffs, at the foot of the Cañon of Desolation. It will be seen that the three tables incline to the north, and are abruptly terminated by cliffs on the south. For want of space the whole view is shortened.

In the three cañons there are three distinct series of beds, belonging to three distinct geological periods. In the Cañon of Desolation we have Tertiary sandstones; in Gray Cañon, Cretaceous sandstones, shales, and impure limestones; between the head of Labyrinth Cañon and the foot of Gray Cañon, rocks of Cretaceous and Jurassic Age are found, but they are soft, and have not withstood the action of the water so as to form a cañon.

These formations differ not only in geological age, but also in structure and color. It will be interesting to notice how these structural differences affect the general contour of the country, and modify its scenic aspects.

In the description of the three cañons in the history of their exploration, the attentive reader has already noticed the great variety of geological and topographic features observed as we passed along.

Let us now take a view of the three lines of cliffs. The Brown Cliffs are apparently built of huge blocks of rock, exhibiting plainly the lines of stratification. The beds are usually massive and hard, and break with an angular fracture. The whole is very irregular, and set with crags, towers, and pinnacles. The upper beds of the Book Cliffs are somewhat like those last described, and they form a cap to extensive laminated beds of blue shales, in which we see exhibited the curious effects of rain sculpture. The whole face of the rock is set with buttresses, and these are carved with a fret-work of raised and rounded lines, that extend up and down the face of the rock, and unite below in large ridges. The little valleys between these ridgelets are the channels of rills that roll down the rocks during the storms, and from one standpoint you may look upon millions of these little waterways.

Labyrinth Cañon is cut through a homogeneous sandstone. The features of the cañon itself have been described, but the cliffs with which it

Figure 61.—Bird's-eye view of the Terrace Cañons.

terminates present characteristics peculiar to themselves. Below, we have rounded buttresses, and mounds and hills of sand, and piles of great, angular blocks; above, the walls are of columnar structure, and sometimes great columns, seen from a distance, appear as if they were elaborately fluted. The brink of this escarpment is a well defined edge. But if these formations extended over the underlying beds at one time, and if they have been carried away by rains and rivers, why has not the country between been left comparatively level, or embossed with hills separated by valleys? It is easy to see that a river may cut a channel, and leave its banks steep walls of rocks; but that rains, which are evenly distributed over a district, should dig it out in great terraces, is not so easy to perceive.

The climate is exceedingly arid, and the scant vegetation furnishes no protecting covering against the beating storms. But though little rain falls, that which does is employed in erosion to an extent difficult to appreciate by one who has only studied the action of water in degrading the land in a region where grasses, shrubs, and trees bear the brunt of the storm. A little shower falls, and the water gathers rapidly into streams, and plunges headlong down the steep slopes, bearing with it loads of sand, and for a few minutes, or a few hours, the district is traversed by brooks and creeks and rivers of mud. A clear stream is never seen without going up to a moister region on some high mountain, and no permanent stream is found, unless it has its source in such a mountain. In a country well supplied with rains, so that there is an abundance of vegetation, the water slowly penetrates the loose soil, and gradually disintegrates the underlying solid rock, quite as fast as, or even faster than it is carried away by the wash of the rains, and the indurated rock has no greater endurance than the more friable shales and sandstones; but in a dry climate, the softer rocks are soon carried away, while the harder rocks are washed naked, and the rains make but slow progress in tearing them to pieces.

When a great fold emerges from the sea, or rises above its base level of erosion,* the axis appears above the water (or base level) first, and is immediately attacked by the rains, and its sands are borne off to form new deposits. It has before been explained that the emergence of the fold is but

---

* For explanation of this term, "base level of erosion," see Chapter XII.

little faster than the degradation of its surface, but, as it comes up, the wearing away is extended still farther out on the flanks, and the same beds are attacked in the new land which have already been carried away nearer the center of the fold. In this way the action of erosion is continued on the same bed from the up-turned axis toward the down-turned axis, and it may and does often happen that any particular bed may be entirely carried away, with many underlying rocks, near the former line, before it is attacked near the latter. Now, as the beds are of heterogeneous structures, some hard and others soft, the harder beds withstand the action of the storms, while the softer beds are rapidly carried away.

The manner in which these beds are degraded is very different. The softer are washed from the top, but the harder are little affected by the direct action of the waters—they are torn down by another process. As the softer beds disappear, the harder are undermined, and are constantly breaking down; are crushed, more or less, by the fall, and scattered over, and mingled with the softer beds, and are carried away with them. But the progress of this undermining and digging down of the cliff is parallel with the upturned axis of the fold, so that the cliffs face such an axis.

When the fold is abrupt, so that the rocks on either side are made to incline at a great angle, ridges are formed, and this topographic structure of a country may be found even in a land of rains, though the ridges will usually be low, rounded, and more or less irregular, while in a dry climate they will be steep and regular, and will usually culminate above in a sharp edge; but where the rocks are slightly inclined, terraces will be formed, with well defined escarpments.

It is interesting to note the manner in which the textures of these hard capping rocks affect the contours of the cliffs. When the hard rocks are separated into well defined layers, or beds, the cliffs will be more or less terraced, as the strata vary in hardness. This is well seen in the Brown Cliffs and the upper portion of the Book Cliffs. In the last mentioned escarpment the harder beds are underlaid by soft, bluish shales, which appear below in the beautifully carved buttresses.

In the Orange Cliffs there are a thousand feet of homogeneous light red sandstone, and this is underlaid by beds of darker red, chocolate, and lilac colored rocks, very distinctly stratified. The dark red rocks are very hard, the chocolate and lilac are very soft, so below we have terraced and buttressed walls and huge blocks scattered about, which have fallen from the upper part of the escarpment. The homogeneous sandstone above is slowly undermined—so slowly that, as the unsupported rocks yield to the force of gravity, fissures are formed parallel to the face of the cliff. Transverse vertical fissures are also formed, and thus the wall has a columnar appearance, like an escarpment of basalt, but on a giant scale; and it is these columns that tumble over at last, and break athwart into the huge blocks which are strewn over the lower terraces.

The drainage of an inclined terrace is usually from the brink of the cliff toward the foot of the terrace above, i. e., in the direction of the dip of the strata. As the channels of these intermittent streams approach the upper escarpment, they turn and run along its foot until they meet with larger and more permanent streams, which run against the dip of the rock in a direction opposite the course of the smaller channels, and these latter usually cut either quite through the folds, or at least through the harder series of rocks which form the cliffs.

In some places the waters run down the face of the escarpment, and cut narrow cañons, or gorges, back for a greater or less distance into the cliffs, until what would, otherwise, be nearly a straight wall, is cut into a very irregular line, with salients and deep re-entering angles.

These cañons which cut into the walls also have their lateral cañons and gorges, and sometimes it occurs that a lateral cañon from each of two adjacent main cañons will coalesce at their heads, and gradually cut off the salient cliff from the ever retreating line. In this way buttes are formed. The sides of these buttresses have the same structural characteristics as the cliffs from which they have been cut. So the buttes on the plains below the Orange Cliffs are terraced and buttressed below, and fluted and columned above. Often the upper parts of these buttes are but groups of giant columns.

The three lines of cliffs, which I have thus described, have been traced to the east but a few miles back from the river. The way in which they terminate is not known; but, from a general knowledge obtained from a hasty trip made through that country, it is believed that they are cut off by a system of monoclinal folds. To the west they are known to gradually run out in plateaus and mountains, which have another orographic origin.

Climb the cliff at the end of Labyrinth Cañon, and look over the plain below, and you see vast numbers of buttes scattered about over scores of miles, and every butte so regular and beautiful that you can hardly cast aside the belief that they are works of Titanic art. It seems as if a thousand battles had been fought on the plains below, and on every field the giant heroes had built a monument, compared with which the pillar on Bunker Hill is but a mile stone. But no human hand has placed a block in all those wonderful structures. The rain drops of unreckoned ages have cut them all from the solid rock.

Between the foot of Gray Cañon and the head of Labyrinth Cañon we descend through many hundred feet of soft shales, sandstones, marls, and gypsiferous rocks of a texture so friable that no cañon appears along the course of the Green, but along the southern border of the terrace above the Orange Cliffs, buttes of gypsum are seen. Sometimes the faces of these buttes are as white as the heart of the alabaster from which they are carved, while in other places they are stained and mottled red and brown.

As we come near to the Book Cliffs the buttes are seen to be composed of the same beds as those seen in the escarpment, and we see the same light blue buttresses and terraced summits.

On the terrace above the Book Cliffs, the buttes are less numerous, but the few seen have the angular, irregular appearance of the Brown Cliffs.

The summit of the high plateau through which the Cañon of Desolation is cut, is fretted into pine clad hills, with nestling valleys and meadow bordered lakes, for now we are in that upper region where the clouds yield their moisture to the soil. In these meadows herds of deer carry aloft with pride their branching antlers, and sweep the country with their sharp outlook, or test the air with their delicate nostrils for the faintest evidence of an approaching Indian hunter. Huge elk, with heads bowed by the weight of ragged horns, feed among the pines, or trot with headlong speed through the undergrowth, frightened at the report of the red man's rifle. Eagles

Figure 62.—Bird's-eye view of the Toom'-pin Wu-near' Tu-weap' looking to the north east, showing the Sierra la Sal ou the right, the cañons through the center, and lines of cliffs on the left.

sail down from distant mountains, and make their homes upon the trees; grouse feed on the pine nuts, and birds and beasts have a home from which they rarely wander to the desert lands below. Among the buttes on the lower terraces rattlesnakes crawl, lizards glide over the rocks, tarantulas stagger about, and red ants build their play house mountains. Sometimes rabbits are seen, and wolves prowl in their quest; but the desert has no bird of sweet song, and no beast of noble mien.

THE TOOM'-PIN WU-NEAR' TU-WEAP'.

We now proceed to the discussion of Stillwater Cañon, Cataract Cañon, and Narrow Cañon, and the region of country adjacent thereto.

At the head of Stillwater Cañon the river turns to a more easterly course, and runs into a fold, which has a northeast and southwest axis, but its central line is never reached. Before coming to it the river turns again to the west, and runs entirely out of the fold, at the mouth of the Dirty Devil River. It will thus be seen that the dip of the formations under discussion is to the northwest. Going down to the middle of Cataract Cañon, we constantly see rocks of lower geological position appearing at the water's edge; and, still continuing from that point to the foot of Narrow Cañon, the same beds are observed in reverse order; that is, we see at the water's edge rocks of later geological age.

Where the upturned axis of this fold is situated is not known; but, looking away to the southeast, mountains are seen—the Sierra La Sal and Sierra Abajo. Looking over the general surface of the country, it appears that the course of the river is from lower into higher lands, and then back again. Observing the present topographic features of the country, it seems strange that it did not find its way directly across from the foot of Labyrinth to the foot of Narrow Cañon, following the low lands. Why should it leave this lower region, and run away out into the slope of a system of mountains, and then return? We must remember that the river is older than the mountains and the cliffs. We must not think of a great district of country, over which mountains were piled, or built, or heaved up, and that when rain fell it gathered into streams along the natural depressions of such a country, and thus attempt to account for the course of the river; but we must understand that the river cut its way through a region that was slowly rising above the level of the sea, and the rain washed out the valleys, and left rocks and cliffs standing, and the river never turned aside from its original course to seek an easier way, for the progress of uplifting was not greater than that of corrasion. Again we see how slowly the dry land has emerged from the sea; no great convulsion of nature, but steady progress.

The Orange Cliffs, which terminate Labyrinth Cañon, extend to the west a few miles, and then change their course to the southwest, running parallel with the axis of the fold we are now discussing, and they cross the Dirty Devil a few miles above its mouth. Thus they are seen, like the other lines of cliffs, to face the axis of a fold. Figure 62 is a bird's-eye view of this country, showing the course of the river through Stillwater, Cataract, and Narrow Cañons. It represents the cutting of the stream into the slope of a mountain range, and out of it again, without crossing the range. On the left it shows two lines of cliffs. Here we have a district inclosed within Titanic walls. On the southeast are great mountains, and from the foot of their slope, on the north side, near Grand River, we find a line of cliffs crossing this stream, and extending to the Green, in a westerly direction; then to the southwest, to the Dirty Devil River, and then broken and confused by buttes and cañon walls, which extend toward the east, until it strikes the southern foot of the mountains. Within this walled area a profound gorge—Cataract Cañon—is seen, with Stillwater Cañon above, and Narrow Cañon below. The lower cañon of the Grand is also seen, and a number of lateral cañons.

Along the general slope of the district between the cañons are vast numbers of buttes. Their origin is the same as that of the buttes previously described. Often they are but monuments, or standing columns of rocks. From them is derived the Indian name *Toom'-pin Wu-near' Tu-weap'*—the Land of Standing Rocks.

Adjacent to the larger cañons, especially near the junction of the Grand and Green, walled coves are found. Each main gulch branches into a number of smaller gulches above, and each of these smaller gulches heads in an amphitheater. The escarpments of these amphitheaters are broken and terraced, and in many places two such amphitheaters are so close together that they are separated only by a narrow gorge of vertical homogeneous sandstone.

This latter, though homogeneous in general structure, is banded with red and gray, so that the walls of the amphitheaters seem painted. In many places these walls are broken, and the coves are separated by lines of monuments. Where these coves or amphitheaters are farther apart, the spaces above are naked, presenting a smooth but billowy pavement of sandstone, in the depressions of which are many water pockets, some of them deep, preserving a perennial supply; but the greater number so shallow that the water is evaporated within a few days after the infrequent showers.

In many places, especially in the sharp angles between gulches, the rocks are often fissured, and huge chasms obstruct the course of the adventurous climber.

These cañons, and coves, and standing rocks, and buttes, and cliffs, and distant mountains present an *ensemble* of strange, grand features. Wierd and wonderful is the *Toom'-pin Wu-near' Tu-weap'*.

GLEN CAÑON.

The deepest part of Glen Cañon is found in the bend to the north, several miles above the mouth of the Paria, where the river runs through the variegated beds.

Its entire course is through rocks of Triassic Age, chiefly red sandstones. These rocks, beautifully exposed in the Orange Cliffs, return to the river down the western bank of the Dirty Devil, and we enter them again immediately below the mouth of that stream; and here we pass around the lower end of the fold which brought up the Carboniferous limestones and sandstones through which Stillwater, Cataract, and Narrow Cañons are excavated. The group of mountains discovered in coming down Narrow Cañon is composed of eruptive rocks in part, but only in part. Quantities of molten matter poured out through some fissures here, and spread over the country before it had been eroded to its present depth; and this harder material, which came from the depths below, protected the sandstones, over which it was spread, from the degradation which befell the extension of the beds beyond the capping trachyte. The base of the

23 COL

mountain is composed of sedimentary beds, and the summit of this, cooled lava. So even, these so called eruptive mountains were not piled up, but were carved from beds of sedimentary and igneous matter.

We have named this group, in honor of the Secretary of the Smithsonian Institution, "Henry Mountains."

A few miles below the mouth of the San Juan River we come to an interesting monoclinal fold, where the dip of the rocks is in a direction a little north of east; that is, the beds are dropped down on the eastern side of the line, which trends nearly north and south, not broken off and dropped down, but flexed, or bent, so that the beds on the western side of the line are found at an altitude many hundreds of feet above those on the east, and farther down the river the rocks exposed at the water edge are of greater age than those above.

Hereafter, in this discussion, I shall more fully explain the nature of these monoclinal folds and faults, and the topographic features to which they give origin.

At the foot of this cañon another monoclinal fold is seen, with the throw, or drop, also on the east side, or the uplift, if one is so pleased to term it, on the west side; and this brings up again Carboniferous sandstones and limestones. The surface of the country immediately outside the cañon, along its whole course, is on the summit of the red Trias; but, away back on either side, we see long lines of towering cliffs, now running in this, now in that direction, still keeping their courses parallel to the axes of folds which are scattered in many directions over the country. A region more desolate, and, for all economic purposes, more valueless, perhaps, cannot be found on the continent.

There are some features of this cañon of great interest, which I have already mentioned in the account of the exploration. These are the chambers, or caves, found along the cañon, at the foot of the wall, here and there, or in the side cañons and gulches; the great mural cliffs, about sweeping curves of the river; terraced glens, where the walls are composed of well defined strata, with springs about which oaks and aspens grow; and the deep, narrow alcoves or side gulches.

The origin of these chambers was explained in the mention of Music

Temple. They are due to the crumbling of softer rocks, which underlie harder beds, the friable material being carried away by springs, or wet weather streams. The greater number are found at the heads of little gulches.

In many places the walls of the cañon are of homogeneous sandstone, and where the river sweeps in a great curve at the foot of the wall, mural cliffs are found.

The oak glens have been excavated by springs, and the alcoves are the channels of intermittent rills.

Away from the river, on either side, there are broad stretches of naked sandstone, carved by the rains into gentle billows or mounds. As the rains gather into streams, the little valleys, or grooves, between the mounds become gulches, and where the smaller streams gather into larger the gulches become cañons, often having vertical or even overhanging walls.

When, in the progress of corrasion, these streams have cut through harder beds, and reach softer, the channels are seen to widen. The manner in which this widening occurs is curious. The streams are everywhere tortuous, and, as the power of the water is constantly exerted in corrasion, the streams are not only made deeper, but the curves are increased by methods well known to those who have studied the origin and change of river channels; so the walls are often undermined on the outer side of curves, and here overhanging cliffs are found.

So these cañons are not only flexuous in horizontal outline, but they are also flexuous in vertical outline, giving them warped or tortuous courses. The streams do not always cut channels with vertical walls. Occasionally, deep water-ways are found, with flaring walls to the very bottom. Such cañons usually occur where the beds of streams are in rocks quite as hard, or even harder, than those above. A good illustration of such a channel is seen in Figure 48. Besides the grooves, gulches, and cañons that head among the mounds, we have another class of water-ways, to which the former are sometimes tributary. Many streams come down from distant mountains, where they receive a more constant supply of water. They often run for many miles through narrow, winding cañons, with walls so precipitous that they cannot be scaled, and they form impassable barriers to the traveler.

Other interesting features of the landscape are found in the great monuments and buttes that are scattered here and there, attesting to a former extension of the beds seen in the more distant cliffs. Of the cliffs more will be said hereafter.

Glen Cañon is the channel which the Colorado River has cut for itself through beds of red and orange sandstones. Its head is at the mouth of the Dirty Devil, and its foot at the mouth of the Paria. It terminates abruptly below by an escarpment which we have called the "Vermilion Cliffs." Along this irregular line, extending from east to west across the Colorado, and far back on either side, the general surface of the country suddenly drops down.

MARBLE CAÑON.

The escarpment, which we call the "Vermilion Cliffs," at the foot of Glen Cañon, exposes the same beds as are seen in the face of the Orange Cliffs, at the foot of Labyrinth Cañon. It will be remembered that the beds exposed in the Terrace Cañons dip to the north. Between the Orange Cliffs and the Vermilion Cliffs the strata are variously dipped by monoclinal folds, having their axes in a northerly and southerly direction, and the red beds are at about the same altitude above the sea at the two points. The Vermilion Cliffs which face the south form a deep, re-entering angle at the mouth of the Paria. On the east side of the Colorado, the line stretches to the southeast for many miles; on the west side, it extends, in a southwesterly direction, about fifteen miles, then turns west, and, at last, to the northwest. The general northerly dip is again observed from the mouth of the Paria to the mouth of the Colorado Chiquito.

The general surface of the country between the two points is the summit of the Carboniferous formation. At the mouth of the Paria this is at the water's edge; at the mouth of the Colorado Chiquito it is 3,800 feet above the river. The fall of the river, in the same distance, is about six hundred feet, so that the whole dip of the rock between the two points is about three thousand two hundred feet. The distance, by river, is sixty five miles; in a direct line, twenty miles less. So we have a dip of the formation of 3,200 feet in forty five miles, or about seventy feet to a mile.

Figure 63.—View of Marble Cañon from the Vermilion Cliffs near the mouth of the Paria. In the distance, the Colorado River is seen to turn to the west, where its gorge divides the twin plateaus. On the right is seen the Eastern Kaibab Displacements, appearing as folds, and, farther in the distance, as faults.

The slope of the country to the north is the same as the dip of the beds, for the country rises to the south as the beds rise to the south.

Stand on the Vermilion Cliffs, at the head of Marble Cañon, and look off down the river over a stretch of country that steadily rises in the distance until it reaches an altitude far above even the elevated point of observation, and then see meandering through it to the south the gorge in which the river runs, everywhere breaking down with a sharp brink, and in the perspective the summits of the walls appearing to approach until they are merged in a black line, and you can hardly resist the thought that the river burrows into, and is lost under, the great inclined plateau.

CHAPTER XII.

THE PHYSICAL FEATURES OF THE VALLEY OF THE COLORADO, CONTINUED.

In the previous chapter, I have made frequent mention of long lines of cliffs, or escarpments, extending across the Colorado, far back into the country on either side. I have attempted to explain the origin of these cliffs, as well as the origin of cañons, as due to the erosion of greater or smaller folds of the stony formations, or beds of rock. To explain the chief characteristics of the Grand Cañon, and the adjacent country, it is necessary to describe other lines of cliffs, due to other causes.

CLIFFS AND SLOPES OF DISPLACEMENT.

The geological formations, or beds of rock, exposed in the Grand Cañon and the tributary gorges, have been fractured, or folded, on an extensive scale. These great fractures, or folds, extend across the cañon in a northerly and southerly direction, and can be traced for scores of miles on either side— not as huge cracks, or chasms, for they are observable only to the eye of the geologist, and are traced by the high steps and great displacements seen along their courses. Along these fractures we find what geologists call faults, *i. e.*, the beds have fallen down on one side of each crack. This displacement, or *throw* of the fault, as it is technically called, is from one or two hundred to two or three thousand feet, and is always noticed to be quite variable along any particular fault which may be studied.

Let us try to obtain a well defined conception of such a fault. Suppose that a fracture should be formed, extending from the shore of Lake Erie, in the northwest corner of Pennsylvania, diagonally through the State to the head of Delaware Bay—a great crack, through the underlying rocks, to unknown depths below—and that the country on the southwestern side

Figure 64.—Section across a simple fault.

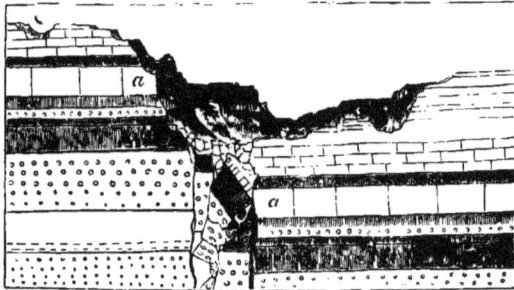

Figure 65.—Section across a fault with walls widely separated, the
intervening space filled with broken rocks.

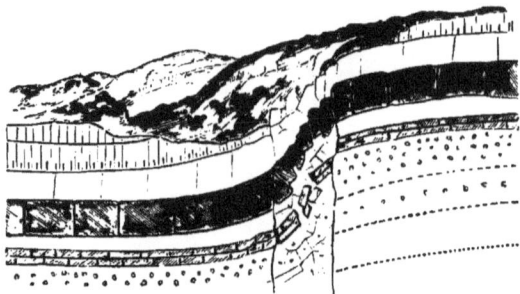

Figure 66.—Section across a fault with walls widely separated, the intervening space filled with broken rock, still exhibiting the original stratification.

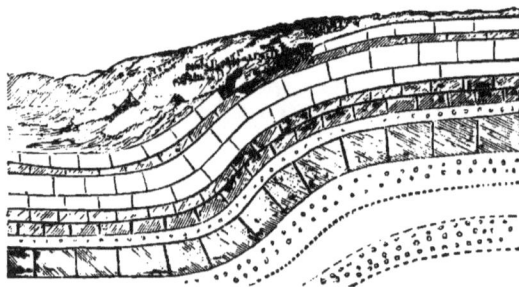

Figure 67.—A monoclinal fold.

of this fracture should drop down many hundreds of feet. Now, to go from the low lands to the high lands it would be necessary to climb a great wall. We must conceive this line to be a somewhat meandering one, so that the wall is turned more or less from a direct course. Again, the throw of the beds is variable, being greater or lesser here and there along the fault—in some places, but two or three hundred feet, perhaps; in others, two or three thousand. For this reason the altitude of the cliffs is greatly variable.

Again, the brink, or edge, of the irregular wall has tumbled down in many places, leaving pinnacles, towers, and crags here and there, and below may be seen a great talus, where the rocks which have tumbled down are piled against the foot of the wall. Then there are streams heading in the upper country, and running down into the lower, which have cut for themselves channels—narrow gulches, or, perhaps, in some places, narrow valleys, so that we have, not a vast, unbroken wall, but an irregular line of cliffs.

Let us turn our attention to these faults, and the topographic features to which they give rise. Sometimes we find that the beds are broken by a well defined fracture, and the plane of separation between the beds which have dropped down and those which have remained in place is clearly marked. Figure 64 is designed to represent a section across such a fault, where the bed *a, a* on the left is seen to lie at a higher level than on the right. Sometimes the fault branches, and the throw, or displacement, occurs along two or more lines, so that a great step may be broken into two or more smaller ones, as represented in Figure 69, where the bed *a, a* is seen in each step. In other places, the beds have fallen down without obstruction for a part of the distance, and have been caught and turned up, as in Figure 71. In many places we find no definite line of separation between the strata in place and the fallen strata, and there is a space of greater or lesser extent, sometimes several hundred feet wide, between the two series, composed of fragments of the same rocks, in some cases, thrown down promiscuously, and found much mixed, as seen in Figure 65; but in others, preserving, in an irregular, broken way, the stratification, by a flexure, from the upper to the lower beds, as seen in Figure 66, where the rocks seem to have been torn asunder by the stretching they received in displacement. Again, we find the rocks intervening between the horizontal beds above and the horizontal beds below, unbroken; the flexure is complete, and we have a *monoclinal* fold, as represented in Figure 67.

Still another variation is found. In the same vertical section we may sometimes see that a bed composed of a somewhat brittle material is broken so as to form a fault, while the bed above or below, composed of a more flexible material, is bent so as to form a fold, and thus a fault and fold will be represented in the same cross section as in Figure 68. Thus it is seen that the transformation of a fold into a fault may occur in two ways—longitudinally along the course of the fault, and vertically in the strata.

The flexures, or monoclinal folds, also change in character, for the dip of the beds may vary greatly—from two or three to ninety degrees—and if we trace such a fold along its course, commencing at its transformation from a fault, we may find the flexure becoming less and less, until it can scarcely be detected by the eye, and then, perhaps, increase gradually into an abrupt fold, and then into a fault, reproducing, in some irregular way, the varieties of faulting above described.

These faults run in lines approximately parallel, and divide the district under consideration into long belts, or blocks, and one edge of each block usually lies at the foot of an escarpment, the other at the summit of an escarpment. In examining the down-throw of these blocks, it is observed that the edge which lies against the foot of an escarpment has usually been thrown down much more than the opposite one, so that the blocks are tilted more or less. The relative amount of the downfall of these two edges is ever changeable. There are cases where the summit edge seems to have preserved its original position without down-throw, and there are other cases where the summit edge seems to have fallen quite as much as the other.

There is yet another change rung on these displacements. In some places the beds, at the edge of the table, lying against the foot of the escarpment, are turned down, while farther back from the fault, toward the summit edge, the beds are approximately horizontal. This is represented in Figure 70. Thus the long, narrow blocks, into which the country is divided by these displacements, are warped, or twisted.

These faults and folds, thus ever changing in their characteristics, produce like changeable features in the topography of the country. A sharp

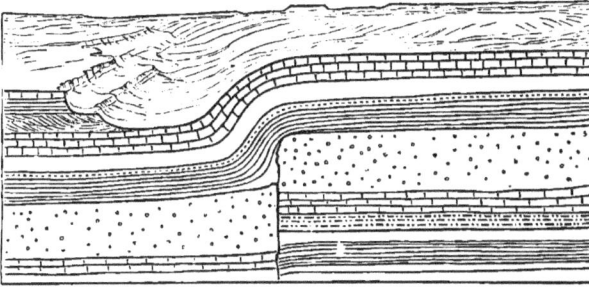

Figure 68.—Fault and fold in same cross-section.

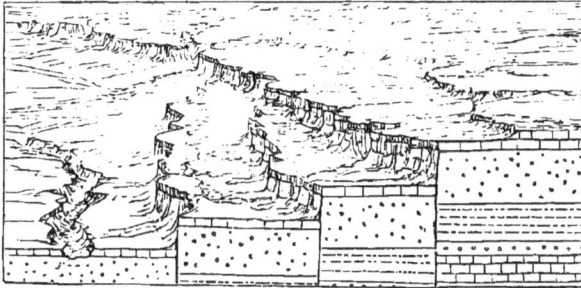

Figure 69.—Section across a branching fault.

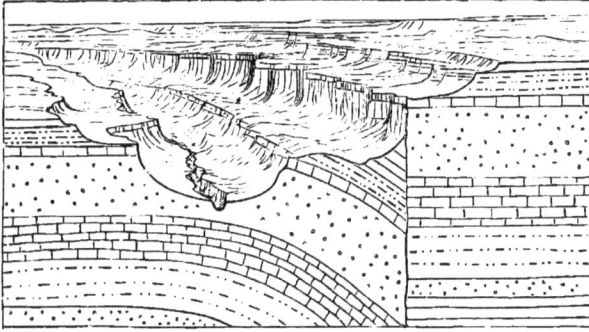

Figure 70.—Fault with thrown beds flexed downward.

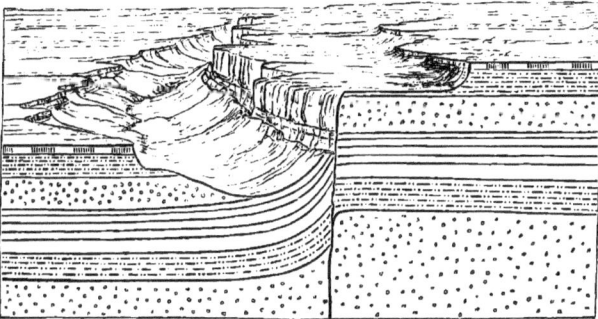

Figure 71.—Fault with thrown beds flexed upward—a dragged fault.

fault, especially where the throw is great and the rocks are indurated, produces precipitous cliffs, with a small talus below, made of the fragments which have fallen from above. Where the down-fallen rocks have caught and have been flexed, we usually find a long slope at the foot of the cliffs, and where the faults change into flexures gentle slopes are observed, stretching from the high lands to the lower country.

The elevated district traversed by the Grand Cañon is broken by a number of such faults, and portions of the country have fallen down, so that, although the general upper surface is formed, in chief part, of the same beds of cherty limestone, the cañon is not cut through one great, unbroken plateau, but through a series of plateaus, or great geographic terraces and tables.

The most elevated portion of the country is a central belt, about twenty five or thirty miles in width, and about eighty miles in length. This is called, by the Indians, *Kaibab*, or "mountain lying down," and we have adopted the name. It is well defined on the east and west by lines of cliffs and steep slopes, which have been formed by displacements, and on the south by the chasm of the Colorado, but on the north it abuts against the Vermilion Cliffs. The lines of cliffs which form its eastern and western boundaries extend to the south beyond the Grand Cañon, for the faults run far to the south, and they define there, in part, a companion, or twin plateau. Had there been no river running there, there would have been but one plateau.

From this central belt the general surface of the country drops by steps to the east and west, and the edge of each step marks the line of a fault, or its equivalent fold.

In the region under discussion there are six of these great displacements, which give rise to important elements in the topography, and deserve special mention. I shall enumerate them in order, from east to west, omitting mention of the faults and folds of minor importance.

East of Marble Cañon, and running in a general northerly and southerly course, so as to cross the Colorado at the mouth of the Paria, we have the Paria Fold, in which the down-fall of the rocky foundation is to the

24 COL.

east of the axis of the flexure. Where it crosses the river the throw is about one thousand eight hundred feet, but it increases toward the south.

Going west across Marble Cañon to the foot of the Kaibab Plateau, we find another great fold. Tracing it from the northern extremity of the plateau to the south, we find that, nearly half way along, it branches so as to form two monoclinal folds. These separate rapidly until they are about four miles apart, and then run parallel to each other for twenty five or thirty miles, when they change into faults. The throw of the displacement is about three thousand feet, and is, approximately, the same, whether it appears as one fold, as two folds, or two faults. We have called these the Eastern Kaibab Faults. The down-fall of the beds, as in the Paria Fold, is to the east of the axis of flexure.

Crossing the Kaibab Plateau, we come to another great monoclinal fold, which changes into a fault in some places, and these faults sometimes branch. The throw is here on the western side of the axis of flexure, and varies from five hundred to two thousand feet. We call this the Western Kaibab Fault.

Continuing to the west, and passing over some minor faults, we reach, at last, the To-ro'-weap Valley. On the eastern side of this valley there is an abrupt wall, eight hundred or nine hundred feet high, which marks another fault, the throw of which is also to the west. This is the To-ro'-weap Fault. Its throw is but little over eight hundred feet, where it crosses the Grand Cañon. Farther to the south it increases somewhat, but to the north it becomes less, and where it crosses the Vermilion Cliffs it is only about two hundred feet.

Twelve or fifteen miles to the west is the Hurricane Ledge Fault. Its throw is also to the west. It has been traced from a point north of Tokerville southward across the Grand Cañon, and out to the brink of the great San Francisco Plateau. The throw varies from two to three thousand feet. Usually it is a sharp, or abrupt, fault, though here and there the strata have been caught below.

Twenty five or thirty miles farther to the west, we find the Grand Wash Fault—a fault in some places, elsewhere a fold. Here, also, the throw is to the west, and it is more than five thousand feet where it crosses the Colorado.

Figure 72.—Bird's-eye view of the Grand Cañon looking east from the Grand Wash. One bird, Echo Cliffs. Two birds, Kaibab Plateau. Three birds, To-ro'-weap Cliffs. Four birds, Hurricane Ledge. Five birds, Shi-vwits Plateau.

So we have selected, for purposes of discussion here, six great displacements—the Paria Fold, the Eastern Kaibab Fault, the Western Kaibab Fault, the To-ro'-weap Fault, the Hurricane Ledge Fault, and the Grand Wash Fault. Let us review them in reverse order, and examine the lines of cliffs to which they give rise, and the table lands which they divide. (See bird's-eye view, Figure 72.)

We will start at the Grand Wash, half a dozen miles north of the river. Here the summit of the Carboniferous rocks is deeply buried beneath sandstones and shales of later origin. At the start we are but five or six hundred feet above the level of the Colorado, and we climb by a gentle slope several miles in length, until we reach an altitude of six or eight hundred feet above the starting point, and are at the foot of the Grand Wash Cliffs. Now we must climb this great wall, one thousand five hundred or one thousand eight hundred feet high; no easy task, as it is not a mountain slope, up which we can walk, but a wall, broken somewhat with gulches, and set with narrow benches, or shelves, here and there, and up some one of these gulches and along the narrow shelves we pass, until we reach the summit of the first great terrace.

Still we go a short distance to the east, and must climb another thousand feet, or more, and we are on the *Shi'-wits* Plateau. This last escarpment of a thousand feet is not due to a fault, but is a line of cliffs formed by erosion. On the plateau there is a dead volcano, and from its crater have poured floods of basalt in great sheets, which now stand as a central and higher table on the plateau.

We go on to the east thirty miles. It is not an easy way, but we stop not here to describe it, and we arrive at the foot of the Hurricane Ledge. We have descended a little, for the *Shi'-wits* Plateau inclines, or dips, from its western margin to the foot of this ledge, or line of cliffs. The Hurricane Ledge is more than two thousand feet high, and we have another hard climb.

It is related that a storm overtook a party of Mormon officials while attempting to explore a route for a wagon road up a gulch which comes down from the upper country, and hence its name, Hurricane Ledge.

It presents a bold, precipitous wall to the west, which forms, along its entire course, an impassable barrier to the traveler, except that here and there it is cut by narrow cañons or gulches, which may be ascended, and in two or three places volcanoes, standing on the plateau above, have poured out streams of lava, that have run over this wall in rugged slopes, which can be climbed with difficulty.

Then we pass on to the east, winding among volcanic cones, and in many places walking over sheets of cooled basalt and beds of cinders, until we reach the foot of the To-ro'-weap Cliffs. Here we have another wall 800 feet high to climb.

Still passing to the east, by a difficult way, crossing cañons and gulches, at last we reach the western foot of the Kaibab Plateau, and again climb 2,000 feet to its summit, where we are 8,000 feet above the level of the sea. To the south, we can see the Grand Cañon of the Colorado; its meandering course can be traced for two hundred miles; far away to the north, we see the ragged lines of Vermillion Cliff, an escarpment due to erosion.

On to the east, for thirty miles, and we reach the eastern brink of the Kaibab Plateau. Descending 1,500 feet, we have a bench three or four miles wide, and make a second descent of fifteen hundred or eighteen hundred feet, when we reach the eastern foot of the plateau, and stand on the plain above Marble Cañon. To the south, these eastern Kaibab steps have escarpments, as the displacements are by faults. To the north, they have slopes, as the displacements are by folds.

Then we cross the plain, and still go on to the east for a distance of thirty five or forty miles, and reach the foot of a line of cliffs facing the west once more.

Climbing this, we find it to be a sharp ridge, with a face also turned to the east, so that we have two lines of cliffs or escarpments, one facing the east, the other the west, brought so close together as to form a sharp ridge. The eastern face is due to erosion; the western face to displacement by folding. I shall hereafter discuss this ridge in a more elaborate manner.

The Grand Wash Valley is a desert of broken rocks and naked sands. There are two or three springs in the valley, and here squalid Indians live, in a region so warm and so arid, that they are not compelled to build themselves even shelter of bark and boughs, but wallow in the sand or seek the shade of the few scrubby cedars that grow from the crevices of the rocks.

The *Shi'-wits* Plateau is naked and desolate, but here and there springs burst from beneath the basaltic cliffs, and deep gulches and cañons are cut from its margin and run into side cañons of the Colorado. About these springs and in the deep gulches the *Shi'-wits* Indians live, cultivating little patches of corn, gathering seeds, eating the fruits and fleshy stalks of cactus plants, and catching a rabbit or a lizard now and then; dirty, squalid, but happy, and boasting of their rocky land as the very Eden of the earth.

In the region above the Hurricane Ledge there are extensive grazing lands, and where there are a few springs, which can be used for irrigation, the Mormon people have succeeded in raising the products of a temperate climate. In the region below there are two or three small towns along the course of the Virgen and Santa Clara Rivers, where the inhabitants have succeeded in cultivating sub-tropical products, and you can throw a stone from the land of the potato and apple to the land of the fig and sugar cane.

On this great table-land, immediately north of the Colorado River, there is a group of mountains and volcanic cones, known as the *U-in-ka-rets*, of which mention will be made hereafter.

The benches I have described are steps in the great stairway to the Kaibab Plateau, where the clouds yield their snows even in July, and the moisture of this upper region has disintegrated the rocks, and formed a soil which gives footing to vast pine forests. Springs of water abound, beautiful lakes are scattered here and there, and meadows, clothed with verdure, give pasturage to herds of deer. This is the summer home of the *Kai-vav'-its*.

The plain between the foot of the Kaibab Plateau and the Echo Cliffs, along the Paria Fold, is naked and desolate. Through its center runs the deep gorge known as Marble Cañon, with its many side cañons and gulches.

On the eastern slope of the Echo Cliffs a number of springs are found, and these are famous watering places for the Navajo Indians.

The western slope of the range is composed of homogeneous, but rather friable, sandstone, and the rain-water rills have corraded deep channels, interrupted by many pot-holes. After a shower, these pot-holes are found filled with water. There is a place, near by the trail which passes from the mouth of the Paria to the province of Tusayan, where there is a collection of these water-pockets, known as the Thousand Wells.

(The plateaus and tables, the faults, and folds, and the escarpments, due to displacement and erosion, are exhibited in bird's-eye view, Figure 72, and also in section and bird's-eye view, Figure 73.)

CLIFFS OF EROSION.

I have said that the upper surface of the district adjacent to the Grand Cañon is the summit of the rocks of Carboniferous Age. North of the Grand Cañon, from forty to sixty miles, we find rocks of later age, standing in cliffs, the escarpments of which face the south. There are four lines of these, preserving, in their courses, a general parallelism. Going north from the Grand Cañon, we first meet with the *Shin-ar'-ump* Cliffs, a step to a bench, low, and much broken. Capping the cliffs, we find conglomerate, over which are scattered many fragments of silicified wood, known to the Indians as the arrows of *Shin-au'-av*, or *Shin-ar'-ump*. Still proceeding north, we come to a second line of cliffs, with soft beds below, and harder beds above, known as the Vermilion Cliffs. The rocks exposed in these two lines of cliffs have been, by courtesy, called Trias, but without sufficient paleontological evidence. The third line of cliffs has a gray, homogeneous sandstone at the base, and a capping of limestone, containing Jurassic fossils. Above this line we have many hills, carved out of beds of Cretaceous Age, and above and beyond these hills, a line of cliffs, the summit of which is of Tertiary Age. The faces of these upper cliffs are stained with red oxide of iron, and they are called the Pink Cliffs. The dip of the beds is to the north: the strike east and west; and as these are cliffs of erosion, they follow the strike in a general way, and hence have an easterly and westerly trend.

The ascent from the foot of the Shin-ar'-ump Cliffs to the summit of the Pink Cliffs is but 4,000 feet; but as the dip is to the north, in the direction of the ascent, the thickness of the beds passed over is much greater, being more than ten thousand feet.

I have said that these lines of cliffs have an easterly and westerly course, but they deviate greatly from this general direction in many places. Wherever a north and south fault is found, the block which has been thrown down has its lines of cliffs carried southward, or toward the axis of upheaval,

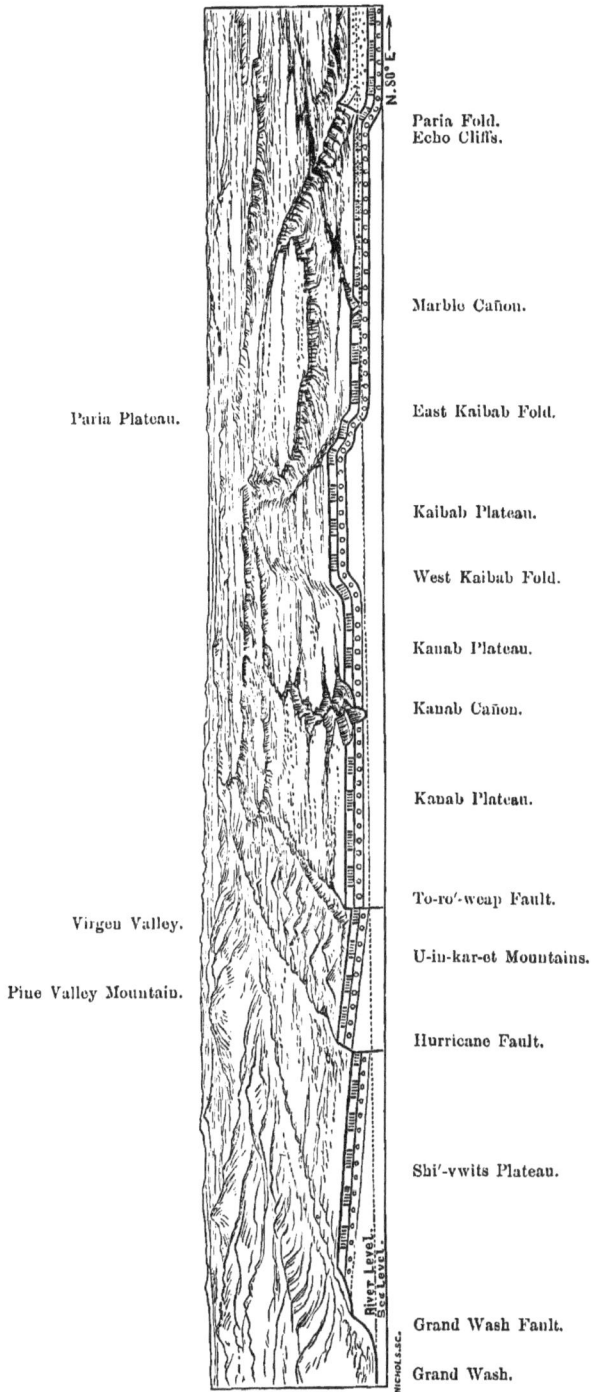

Paria Fold.
Echo Cliffs.

Marble Cañon.

East Kaibab Fold.

Paria Plateau.

Kaibab Plateau.

West Kaibab Fold.

Kanab Plateau.

Kanab Cañon.

Kanab Plateau.

To-ro'-weap Fault.

Virgen Valley.

U-in-kar-et Mountains.

Pine Valley Mountain.

Hurricane Fault.

Shi'-vwits Plateau.

River Level.
Sea Level.

Grand Wash Fault.

Grand Wash.

N. 80° E.

Figure 73.—Section from west to east across the plateaus north of the Grand Cañon, with bird's-eye view of terraces and plateaus above. Horizontal scale, 16 miles to the inch; vertical scale, 4 miles to the inch.

Figure 74.—Bird's-eye view of cliffs of erosion, showing the Shin-ar'-ump Cliffs, Vermilion Cliffs, and Gray Cliffs, in order from right to left.

Figure 75.—Bird's-eye view of cliffs of erosion thrown forward by a fault.

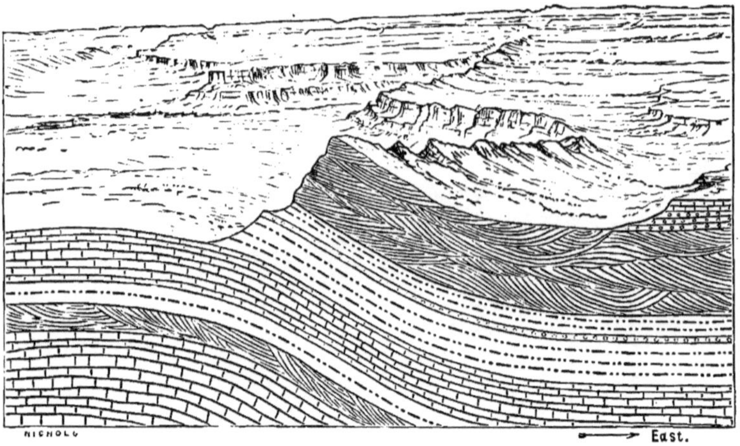

Figure 76.—Section through Echo Cliffs.

or, if we are to consider the displacement as caused by upheaval, the blocks uplifted have their lines of cliffs set farther back to the north; and the amount of this backward or forward displacement is in direct ratio to the amount of vertical displacement in the fault or monoclinal fold. The higher region has suffered a greater amount of erosion, and as erosion progresses chiefly by undermining, as I have explained in the discussion of the Terrace Cañons, the cliffs of the higher blocks stand farther back from the axis of upheaval than those of the lower blocks.

The general line of these cliffs is broken in another way. Streams, heading on the high plateaus to the north, run southward into the Grand Cañon, and have carved out cañons through the cliffs, and turned the escarpment far back into the several benches, so that instead of four unbroken walls facing the south, and having an easterly and westerly direction, we have, in fact, a series of salients and re-entering angles.

Entering this country from the east or west, it is necessary to climb great benches, due to displacements along faults, and crossing it from south to north, it is necessary to climb great benches, but these are due to erosion; so we have two systems of cliffs—cliffs of displacement, having a northerly and southerly trend, and cliffs of erosion, having an easterly and westerly trend.

The first—cliffs of displacement—are of two classes: those facing the west, where the throw of the beds is on the western side of the fracture, and those facing the east, where the throw of the beds is on the eastern side of the fracture.

The cliffs of erosion are very irregular in direction, but somewhat constant in vertical outline; and the cliffs of displacement are somewhat regular in direction, but very inconstant in vertical outline. This inconstancy is due to the frequent changes in the character of the faults, which I have previously described.

In the Echo Cliffs, east of Marble Cañon, a line of cliffs, due to erosion, and a slope due to displacement, have come together, back to back. The position of the slope is essentially unchangeable, as it is due to a flexure; but the escarpment, due to erosion, has doubtless been carried back from Marble Cañon to the east, until it has just reached this slope. Figure

76 is a cross section, intended to represent the structure of these interesting cliffs. In some places, the erosion of the western escarpment has been carried back farther than the line of displacement; in other places, not quite up to it. But wherever the line of erosion has been brought up to the line of displacement, or near it, we find the rocks standing in sharp crags.

I have heretofore explained that one of the conditions essential to the cliff structure is that the beds of the summit must be comparatively hard, and the beds below, at the foot of the cliffs, very soft; and this condition is well illustrated in these cliffs. Now the lower beds are turned down, by the monoclinal fold, below the reach of the waters employed in degradation, as you pass across the fold from west to east, and hence these cliffs cannot be carried farther to the east, by the progress of undermining, as long as the present conditions exist; and now the agency of erosion can only be exerted in obliterating the ridge. For this reason the ridge disappears in those places along its line where the undermining erosion from the west has progressed the farthest.

On the western side of the Paria Plateau there is an escarpment, facing the west, due to erosion, and the line of the escarpment, on its northern end, coincides with the line of flexure of the Eastern Kaibab Fault. Here, again, we have a line of crags or peaks, forming an irregular ridge, like that in the Echo Cliffs; but this stands on the brink of a well defined plateau, and is higher than the general surface of the table. The crags and peaks are carved from the upturned edges of the beds. The slope due to displacement is seen farther to the west, and is the slope of the Kaibab Plateau, and faces the escarpment. Only a small portion of this slope is seen in the edge of the plateau, where stands the line of crags. The softer beds at the bottom, which constitute one of the conditions on which the escarpment depends, are still exposed to the action of rains and streams, and the cliff condition is not terminated, as in the section previously given, and future erosion will carry this line of cliffs back to the east, as long as the present conditions are preserved.

Figure 77 is a section extending from the Paria Plateau, on the east, across House Rock Valley, to the Kaibab Plateau, on the west, and shows the upturned edges of the rocks on the brink of the Paria Plateau. The

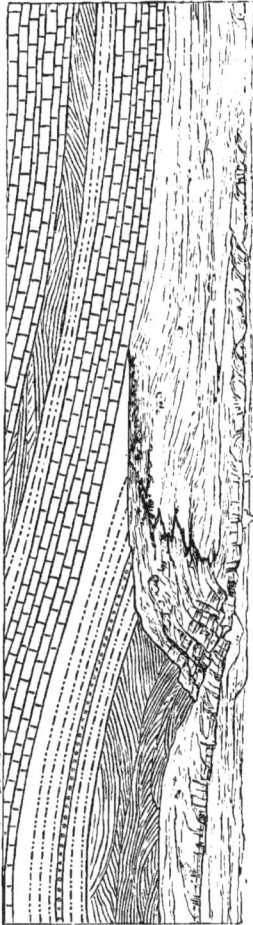

Figure 77.—Section across House Rock Valley.

sharp crags and peaks seen along this edge of the Paria Plateau are not well represented in the section, as it was taken along the line a little too far to the south for that purpose.

So the district of country through which the Grand Cañon is cut, is divided into blocks by cliffs and cañons, and to each of the greater blocks we have given a name, and called it a plateau. Only a few of these, like the Kaibab, are well defined as tables, i. e., blocks of land bounded on all sides by escarpments and slopes, which descend to lower lands. Many of them have escarpments and slopes to lower lands only on two or three sides, while the escarpments on the other sides are ascents to other plateaus. I shall not linger here to describe these plateaus in detail, but shall defer a more thorough discussion of the subject to the detailed report on the geology of the district.

THE GRAND CAÑON.

Through these tables the Colorado runs, in an easterly and westerly direction, in a deep gorge, known as the Grand Cañon.

The varying depths of this cañon, due to the varying altitudes of the plateaus through which it runs, can only be seen from above. As we wind about in the gloomy depths below, the difference between 4,000 and 6,000 feet is not discerned, but the characteristics of the cañon—the scenic features—change abruptly with the change in the altitude of the walls, as the faults are passed. In running the channel, which divides the twin plateaus, we pass around the first great southern bend. In the very depths of the cañon we have black granite, with a narrow cleft, through which a great river plunges. This granite portion of the walls is carved with deep gulches and embossed with pinnacles and towers. Above are broken, ragged, non-conformable rocks, in many places sloping back at a low angle. Clambering over these, we reach rocks lying in horizontal beds. Some are soft; many very hard; the softer strata are washed out; the harder remain as shelves. Everywhere there are side gulches and cañons, so that these gulches are set about ten thousand dark, gloomy alcoves. One might imagine that this was intended for the library of the gods; and it was. The shelves are not for books, but form the stony leaves of one great book. He who would read the language of the universe may dig out letters here and

25 COL

there, and with them spell the words, and read, in a slow and imperfect way, but still so as to understand a little, the story of creation.

These rust colored shelves have above them soft shales, of a lemon color, and in ascending the wall we climb them by passing up a steep slope, curiously carved by innumerable rainy-day rills. Above these we find homogeneous limestone a thousand feet in thickness, standing in vertical cliffs. On top of this great bed we find soft sandstones, so washed away as to leave comparatively flat spaces of solid rock above—a bench on which we can walk on the side of the Grand Cañon, more than four thousand feet above the river. In this part of its course the channel is very tortuous. Many streams head in the Kaibab Plateau, to the north, and the Coanini Plateau, to the south, and run down into the Grand Cañon; and these have their lateral cañons, and a third and fourth system of side gulches are seen, all having winding ways. Now suppose that we start on this bench, where the Grand Cañon cuts through the second of the Eastern Kaibab Faults, and follow it down the cañon until we come to the Western Kaibab Fault. We start on the north side of the river, and the Kaibab Plateau is on our right. At once we walk around a great amphitheater, the head of a side gulch, and then another, and another, until we come to a lateral cañon coming down the Kaibab, which has its beginning many miles back. Now we must head this. In doing so we must walk around the brink of a great amphitheater, the head of a side gulch, then another, and still another, until we come to a side cañon lateral to the one we are attempting to head, and around it we must go. In doing so, still following the bench on the summit of the limestone, we pass around, in gentle curves, by many of these amphitheaters, and so on we go, everywhere traveling in half circles, which are arranged about side cañons. At last we head the first side cañon, and return to the brink of the Grand Cañon, at a point only a mile or two to the west of where we started, and so head side cañons with side cañons, all set with amphitheaters, and travel day by day, and must walk hundreds of miles to reach the western edge of the Kaibab Plateau, not more than thirty miles in a direct line from where we started. So this great bed of rock, a thousand feet in thickness, is elaborately carved into a series of amphitheaters.

Figure 78.—The Grand Cañon of the Colorado showing ampitheaters and sculptured buttes.

Above this bed of limestone we have beds of bright red sandstones, weathered so as to form shelves on a scale even greater than in the rust colored rocks below, but in many places they break down in steep slopes. Then above we have buff and gray sandstones, and limestones heavily bedded, and near the summit, where the limestone prevails, they are full of nodules of chert. This cherty limestone weathers in columns, and towers, and pinnacles; curious forms of standing rock are arranged all along the brink of the cañon wall.

So below we have granite buttresses, themselves set with pinnacles and towers, then broken slopes, then somber recesses, set with ragged shelves, then strangely carved and fretted slopes, and lemon colored shales, then vast amphitheaters of marble, then red slopes and sandstone shelves, then cliffs of ragged limestone, set with towers.

The wonderful elaboration and diversity with which this work has been done is only equaled by the vast scale on which the plan was laid.

In many places the conditions of erosion have been such that great blocks have been severed from the main plateau and stand as outliers, their sides having all the elaborate sculpture of the walls of the cañon. Lieutenant Ives, who explored the lower Colorado, made a land trip, from a point below the Grand Cañon around to the southwest, and climbed the San Francisco Plateau, and from an elevated point he could look off to the northeast and see the region of which we are now speaking. Of this country he says: "The extent and magnitude of the system of cañons in that direction is astounding. The plateau is cut into shreds by these gigantic chasms, and resembles a vast ruin. Belts of country, miles in width, have been swept away, leaving only isolated mountains standing in the gap—fissures, so profound that the eye cannot penetrate their depths, are separated by walls whose thickness one can almost span, and slender spires, that seem tottering upon their base, shoot up a thousand feet from vaults below."

In other regions, the rocks, when not covered with soil, or more vigorous vegetation, are at least lichened, or stained, and the rocks themselves of somber hue, but in this region they are naked, and many of them brightly colored, as if painted by artist gods; not stained and daubed with inharmonious hues, but beautiful as flowers, and gorgeous as the clouds. Such are the walls of the Grand Cañon of the Colorado, where it divides the twin plateaus.

Having crossed the Western Kaibab Fault, the cañon suddenly changes in character. The throw of the rocks being more than one thousand five hundred feet, we lose the granite, and the bed of the river is in the lemon colored rocks, and now for many miles the cañon is comparatively straight, and the walls are much more regular. At the bottom we have the rusty beds, and then the lemon colored beds, and then the marble cliffs, and when we reach the summit of this limestone we find the same bench as above, under the Kaibab Plateau, but here it is wider, ranging from two or three hundred yards to two or three miles. Then comes a sloping, bright red terrace, and back of it the cliffs of the cherty limestone, with standing rocks on the brink.

You can stand on the southwestern corner of the Kaibab Plateau, and look over this straight stretch of cañon for sixty miles. There seems to be a valley enclosed with walls one thousand five hundred or two thousand feet high, five to ten miles in width, with a narrow, winding gorge down its center.

A few lateral cañons come in on either side; so the walls are broken here and there, but the general outline is well preserved.

Just before the river wheels again to the south, in the second great bend, it passes the To-ro'-weap Fault, which extends across the cañon. The rocks have dropped down about eight hundred feet, and let the homogeneous limestone nearly down to the water. The fissure of this fault has been the channel through which floods of lava have been forced from depths below into the upper world.

Many volcanic cones are seen standing along the line of the fault, or on the branches of the fissure. One of these volcanic cones stands on the very brink of the cañon, and is the one of which mention was made in the account of the exploration.

Passing this, the course of the river is southward, and once more the channel enters the granite. At the very apex of this bend, Diamond Creek makes its contribution from the south, and it was here that Lieutenant Ives and Doctor Newberry came down to the depths of the Grand Cañon.

Turning here again to the north, the river soon passes out of the granite, and then, at last, out of the cañon, where the Grand Wash comes down from the north. Around this second great bend the walls of the cañon have a more simple structure than in the first, but there are many points where views can be obtained of a simple gorge, much more impressive as such, than in the complex region above.

LATERAL CAÑONS.

Many other streams, heading to the north and south, are tributaries of the Colorado, and have cañons which are lateral to the Grand Cañon. The Kanab heads away to the north, at the foot of the Pink Cliffs, and runs south into the Grand Cañon, passing through a series of gorges. Where it cuts through the successive lines of cliffs, it presents another series of terrace cañons, in many respects like the series on Green River; but the lower cañon of the Kanab, which comes down to the Colorado River, is carved through the harder limestones and sandstones of Carboniferous Age, and its general characteristics are the same as those of Marble Cañon.

The Little Colorado, heading away off to the southeast, enters the Grand Cañon by a profound gorge of its own.

From the south, the most important stream is Coanini Creek, which heads near the San Francisco Mountain, and rapidly finds its way into great depths.

Besides these streams, the plateaus are cut by the Rio Virgen, in its upper course, which empties into the Colorado below the Grand Cañon, and by the Paria, which heads in the Pink Cliffs, and enters the Colorado at the head of Marble Cañon.

All these streams, and many others of lesser importance, have cut gorges of their own; and they all have wet-weather affluents, that run in deep cañons. It is a cañon land.

THE CAÑONS CARVED BY RUNNING WATERS.

I have stated, and assumed, from time to time, in the above discussion, that these cañons have been cut by running waters. Professor Newberry, who first studied this region, in his report on the geology of the country which he visited, says: "Having this question constantly in mind, and examining, with all possible care, the structure of the great cañons which we entered, I everywhere found evidence of the exclusive action of water in their formation. The opposite sides of the deepest chasm showed perfect correspondence of stratification, conforming to the general dip, and nowhere displacement; and the bottom rock, so often dry and bare, was perhaps deeply eroded, but continuous, from side to side, a portion of the yet undivided series lying below."

Professor Newberry saw the great cañon region which I have described only on its southern border, but where the cañon features are developed on the grandest scale. My own observations overlap his, and extend to the north many hundreds of miles; and during the last six years I have explored many thousands of miles of cañons, and everywhere the facts observed confirm Professor Newberry's conclusions, as stated above.

Though the entire region has been folded and faulted on a grand scale, these displacements have never determined the course of the streams. The cañons are seen to cut across them, either directly or obliquely, here and there, and in a few instances, I have observed cañons to follow the course of faults for a short distance. They have also been observed to run back and forth across a fault; but such instances are surprisingly rare. In all the cañons where the streams are not so large as to cover the bottom, the continuity of the strata below has been apparent; and in the cañons traversed by the larger streams, the beds on either side have been found at the same altitude; and if it is supposed that these water-ways were determined by fissures, then such fissures were made without displacement, and did not extend to the depths now reached by the streams. If it is possible to conceive of such fissures, they must have been quite narrow; in fact, the whole supposition is evidently absurd. All the facts concerning the relation of the water-ways of this region to the mountains, hills, cañons, and cliffs, lead to the inevitable conclusion that the system of drainage was determined antecedent to the faulting, and folding, and erosion, which are observed, and antecedent, also, to the formation of the eruptive beds and cones.

THE U-IN-KA-RET MOUNTAINS.

The plateaus are yet modified in another way. Eruptive mountains, beds of black basalt, and volcanic cones are found here and there, and scoria and ashes are scattered over the land. There are three great, irregular mountains standing on the bench between the To-ro'-weap Fault and the Hurricane Ledge Fault. These great, complex masses of rock, or irregular mountains, are called by the Indians *U-in-ka'-rets*, (Pine Mountains.)

Lieutenant Whipple, on the first of January, 1854, while making a reconnaissance for a railroad route to the Pacific Ocean, camped at a spring about thirty miles to the southwest of the San Francisco Mountain, to which he gave the name "New Year's Spring." From this elevated position on the plateau he looked north, and over the chasm, in the distance, 200 miles away, he saw these mountains. Perhaps he discovered but a single peak, but on the map of the country over which the reconnaissance was made, he has indicated these peaks, and called them "High Mountains." Probably he intended this as a provisional name only.

In the winter of 1857–'58, when Lieutenant Ives explored the Lower Colorado, he reached, with a boat, a point on the river about ten miles below the Rio Virgen, and about eighty miles below the Grand Cañon. Being unable to proceed farther in his boat, a land expedition was organized, and he explored the plateaus to the south, descending to the mouth of Diamond Creek, as I have mentioned. His first view of the cañon, and the great plateaus through which it is carved, was obtained April 3, 1858, and is thus described: "At the end of ten miles the ridge of the swell was attained, and a splendid panorama burst suddenly into view. In the foreground were low table hills, intersected by numberless ravines; beyond these a lofty line of bluffs marked the edge of an immense cañon; a wide gap was directly ahead, and through it were beheld, to the extreme limit of vision, vast plateaus, towering one above the other, thousands of feet in the air, the long, horizontal bands broken, at intervals, by wide and profound abysses, and extending a hundred miles to the north, till the deep azure blue faded into a light cerulean tint, ·that blended with the dome of the heavens. The famous Big Cañon was before us, and for a long time we paused in wondering delight, surveying the stupendous formation through which the Colorado and its tributaries break their way."

On the 12th of April he obtained another good view across the country to the north, and, in his account of the day's journey, he makes this remark: "On the north side of the Colorado appeared a short range of mountains, close to the cañon, which had been previously hidden by the intervening plateaus."

On the map of the country embraced in this reconnaissance, a group of mountains are indicated, and called, by him, "North Side Mountains"—a name doubtless intended by him as provisional. They are the same as those mentioned by Lieutenant Whipple, and the same that we have described as standing on the bench between the To-ro'-weap Cliffs and the Hurricane Ledge. The Indian name *U-in-ka'-rets* has been adopted by the people who live in sight of the highest peaks, and so I have adopted the name which will doubtless live among those who use it daily.

The most northern of these mountain masses I have called Mount Trumbull, the next Mount Logan, and the one standing nearest to the Grand Cañon Mount Emma.

The great mountain masses themselves are covered with volcanic cones, and groups of volcanic cones are scattered over the benches. Let us see how these mountains were formed.

We have seen that the Uinta Mountains were not thrust up as peaks, but were carved from a vast, rounded block left by a retiring sea, or uplifted from the depths of the ocean, and its present forms are due to erosion! But these are volcanic cones. Have they, then, been built up as mountains? We shall see. The beds of sedimentary rocks, on which these mountains stand, run under the Vermilion Cliffs, to the north, and the beds seen in the Vermilion Cliffs at one time extended far away to the south, over this country and beyond the Grand Cañon. Shales, sandstones, and limestones, several thousand feet in thickness, have been washed away from the summit of all these benches south of the cliffs.

When this denudation commenced, there were no faults and no benches, and streams ran down from the north, heading in the Mar-ka'-gunt and Pauns-a'-gunt Plateaus, and found their way into the Colorado, and probably there were valleys along their courses. Other streams had their sources far away to the south, and came down into the Colorado, and it is probable that they also ran through valleys. Then these displacements began; they were not formed suddenly; the rocks were not flung down during some great convulsion, but settled slowly, so that this change in the contour of the surface had no effect on the course of the streams. Thus the downfall of the beds was not faster than the wearing away of the channels, for the displacements by faults and folds has not determined nor modified the direction of the principal streams. As the rocks fell, molten lava was thrust up, not suddenly, nor all at once, but from time to time—now here, now there—pouring out a sheet of molten rock in one eruption, and again in another, and this commenced away back in that time before the shales and sandstones seen in the Vermilion Cliffs had been carried away from the benches and plateaus to the south. Doubtless these first floods of lava found their ways into valleys—valleys in that elder time—and covered great beds of these sandstones and shales. When the lavas cooled, the rocks which they formed were much harder than the sandstones by which they were underlaid, and the beds which formed the surface of the country elsewhere; and as the degradation of this region by rains and rivers continued, the surrounding country was carried away, and the sandstones and shales, protected by the harder beds of basalt, remained; and now mountains stand in such places, doubtless marking the sites of ancient valleys. So the uncovered sandstones wasted away, and the lava-capped beds remained, leaving at first low tables, covered with sheets of basalt. Still, from time to time, new beds of lava were poured out—not over the old beds, usually, but on their borders, increasing their protected area; and, as the surrounding sandstones were still farther carried away, still, *pari passu* with erosion, came floods of lava, and thus the mountains which remain have a strangely complex constitution. We may call them eruptive mountains, for, had no eruption occurred, no mountains would have been left; all of the sandstones would have been carried away. But yet the great mass of the material of which the mountains are made is not eruptive matter; the mountains are great beds of sandstone and shale, covered with blankets of basalt, and, in a general way, the older beds of lava have the higher position on the mountains.

26 COL.

Since these vermilion beds were stripped from the adjacent country, the few showers of this arid region condense chiefly about the summits of the mountains, and the waters, gathering into streams, and running down into the lower region, have cut deep gulches through the sheets of basalt, in many places revealing the structure of the mountains themselves. The last puff in these eruptive vents tossed high into the air scoria and ashes; the lighter materials were carried away by the winds, the heavier fragments fell, and thus cinder-cones were piled up; and in many of these cinder-cones the outlines of the craters are still preserved.

The beds of lava are of various ages. The first were poured out in that ancient time before the sandstones had been carried away. From time to time new beds were formed, and the latest beds have been poured out in a time so recent, that the very waves of the congealed floods are still preserved, and there is no reason to suppose that this action is completed. In time another vent may be opened, and another river of red hot rock gush from the earth. Nor are all the cones of late origin; each outflow of molten matter seems to have ended in the formation of a cone. In the elder beds the cones have been washed away, but their sites are marked by scattered cinders. In the very latest cones the craters are still preserved, and their cinders are angular fragments of slag, that show that many storms have not fallen upon them since they broke in cooling.

So, even these eruptive mountains were hewn from the rock, and only the cinder-cones, scattered here and there, small in comparison to the great mountain masses, were piled up in their present forms.

It is probable that the cones have cores which extend to great depths, and perhaps connect the sheets of basalt above with masses of like material below, and thus the more enduring and protecting beds to which these mountains owe their preservation are anchored to the heart of the earth.

METHODS OF EROSION.

In this and the foregoing chapter I have attempted to describe the agencies and conditions which have produced the more important topographic features in the Valley of the Colorado. These features are mountains, hills, hog-backs, bad-lands, alcove lands, cliffs, buttes, and cañons. The primary agency in the production of these features is upheaval, *i. e.*, upheaval in relation to the level of the sea, though it may possibly be down-throw in relation to the center of the earth. This movement in portions of the crust of the earth may be by great folds, with anticlinal or synclinal axes, and by monoclinal folds and faults.

The second great agency is erosion, and the action of this agency is conditioned on the character of the displacements above mentioned, the texture and constitution of the rocks, and the amount and relative distribution of the rains.

In a district of country, the different portions of which lie at different altitudes above the sea, the higher the region the greater the amount of rainfall, and hence the eroding agency increases in some well observed, but not accurately defined, ratio, from the low to the high lands. The power of running water, in corrading channels and transporting the products of erosion, increases with the velocity of the stream in geometric ratio, and hence the degradation of the rocks increases with the inclination of the slopes. Thus altitude and inclination both are important elements in the problem.

Let me state this in another way. We may consider the level of the sea to be a grand base level, below which the dry lands cannot be eroded; but we may also have, for local and temporary purposes, other base levels of erosion, which are the levels of the beds of the principal streams which carry away the products of erosion. (I take some liberty in using the term level in this connection, as the action of a running stream in wearing its channel ceases, for all practical purposes, before its bed has quite reached the level of the lower end of the stream. What I have called the base level would, in fact, be an imaginary surface, inclining slightly in all its parts toward the lower end of the principal stream draining the area through which the level is supposed to extend, or having the inclination of its parts varied in direction as determined by tributary streams.) Where such a stream crosses a series of rocks in its course, some of which are hard, and others soft, the harder beds form a series of temporary dams, above which the corrasion of the channel through the softer beds is checked, and thus we may have a series of base levels of erosion, below which the rocks on either side of the river, though exceedingly friable, cannot be degraded. In these districts of country, the first work of rains and rivers is to cut channels, and divide the country into hills, and, perhaps, mountains, by many meandering grooves or water-courses, and when these have reached their local base levels, under the existing conditions, the hills are washed down, but not carried entirely away.

With this explanation I may combine the statements concerning elevation and inclination into this single expression, that the more elevated any district of country is, above its base level of denudation, the more rapidly it is degraded by rains and rivers.

The second condition in the progress of erosion, is the character of the beds to be eroded. Softer beds are acted upon more rapidly than the harder. The districts which are composed of softer rocks are rapidly excavated, so as to become valleys or plains, while the districts composed of harder rocks remain longer as hills and mountains.

Where the beds are of stratified material, so that the change from harder to softer materials is from bed to bed, rather than from district to district, and in a vertical or inclined direction, rather than a horizontal, the topographic features, which I have described as hog-backs and cliffs of erosion, are produced. The difference between hog-backs and cliffs of erosion is chiefly due to the amount of dip or inclination of the beds.

But there is another condition necessary to the production of cliffs and hog-backs in their typical forms. The country must be arid, for where there is a great amount of rain-fall, the water penetrates and permeates the rocks, and breaks them up, or rots them, to use an expression which has been employed with this meaning; and the difference between the durability of the harder beds and that of the softer, is, to some extent, compensated for by this agency, though doubtless ridges and cliffs may be produced in less arid climates, as we find them in the Appalachian System, but not so well marked. In a region of country where there is a greater amount of rain-fall, the tendency is to produce hills and mountains, rather than plateaus and ridges, with escarpments.

Now let us examine the character of the channels which running streams carve. Where the rocks to be carved are approximately horizontal, and composed of stratified beds of varying thickness, the tendency is to cut channels with escarpments or cliffs; but if the beds are greatly inclined, or composed of unstratified material, the tendency is to cut channels with more flaring and irregular walls. These tendencies are more clearly defined when the meteorologic conditions are favorable—that is, if a stream cuts through stratified rocks, in an arid region, and carries the waters from a district more plentifully supplied, the cliff character of the walls is increased; and where a stream runs through unstratified rocks, in a district well supplied with rains, the walls or banks of the stream are cut down in more gentle slopes.

For purposes of discussion, it will be convenient to call the deep channels of streams through table-lands, in arid climates, cañons; and the deep channels of streams through heterogeneous beds, in a moist climate, water-gaps, or narrows, and ravines.

Having in view the forms which are produced by erosion, it will be convenient to classify the methods of erosion as follows: First, corrasion by running streams, and, second, erosion by rains; the first producing channels along well defined lines, the second producing the general surface features of the landscape.

Of the first class we have two varieties:

A. The corrasion of water-gaps.

B. The corrasion of cañons.

Of the second class we have three varieties:

A. Cliff erosion, where the beds are slightly inclined, and are of heterogeneous structure, some soft and others hard; and for the production of the best marked forms, the climate should be arid. Here the progress of erosion is chiefly by undermining.

B. Hog-back erosion, where the beds have a greater inclination, but are still of heterogeneous structure. Here the progress of erosion is by undermining and surface washing, and the typical forms would require an arid climate.

C. Hill and mountain erosion, where the beds may lie in any shape, and be composed of any material not included in the other classes, and the progress of erosion is chiefly by surface washing. The typical forms are found in a moist climate.

There is still another agency in the production of topographic features, viz, the eruption of molten matter from below the general surface. The beds formed are soon modified by erosion, and then the forms produced are due to that agency, and fall under the general series. But there is a time, immediately after the eruption, when these beds lie in forms due to igneous dynamics, and the most important features produced are cones. These cones are very conspicuous features of the landscape over much of the region drained by the Colorado River.

The district of country drained by the Colorado and its tributaries is divided into two parts, by a well marked line of displacements. The lower third of the valley, which lies southward from this line, is but little above the level of the sea, except that here and there ranges of mountains are found. From this region, there is usually a bold step to a higher.

The upper two-thirds of the area drained by the Colorado is from four to eight thousand feet above the level of the sea, with mountain ranges on the east, north, and west, of greater altitude. The bold step from the lower country to the table lands is usually an escarpment in rocks of Carboniferous Age, marked, here and there, by beds of lava, and along its margin stand many volcanic cones. San Francisco Mountain is made up of a group of these beds of eruptive matter, covering stratified rocks. This higher region is the one to which we have given especial attention in the previous discussion.

The principal condensation of moisture occurs on and about the mountains standing on the rim of the basin, the region within being arid.

Bad-lands, alcove lands, plains of naked rock, plains of drifting sands, *mesas*, plateaus, buttes, hog-backs, cliffs, volcanic cones, volcanic mountains, cañons, cañon valleys, and valleys are all found in this region and make up its topographic features. Mountains, hills, and small elevated valleys are the features of the irregular boundary belt.

No valley is found along the course of the Colorado, from the Grand Wash toward the sources of the river, until we reach the head of Labyrinth Cañon. For this entire distance the base level of erosion is below the general surface level of the country adjacent to the river, but at Gunnison's Valley we have a local base level of erosion which has resulted in the production of low plains and hills for a number of miles back from the stream. North of the Cañon of Desolation and south of the Uinta Mountains, another local base level of erosion is found, so near to the general surface of the country that we find a district of valleys and low hills stretching back from Green River, up the Uinta to the west, and White River to the east, for many miles. North of the Uinta Mountains a third local base level of erosion is seen, but its influence on the topographic features is confined to a small area of two or three hundred square miles. Going up the chief lateral streams of the Colorado, we find one or more of these local base levels of erosion, where the streams course through valleys.

Where these local base levels of erosion exist, forming valley and hill regions, the streams no longer cut their channels deeper, and the waters of the streams, running at a low angle, course slowly along and are not able to carry away the products of surface wash, and these are deposited along the flood-plains, in part, and in the valleys, among hills, and on the gentler slopes. This results in a redistribution of the material in irregular beds and aggregations.

In this region, there are occasional local storms of great violence. Such storms may occur in any particular district only at intervals of many years, possibly centuries. When such a one does occur, it reopens great numbers of channels that have been filled by the ordinary wash of rains, and often cuts a new channel through beds which have accumulated in the manner above described. The structure of these beds is well exposed, and we find beds of clay, beds of sand, and beds of gravel occurring in a very irregular way, due to the vicissitudes of local wash, and, where the progress of erosion has been more or less by undermining, larger fragments or boulders are found, and these boulders are sometimes mixed with clay, and sometimes with sand and gravel, and where thin sheets of eruptive rocks have been torn to pieces, more or less by undermining, (for such is the usual way in this country,) the beds appear to contain erratics, and in fact some of the rocks are erratics, for in the various changes in the levels produced they have often been transported many miles, not by sudden and rapid excursions, but moved a little from time to time.

Again, the beds from which they were derived, doubtless, in many cases have been broken up or lost, and these fragments only remain to attest to the existence of such beds in some former time, and all stages may be observed, from the beds the edges only of which have been broken up, to those that have only fragments remaining or have entirely disappeared. Another interesting fact has been observed, that these erratics or boulders are often found distributed somewhat in lines due to the undermining of lines of cliffs. Often where we have cliffs capped with a bed of lava, former and more advanced positions of these lines of cliffs can be recognized by the position of lines of lava fragments which are seen in the valley or plains in front of the cliffs. It will be seen that these local accumulations of material, due to the excess of erosion over that of transportation, greatly resemble the accumulations of "the Drift." Especially is this true where I have studied the latter in the valley of the Mississippi, and I have been led to query whether it may not be possible to refer the origin of the Drift of the Valley of the Mississippi, in part at least, to some such action as this ; not that I question the evidence of extended glacial action in that region, but may it not be that this glacial action has only resulted in somewhat modifying a vast accumulation of irregularly bedded material, originally due to the fact that the grand base level of erosion had been reached by the running streams of that region, and hills and mountains had been degraded by having the material of which they were composed scattered over lower lands, without being carried away by streams to the sea?

All the mountain forms of this region are due to erosion ; all the cañons, channels of living rivers and intermittent streams, were carved by the running waters, and they represent an amount of corrasion difficult to comprehend. But the carving of the cañons and mountains is insignificant, when compared with the denudation of the whole area, as evidenced in the cliffs of erosion. Beds hundreds of feet in thickness and hundreds of thousands of square miles in extent, beds of granite and beds of schist, beds of marble and beds of sandstone, crumbling shales and adamantine lavas have slowly yielded to the silent and unseen powers of the air, and crumbled into dust and been washed away by the rains and carried into the sea by the rivers.

The story we have told is a history of the war of the elements to beat back the march of the lands from ocean depths.

And yet the conditions necessary to great erosion in the Valley of the Colorado are not found to exceed those of many other regions. In fact, the aridity of the climate is such that this may be considered a region of lesser, rather than greater, erosion. We may suppose that, had this country been favored with an amount of rain-fall similar to that of the Appalachian country, and many other districts on the surface of the earth, that the base level of erosion of the entire area would have been the level of the sea; and, under such circumstances, though the erosion would have been much greater than we now find, the evidences of erosion would have been more or less obliterated. As it is, we are able to study erosion in this country, and find evidences of its progress and its great magnitude, from the very fact that the conditions of erosion have been imperfect.

It is proper to remark here that erosion does not increase in ratio to the increase of the precipitation of moisture, *cæteris paribus*, as might be supposed; for, with the increase of rains there will be an increase of vegetation, which serves as a protection to the rocks, and distributes erosion more evenly, and it may be that a great increase of rains in this region would only produce a different series of topographic outlines, without greatly increasing the general degradation of the Valley of the Colorado.

To a more thorough discussion of this subject I hope to return at some future time.

From the considerations heretofore presented, it is not thought necessary to refer the exhibition of erosion shown in the cañons and cliffs to a more vigorous action of aqueous dynamics than now exists, for, as I have stated, a greater precipitation of moisture would have resulted in a very different class of topographic features. Instead of cañons, we should have had water-gaps and ravines; instead of valleys with cliff like walls, we should have had valleys bounded by hills and slopes; and if the conclusions to which we have arrived are true, the arid conditions now existing must have extended back for a period of time of sufficient length to produce the present cañons and cliffs. But there are facts which seem to warrant the conclusion that this condition has existed for a much longer period than that necessary for the production of the present features; that is, the characteristics of the present topography have existed for a long time. There are

27 col.

evidences that the lines of cliffs themselves have been carried back for great distances as cliffs by undermining, which is a process carried on only in an arid region.

The evidence is of this character. I have stated that the drainage of the inclined plateaus is usually from the brink of the cliffs backward; *i. e.*, the water falling on the plateau does not find its way immediately over the cliffs, but runs from the very brink or edge of the plateau back toward the middle or farther side, which is usually found against the foot of another line of cliffs, and here the waters are turned toward some greater channel, which runs against the dip and cuts through the cliffs. Now the water-ways at the heads of these streams that have their sources near the brink of the cliffs would always be small, shallow, and ramifying into many minute branches if the line of cliffs were a fixed or immovable line, but we often find that the cliffs have been carried back by the undermining process until all these minute ramifications have been cut off; and we find cañons opening on the faces of the cliffs, the waters of which run backward as above described.

Let us suppose that we have a line of cliffs with an escarpment facing the south. The rain, falling on the escarpment and in the region south of the cliffs, would run toward the south or along the foot of the cliffs until it reached some more important water channel; the rain falling on the plateau, from the brink of the cliffs backward, would run toward the north, and the waters falling on this upper region would excavate channels for themselves, and, under proper conditions, cañons would be cut. As the cliffs are undermined and this line carried back into the plateau, the area with a southern drainage would be increased, the area with a northern drainage correspondingly diminished, and, when the process had continued for a sufficient length of time, we would find the southern edge of the plateau carried away by this undermining process, until all the heads of the streams were cut off and until the line had reached the cañons.

Gradually, during the progress of erosion, the excavation of the bottom of the cañons would cease, as the supply of water running through them would be cut off, and such cañons would have to be considered as comparatively ancient. Such facts are frequently observed in this cañon and cliff country.

From such considerations, it seems that we may safely conclude that the cliff topography has prevailed in that region for a long time. There are evidences also that there were cañons here before the present cañons were carved. The facts in relation to this matter can be better stated when we come to discuss the geology of the region.

Mr. G. K. Gilbert, a geologist of Lieutenant Wheeler's corps, in a paper communicated to the Philosophical Society of Washington, in 1873, deduced a similar conclusion from an independent series of facts observed in Western Utah. The basin of Great Salt Lake, a portion of what Frémont designated the "Great Basin," has now so dry a climate that its waters gather in its lowest parts and evaporate and have no outlet to the sea. In a former period, however, there was more rain, the valley was filled with water to its brim, and in place of the Salt Lake Desert, there was a broad and deep fresh lake, discharging its surplus into the Columbia River. The epoch of this lake Mr. Gilbert finds reason to consider identical with the Glacial Epoch, and it was of limited duration. Among its vestiges are deposits of fossiliferous marl, which are conspicuously contrasted with the gravels and sand that now slowly accumulate in the same region, borne by the intermittent streams that descend from the mountains. Where the beds are superposed, the marls testify to a moist climate and the gravels to a climate so dry that the basin was never filled with water. But above the marls are found only scattered and thin deposits of gravel, while below them the gravel beds are omnipresent and of great depth, and hence it was reasoned that the arid period that preceded the Glacial Epoch was many times longer than that which has followed it.

Even during the Glacial Epoch, Mr. Gilbert considers that "the Atlantic slope, and the region of the Great Basin, were contrasted in climate, just as now. The general causes that covered the humid east with a mantle of ice, sufficed, in the arid west, only to flood the valleys with fresh water, and send a few ice streams down the highest mountain gorges."*

RECORDS OF MORE ANCIENT LANDS.

The summit of the Kaibab Plateau is more than six thousand feet above the river, and I have already mentioned that the summit of the plateau is also the summit of rocks of Carboniferous Age. These beds are about three

---

* Bulletin Phil. Soc., Washington, 46th meeting, April 26, 1873.

thousand five hundred feet in thickness, and beneath them we have a thousand feet of conformable rocks of undetermined age. This gives us 4,500 feet, from the summit of the plateau down to the non-conformable beds. Still beneath these we have 1,500 feet, so that we have more than one thousand five hundred feet of other rocks exposed in the depths of the Grand Cañon. Standing on some rock, which has fallen from the wall into the river—a rock so large that its top lies above the water—and looking overhead, we see a thousand feet of crystalline schists, with dikes of greenstone, and dikes and beds of granite. Heretofore we have given the general name granite to this group of rocks; still, above them we can see beds of hard, vitreous sandstone of many colors, but chiefly dark red. This group of rocks adds but little more than five hundred feet to the height of the walls, and yet the beds are 10,000 feet in thickness. How can this be? The beds themselves are non-conformable with the overlying Carboniferous rocks; that is, the Carboniferous rocks are spread over their upturned edges.

In Illustration 79 we have a section of the rocks of the Grand Cañon. *A, A* represents the granite; *a, a*, dikes and eruptive beds; *B, B*, these non-conformable rocks. It will be seen that the beds incline to the right. The horizontal beds above, *C, C* are rocks of Carboniferous Age, with underlying conformable beds. The distance along the wall marked by the line *x, y*, is the only part of its height represented by these rocks, but the beds are inclined, and their thickness must be measured by determining the thickness of each bed. This is done by measuring the several beds along lines normal to the planes of stratification; and, in this manner, we find them to be 10,000 feet in thickness.

Doubtless, at some time before the Carboniferous rocks *C, C* were formed, the beds *B, B* extended off to the left, but between the periods of deposition of the two series, *B, B* and *C, C* there was a period of erosion. The beds, themselves, are records of the invasion of the sea; the line of separation, the record of a long time when the region was dry land. The events in the history of this intervening time, the period of dry land, one might suppose were all lost. What plants lived here, we cannot learn; what animals roamed over the hills, we know not: and yet there is a history which is not lost, for we find that after these beds were formed as sediments beneath the sea, and still after they had been folded, and the sea had left them, and

Figure 79.—Section of wall in the Grand Cañon.

the rains had fallen on the country long enough to carry out ten thousand feet of rocks, the extension of these beds to the south, which were cut away, and yet before the overlying Carboniferous rocks were formed as sediments of sand and triturated coral reefs, and ground shells and pulverized bones, some interesting events occurred, the records of which are well preserved. This region of country was fissured, and the rocks displaced so as to form faults, and through the fissures floods of lava were poured, which, on cooling, formed beds of trap, or greenstone. This greenstone was doubtless poured out on the dry land, for it bears evidence of being eroded by rains and streams prior to the deposition of the overlying rocks.

Let us go down again, and examine the junction between these red rocks, with their intrusive dikes and overlying beds of greenstone, and the crystalline schists below.

We find these lower rocks to be composed chiefly of metamorphosed sandstones and shales, which have been folded so many times, squeezed, and heated, that their original structure, as sandstones and shales, is greatly obscured, or entirely destroyed, so that they are called metamorphic crystalline schists.

Dame Nature kneaded this batch of dough very thoroughly. After these beds were deposited, after they were folded, and still after they were deeply eroded, they were fractured, and through the fissures came floods of molten granite, which now stands in dikes, or lies in beds, and the metamorphosed sandstones and shales, and the beds of granite, present evidences of erosion subsequent to the periods just mentioned, yet antecedent to the deposition of the non-conformable sandstones.

Here, then, we have evidences of another and more ancient period of erosion, or dry land. Three times has this great region been left high and dry by the ever shifting sea; three times have the rocks been fractured and faulted; three times have floods of lava been poured up through the crevices, and three times have the clouds gathered over the rocks, and carved out valleys with their storms. The first time was after the deposition of the schists; the second was after the deposition of the red sandstones; the third time is the present time. The plateaus and mountains of the first and second periods have been destroyed or buried; their eventful history is lost; the rivers that ran into the sea are dead, and their waters are now rolling as

tides, or coursing in other channels. Were there cañons then? I think not.
The conditions necessary to the formation of cañons are exceptional in the
world's history.

We have looked back unnumbered centuries into the past, and seen the
time when the schists in the depths of the Grand Cañon were first formed as
sedimentary beds beneath the sea; we have seen this long period followed
by another of dry land—so long that even hundreds, or perhaps thousands,
of feet of beds were washed away by the rains; and, in turn, followed by
another period of ocean triumph, so long, that at least ten thousand feet of
sandstones were accumulated as sediments, when the sea yielded dominion
to the powers of the air, and the region was again dry land. But aerial
forces·carried away the ten thousand feet of rocks, by a process slow yet
unrelenting, until the sea again rolled over the land, and more than ten
thousand feet of rocky beds were built over the bottom of the sea; and then
again the restless sea retired, and the golden, purple, and black hosts of
heaven made missiles of their own misty bodies—balls of hail, flakes of
snow, and drops of rain—and when the storm of war came, the new rocks
fled to the sea. Now we have cañon gorges and deeply eroded valleys, and
still the hills are disappearing, the mountains themselves are wasting away,
the plateaus are dissolving, and the geologist, in the light of the past history
of the earth, makes prophecy of a time when this desolate land of Titanic
rocks shall become a valley of many valleys, and yet again the sea will
invade the land, and the coral animals build their reefs in the infinitesimal
laboratories of life, and lowly beings shall weave nacre-lined shrouds for
themselves, and the shrouds shall remain entombed in the bottom of the sea,
when the people shall be changed, by the chemistry of life, into new forms;
monsters of the deep shall live and die, and their bones be buried in the
coral sands. Then other mountains and other hills shall be washed into the
Colorado Sea, and coral reefs, and shales, and bones, and disintegrated
mountains, shall be made into beds of rock, for a new land, where new
rivers shall flow.

Thus ever the land and sea are changing; old lands are buried, and
new lands are born, and with advancing periods new complexities of rock
are found; new complexities of life evolved.

PART THIRD.

ZOOLOGY.

By ELLIOTT COUES.

CHAPTER XIII.

ABSTRACT OF RESULTS OF A STUDY OF THE GENERA GEOMYS AND THOMOMYS.*

BY DR. ELLIOTT COUES, U. S. A.

These two genera are closely allied; the principal difference being in the character of the sulcation of the superior incisors. In *Geomys*, the upper front teeth have a deep groove along the front face, at or near the middle, with or without a fine groove along the inner margin. In *Thomomys*, the latter groove exists, but there is no other. The fore feet of *Geomys* are more decidedly fossorial than those of *Thomomys*, owing to greater development of the claws. In *Geomys*, the external ears are a mere rim surrounding the auditory orifice; in *Thomomys*, there is a decided, though small, auricle. The two genera constitute a perfectly natural group, of the grade of a family, which may be called *Geomyidæ*, equivalent to the subfamily *Geomyinæ* of Baird, or the *Sciuro-spalacoides* of Brandt. Their closest affinities are with the *Saccomyidæ* (*Dipodomys*, *Perognathus*, &c.), under which they have been placed as subfamilies by Waterhouse and Baird. These authors are certainly right in differing from those who, like Brandt and others, widely dissociate the two groups; for, as Baird has insisted, they are very closely allied in all essential respects, notwithstanding their remarkable dissimilarity in contour and other superficial points. Still, I do not go to the length of the authors named in associating *Geomys* and *Thomomys* with *Dipodomys*, *Perognathus*, &c., in one; preferring to follow Gill in considering them as a distinct, though the

---

* Based on the material contained in the National Museum, Smithsonian Institution, Washington, D. C.

28 COL

most nearly allied, family. The *Saccomyidæ* are extremely lithe, agile, graceful animals; jerboa-like, with long saltatorial hind limbs, elongated and often tufted tail, large ears, and full eyes, and are not specially nocturnal or subterranean in habits. The *Geomyidæ*, on the other hand, are hamster-like, or rather an exaggeration of that kind of structure; they are among the heaviest for their inches of any animals of this country, of squat, bunchy shape, with short, thick limbs, a short tail, very small or rudimentary ears, small eyes, no appreciable neck, and thick, blunt head; and they are as completely subterranean as the mole itself. They are rarely and only momentarily seen above ground; they excavate endless galleries in the earth in their search for food, frequently coming to the surface to throw out the earth in heaps, but plugging up these orifices as soon as they have served their purpose.

Both families agree in possessing enormous cheek-pouches, overlying the whole side of the head, in some species even reaching over the neck and shoulders. The nature and construction of these sacs was long misunderstood. They were supposed for many years to be external pendulous bags opening into the mouth, and thus to differ only in degree of development from the ordinary "cheek-pouches" of many other rodents—an enlargement of the mucous membrane of the mouth and skin of the cheeks. But, as now well known, they have no connection with the mouth; at least, no more than the abdominal pocket of an opossum has with the genitalia. Their chief purpose is not even related to the food of the species; they are sacs that the animals use chiefly in carrying out dirt from their burrows to deposit it on the surface of the ground. They are fully described beyond.

Several circumstances have conspired to obscure the history of the *Geomyidæ*, and to involve the determination of the species in doubt. In the first place, the animals are largely withdrawn from ordinary observation, and the acquisition of specimens is difficult. Their geographical distribution is limited to a portion of America. Very few specimens, comparatively, have ever reached Europe, and very few foreign naturalists have written about them from anything like sufficient means of observation. In fact, they are among the rarest sets of specimens in any museums; and I think it probable that there are before me, as I write, more prepared specimens than have before been examined by all naturalists put together. This shows the difficulty of getting material to work upon on this family, though the animals fairly swarm in certain regions, becoming a serious hinderance to agriculture. There is another point to be considered here : the shapelessness of the species, so to speak, with the looseness and distensibility of the skin, renders them peculiarly susceptible of atrocious taxidermy, with the result of scarcely leaving a hint of their actual appearance and true dimensions. One result of all this is that a mass of pointless, if not erroneous, descriptions and conflicting accounts forms a large part of the written history of the species. There appears to have been an unusually large amount of compilation done in this group; more than half of everything extant upon the subject is of this character.* The 'systematic" accounts given by Fischer, Schinz, Wagner, Giebel, and some others that might be named, are simply worthless for any practical purpose. The special papers upon the subject are so few that it was not thought necessary to enumerate them. Aside from the descriptions of "new species" which it is necessary to examine, the authorities which need be consulted are very few. Waterhouse's and Brandt's articles; especially Richardson's, in the Fauna Boreali-Americana; LeConte's monographic sketch of the family ; and Baird's later, more elaborate, memoir, with Audubon's and Bachman's figures, represent the gist of the matter. The synonymy collated in this paper is believed to represent very nearly all the literature of the subject.

It is not within the scope of the present article to treat fully of the characters of the family. I confine myself here almost entirely to the determination of the species and their full description, with the necessary bibliographical matter. The number of species I find to have been, much as usual, largely overstated. This is particularly the case in the genus *Thomomys*, where the three recognizable races of the single known species have been described as a dozen distinct species, and been referred to half as many different genera. Most late authors recognize at least six or eight species of the genus. *Geomys* makes out a better case ; out of the seven species admitted by Baird, five are unquestionably valid. It is very curious and interesting to note how differently *Geomys* and *Thomomys* have become differentiated into species. The former genus has developed into at least five

---

* *Cf.* the synonymy of *Thomomys talpoides et aff.* in the following pages.

perfectly well-discriminated species, the early links between which have entirely disappeared, leaving the forms as stable as possible. *Thomomys* is still in a transition-stage at present. Setting aside the peculiar *T. clusius*, described as new beyond, all the known forms of that genus are still only incompletely separated, and the links binding them are plainly before our eyes. The genus appears to be making into a number of species, but the process is still far from completion. In talking over this singular difference in the natural history of these two closely-allied genera with Professor Baird, he threw out a suggestion, which, perhaps, may account for the facts. While we have no means of knowing which is the older of the two genera, so as to compare the rates of progress they respectively made in developing their species, yet we may fairly infer, upon geographical considerations, that *Geomys* has been longer about it than *Thomomys*. *Geomys*, though found to a certain longitude westward, is essentially a form of Eastern North America, extended thence to Central America, and it is presumably upon older ground than the late deposits in the West, where *Thomomys* occurs. In the cases of many mammals and birds of this continent, it will be recollected there is a perfectly stable eastern species of a genus which in the West is represented by a number of "varieties." *Junco, Melospiza, Passerella, Picus*, are good illustrations. But be the explanation what it may, there is no doubt about the fact that *Geomys* has made itself into five or six firm species before *Thomomys* has succeeded in turning out more than one or two.

With these few observations by way of introducing the species, I shall proceed at once to give an account of them, reserving many details which contributed to the result of my investigation, as well as all general considerations respecting the family, for publication in a different connection.

GENUS GEOMYS. (*emend. ex* Raf.)

Mus, sp. SHAW, *et al., l. c. infra.*
Cricetus, sp. DESM., *et al., l. c. infra.*
Geomys, RAF., Am. Month. Mag. ii, 1–17, 45.
Diplostoma, RAF., *op. et loc. cit.* (char. plerumq.: inept.), *nec* RICH.
Saccophorus, KUHL, Beitr. 1820, 65.
Pseudostoma, SAY, Long's Exp. R. Mts. i, 1823, 406.
Ascomys, LICHT., Abhand. Berl. Acad. 1822–'3, 1825, 20.

GEOMYS BURSARIUS, (Shaw) Rich.

Mus bursarius, SHAW, Linn. Trans. v, 1800, 227, fig. 8; Gen. Zool. ii, 1801, 100, pl. 138 (the plate clearly
shows the grooved incisors; the pouches are everted).—MITC., Am. Journ. Sci. iv, 1822, 183.
Cricetus bursarius, DESM., Nouv. Dict. d'Hist. Nat. xiv, ——, 177 ; Ency. Méth. Suppl. pl. 10, f. 4 ; Mamm. ii,
1822, p. 312 (*bursarcus*).—F. CUV., Dict. Sc. Nat. xx, ——, 257.—DESMOUL., Dict. Class. viii,
——, 37.—GRIFF., Anim. Kingd. iii, 1827, 138, pl. — ; v, 1827, 235, No. 612.
Saccophorus bursarius, KUHL, Beiträge, 1820, 65.—FISCH., Synop. 1827, 304.
Pseudostoma bursarius, SAY, Long's Exp. R. Mts. i, 1823, 406 (*bursaria*).—HARLAN, Fn. Amer. 1825, 153.—
LESS., Man. 1827, 259.—GODMAN, Am. Nat. Hist. ii, 1831, 90 (*bursarium*).—DEKAY, N. Y. Fn.
i, 1842, 92.—AUD. & BACH., Q. N. A. i, 1849, 332, pl. 44.
Geomys? bursarius, RICH., F. B. A. i, 1829, 203 ; Rep. Brit. Assoc. for 1836, v, 1837, 156 (*nec* Gray).
Ascomys bursarius, EYD. & GERV., Voy. Favorite, v, 1839, 23.—SCHINZ, Syn. ii, 1845, 132.—GIEB., Odon-
tog. 53, pl. 23, f. 8.
Geomys bursarius, WOODH., Zuñi and Col. R. 1853, 50.—PARVIN, Ann. Rep. Smiths. Inst. for 1854, 1855,
293 (habits).—KENN., Trans. Illinois Agric. Soc. for 1853–'4, 1855, 580.—BD., M. N. A. 1857,
372, pl. 22, fig. 1 *a–h*, and pl. 50, fig. 2 *a–g*.—MAXIM., Arch. Naturg. 1861, —— ; Verz. Reise
N.-Am. Säug. 1862, 147.—GERR., Cat. Bones Br. Mus. 1862, 223.—LEIDY, Proc. Acad. Nat. Sci.
Phila. 1867, 97 (skull from loess of Missouri).—AMES, Bull. Acad. Minnesota, i, 1874, 70.
Geomys (Saccophorus) bursarius, GIEBEL, Säng. 1855, 529.
"? *Mus ludovicianus*, ORD, Guthrie's Geog. 2d Am. ed. ii, 1815, 292. (Not determinable.)"
? *Diplostoma fusca*, RAF., Am. Month. Mag. ii, 1817, 44.—DESM., Mamm. ii, 1822, 315.—LESS., Man. 1827, 261.
? *Diplostoma alba*, RAF., Am. Month. Mag. ii, 1817, 44 (albino).—DESM., Mamm. ii, 1822, 315.—LESS., Man.
1827, 261.
Saccophorus? albus, FISCH., Synop. 1827, 305.
? *Geomys cinereus*, RAF., Am. Month. Mag. ii, 1817, 45.
Mus saccatus, MITCH., N. Y. Med. Repos. xxi, 1821, 249.
Ascomys canadensis, LICHT., Abh. Acad. Wiss. Berl. 1823, 13, fig.—BRANTS, Muizen, 1827, 24.—WAGN.,
Suppl. Schreb. iii, 1843, 383; Abh. K. Baier. Akad. München. xxii, 1846, 327, fig. (skeleton).
Geomys canadensis, LEC., Proc. Acad. Nat. Sci. Phila. vi, 1852, 158.
Geomys oregonensis, LEC., Proc. Acad. Nat. Sci. Phila. vi, 1852, 160 (no probability that the assigned local-
ity is correct).
Geomys breviceps, BD., Proc. Acad. Nat. Sci. Phila. 1855, 334 ; M. N. A. 1857, 378, pl. 52, f. 2 *a–g*.—GERR.
Cat. Bones Br. Mus. 1862, 223.
Canada Rat, SHAW, *ll. cc.*
Canada Pouched Rat, RICHARDSON, *l. c.*—AUD. & BACH., *l. c.*
Hamster du Canada, DESM., *l. c.*
Pseudostome à bourse, LESS., *l. c.*
Diplostome brun, D. blanche, DESM., LESS., *ll. cc.*
Canadian Hamster, GRIFFITH, *l. c.*
Goffer, Taschenmaus, SCHINZ, *l. c.*
Pouched Rat, Sand Rat, Camas Rat, Pocket Gopher, Salamander, Vulg.
Gaufre, French (whence English "gopher," and German "goffer").
Quid Geomys drummondii, RICH., Rep. Brit. Assoc. v, 1837, 157 (*Ascomys drummondii* apud Wagn., Suppl.
Schreb.), species indet. dentibus prim. bisulcatis ?

DIAGNOSIS.—Superior incisors bisulcate, with a fine sharp groove along
the inner margin, and another much larger bisecting the remaining plane surface. Check-pouches ample, extending to the shoulders. Hands (including
claws) longer than feet. Tail and feet hairy. Pelage soft, sleek, mole-like.
Color dull reddish-brown, muddy-gray or hoary beneath, the basal portion

of the fur plumbeous throughout; or blackish-gray; feet and tail, for the most part, white or colorless. Average dimensions of adult, 7 to 8 inches; tail, 2 or 3 inches; fore foot, about $1\frac{1}{2}$ inches; hind foot, about $1\frac{1}{4}$ inches; longest fore claw, about 0.75 inch.

Habitat.—Valley of the Mississippi and its tributaries in a broad sense, and somewhat beyond to the northward. "Canada." "Oregon" (!!!).

Description.—I shall draw up my account of this species from the large amount of material, both dry and alcoholic, before me. The specimens are from the whole immediate valley of the Mississippi, from the State of that name to Minnesota; also, from Texas; from the Platte, Washita, and Niobrara Rivers, &c.; but not from west of the Rocky Mountains, where the genus has yet to be satisfactorily determined to occur. Descriptions of form and proportions are taken from alcoholic specimens in the flesh; of color, from dried specimens. The present being taken as the standard of comparison for other species, succeeding descriptions of the rest may consequently be abridged to present in stronger light their own peculiar characters. The present account, besides being descriptive of the particular species, is rendered supplementary to the characters of the genus.

The "pocket-gopher" is about the size of a house-rat (*Mus decumanus*), but less in linear dimensions and much more stoutly built, with a heavy, lumpy body, on which the skin slips loosely; no appreciable neck; a rapidly narrowed blunt head; small eyes; no obvious external ears; short limbs; strong fore feet, somewhat like those of a mole, with enormous claws; and a short, thick, stumpy tail, issuing from a conical prolongation of the rump. The side of the body, before the shoulder, is occupied by an enormous sac, opening by a wide slit along the side of the jaws, but not directly communicating with the mouth. These sacs, fully distended, represent the greatest crosswise dimension of the animal. To sum the generalities, the gopher is a mole-like rat, *plus* these great bags. The general habits bear out the simile: of all rodents, the gopher is probably the most completely fossorial and subterranean; and its underground operations are conducted with the aid of these sacs.

The head is short, wide, deep, and blunt; not separated from the body by any appreciable constriction of the neck. The frontal region is broad and flat; the sides rapidly converge; the under side and mouth parts are anomalous in their peculiar configuration. The muffle is entirely hairy, excepting a small, definitely naked nose-pad, somewhat T-shaped, with long arms and a short leg; the nostrils opening obliquely between these. There is a considerable hairy interval between this pad and the incisors, and a fringe of long hairs hangs down over these teeth. The upper incisors appear to be situated remote from the mouth; for beneath them is a long strip of finely furry skin, longitudinally vaulted, with sides sloping upward to a median line, like the roof of a house with its ridge. This great space, near an inch long, bounded on either side by the swollen furry ridges which constitute the external lips, leads to the contracted orifice of the mouth proper, or that part of the buccal cavity lined by mucous membrane, to which the parts just described are merely the vestibule. The mucous membrane only comes to the border of the thick external lips in a small patch on each side. The lip laps loosely around the base of the under incisors, and the opposite sides meet behind the teeth. In fact, the curious conformation is such that the mouth actually shuts sideways by approach and meeting of the thick lips from either side; further closure of the jaws resulting in merely a folding back of the thus apposed lips. When the mouth is closed, the incisor teeth are entirely shut out of the buccal cavity, and surrounded behind, as well as elsewhere, by furry integument; in a large specimen, with the tips of the incisors in apposition, the end of one's finger may be passed behind them, yet not into the mouth at all. On wrenching open the jaws, the fleshy tongue is seen largely filling the remarkably contracted true orifice of the mouth; but so constricted is the opening that the molar dentition can scarcely be brought into this view. This particular condition of the parts is probably not met with outside the present family.

The pouches of this species—at first supposed to be pendulous bags hanging from the mouth, then with some correction found to be not pendulous, yet believed to open into the mouth from within—are wholly external, and have no more connection with the buccal cavity than the belly-pouch of a kangaroo or opossum has to do with the genital organs. These sacs are simply a purse-shaped duplicature of the loose skin of the side of the head and neck. The free margin of the pouch arises from the side of the upper jaw, about half-way from nose to eye, just underneath the whisker-patch, and curves loosely around the side of the head to the angle of the jaw. The general outline of the orifice is semicircular (or rather semipyriform, since the broadest part sags down a little); the inner border being the proper integument of the side of the head. The lining of the sac is ordinary integument, of rather more delicate texture; it is clothed with fine fur. On the side next the head, the ordinary fur of the parts makes directly into the pouch; on the outside, the fine fur continues to the brim, where it is met by the ordinary external pelage. Between the two layers of skin rests a thin bed of muscular fibers (perhaps a modified platysma myoides), serving for such contractile movements as the receptacle may be susceptible of. But the connection between the folds of skin is so slight and loose that the pouch may, with little force, be turned completely inside out, though it does not appear that this ever occurs in life. A full-sized pouch will admit three fingers as far as the first joint.

The small eyes are situated midway between the nose and ears, below the line between these two; and, if anything, they are rather nearer the latter than the former. The ears have been described in varying terms, leaving a doubt whether there was an auricle or not; but it is proper to say that the auricle is obsolete. The large circular orifice of the meatus externus is surrounded by a raised brim, rather thicker, if not higher, behind than before, and, as such, constituting a rudimentary pinna; but there is nothing to be called a flap (which is something that may be *turned over*).

The large, strong, and eminently fossorial fore feet recall those of the mole in some respects, though they occupy the usual position with reference to the axis of the limb—sole downward instead of tilted over. The hand itself is shorter than the hind foot; but the immense claws reverse the proportion of the two as a whole. The palm is broader than the sole, and perfectly naked. At the juncture with the wrist, it presents two great movable callous tubercles, which probably have a bearing upon the great force of flexion of the member; otherwise the palm is flat, devoid of special pads or callosities, and may be thrown into indeterminate rugæ or sulci, according to the movements of the parts. There are five digits, whose relative lengths are nearly the same as those of the claws they respectively bear. All the claws, excepting the first one, are longer than their respective digits; they are much compressed, single-edged underneath, curved, and acute. Their tips are regularly graduated in position with decreasing disparity from 3d to 1st; 3d–4th–2d–5th–1st; the 3d being much the largest, the 1st a mere stump. The back of the hand is clothed with rather bristly hairs, which fall as a fringe over the sides of the hand, and of the individual digits as well.

As usual in cases of excessive growths of any kind, these great claws of the hand vary a good deal in size and shape, according to the age and vigor of the animal—in other words, according to the degree of use to which they are put. The hind foot is not remarkable, having an ordinary murine character. The sole is perfectly naked, like the palm, and devoid of special pads or tubercles; the skin being everywhere smooth. The toes are short; the claws still shorter, weak, excavated underneath (like a badger's), little curved, and rather acute. The 3d is longest; then come 2d–4th–1st–5th; the digit of the latter being a mere stump, and that of the 1st too short to carry the tip of its claw opposite the base of the 4th.

The tail has an unfinished, or rather neglected, appearance, as if it were of no particular use. It is remarkable, however, for appearing to spring from a peculiar conical backward prolongation of rump, so that it is difficult to determine its true base. This enlarged basal portion is clothed like the rest of the body. From its apex, the tail continues with a shorter and more scanty furring. The tail is rather thick (in comparison with allied rodents) and somewhat quadrangular, the flattening of the under side being especially noticeable; it tapers gradually to an obtuse tip. It is perhaps rather unusually variable in length, averaging in its scant-haired portion about one-third of the length of head and body.

The conical prolongation of the body above mentioned is that portion which protrudes beyond the ischia, which may be plainly felt on either side; and on its under side appear the orifices of the digestive and genito-urinary systems, in close juxtaposition, and both directly at the base of the tail proper. In the rutting-season, however, the topography of the parts is changed, owing to the great distention of the perinæum from the turgid organs within. In the female, there are three pairs of teats—two inguinal, near together along the inside of the thighs; and another pair, pectoral, at a

29 COL

considerable distance. I have not been able to discover any more; and as the same number and position have been found to hold in *G. tuza, mexicanus,* and *hispidus,* such is probably the normal case in this genus; though in species of *Thomomys* I have distinctly recognized six pairs.

The character of the incisor dentition remains for special notice, as a diagnostic feature of the species among all its congeners. Two grooves upon each upper incisor always persist distinctly. One of these is a sharp, fine line of impression, running along the inner margin of the tooth, about the distance of its own width from the edge. The other is a much larger, more profound, and wider sulcus, which fairly bisects the remaining surface, leaving an equal plane area on either side, exclusive of the small portion cut off by the fine marginal groove. This main groove varies a good deal in depth and width in different specimens, and, moreover, is itself sometimes sulcate; that is to say, this excavation sometimes presents, on the outer side, a fine ridge, which marks off a secondary groove within the first. The same thing occurs in the single-grooved species—*castanops, mexicanus,* and *hispidus.* But this supplementary carination of the main groove is not always perceptible, and is generally liable to be overlooked, it is so fine. When most strongly marked, it is just like the inner marginal groove itself; and each tooth seems to consist of two similar halves.

Coloration.—Throughout this family, the coloration is general and diffused; there are no strong special areas of parti-coloration. Most of the species (if not all) of both *Geomys* and *Thomomys* occur under two states of pelage, which we may call the chestnut and the plumbago. The difference is much like that between the gray or cinereous states of young *Hesperomys, Neotoma,* &c., and the brighter-colored adults of the same. But, in the present case, it does not appear to be a matter of age, since full-sized, if not mature, specimens are plumbago-colored. If the dark style of pelage be not wholly fortuitous—*i. e.,* pure melanism—it is, at any rate, as yet unexplained. To these generalities of coloration, it is to be added, that there is a tendency to indefinite albinism of the tail, feet, and parts about the mouth. Whatever the phase of coloration may be, the character of the pelage is constant. As in all the other species, excepting *G. hispidus,* the fur is remarkably soft, fine, and lustrous, reminding one of that of the mole; yet not of the short, close, velvetypilous character seen in that animal, but long and fluffy. The coat appears to be shed from before backward by a steadily progressing process, as witnessed by the definite lines of demarcation frequently observed.

The plumbeous basal portions of the hairs, uniform to the very roots all over the body, are of such extent, and the colored terminal parts so short to correspond, that more or less of this color appears on all but the most daintily prepared specimens, and plumbeous is the prevailing tone of the under parts. The normal coloration is a dull reddish-brown, or impure chestnut, of varying intensity, frequently with a still duller muddy-brown superficial cast difficult to describe.   This is the character of the upper parts, where a dusky dorsal area may or may not be appreciable.   It gives way on the sides to the plumbeous of the under parts, which is overlaid with a hoary-brown or muddygray.   The lips, chin, feet, and even legs, and the tail, are usually more or less white, the extent and purity of this white being wholly indeterminate; it is sometimes wanting; sometimes the tail is variegated with white and brown.   There are also liable to be irregular white patches on the belly. The soles and palms, when not soiled by adventitious substances, are nearly colorless.   The incisors, as usual, are orange-faced in the adult state.   The claws are of an indefinite pale-brown color, often variegated with extravasated blood.

The plumbago state, in which some specimens as large as any others are found, is entirely different, and does not appear to shade into the normal phase.   Here the color is exactly that of a lead-pencil mark on white paper; but such is the gloss of the fur that violet, purplish, or even brassy reflections are shown with different lights.   It is an intensification of the ordinary plumbeous basal portion of the hairs, and its extent over the whole fur.   In this condition, white paws and tail, and other irregular patches of albinism, also occur.   The plumbeous is seen in its purity only above; below, the fur is pointed with muddy-brown or gray.

HISTORY.—Although its written history does not date so far back as the early notices of the "Tucan" (*G. mexicanus*), this species was the first to be introduced to notice under a scientific name, and with a (supposed) scientific description.   Dr. George Shaw was the physician who attended at the birth of the species, which he called *Mus bursarius*, giving a recognizable descrip-

tion indeed, but accompanying it with a grotesque figure from a drawing by
Major Davies, representing an amorphous creature with a pair of great skinny,
veiny bags hanging loosely from the mouth; the pouches of his specimen having everted, and this being their supposed natural state. The original figure
in the Linnæan Transactions is somewhat improved upon in the General Zoology, but is still a very ludicrous object. The animal is said to have come from
"Canada," where it was taken by some Indians in 1798, and afterward presented to Governor Prescott's wife. According to the description, the animal
was in the plumbago state of pelage. There is no doubt whatever about the
species (though some writers have refused to recognize it) ; even the wretched
figure in the General Zoology shows the grooved incisors clearly. Moreover,
this identical specimen, which once formed part of the Bullock collection in
London, and subsequently passed into the hands of Temminck, seems to have
been examined both by Kuhl and Lichtenstein ; and, at about the same time,
each of these naturalists made a new genus for its special benefit, Kuhl calling it *Saccophorus bursarius*, after Shaw, and Lichtenstein renaming it *Ascomys
canadensis*. This title prevailed with most German authors. Contemporary
French authorities considered it a Hamster, and referred it to *Cricetus*. Say
established, in 1823, the genus *Pseudostoma*, generally accepted by American
writers.

The original mistake (arising from faulty taxidermy, that prolific source
of error with the dermatomaniacs) of supposing the pouches were pendulous
sacs opening into the mouth was scotched several times before it was finally
killed. Meanwhile, before Kuhl, Lichtenstein, and Say had severally made
their new genera, species of the genus had already entered the peculiar field
of vision, or supposed vision, of M. Rafinesque, who furnished two new
names. The *Diplostoma* of this writer is diagnosticated by an expression
few terms of which are founded in fact ; for he denies the animal tail, ears, and
open eyes, and only credits it with four toes to each foot, whereas it has a
tail, ears, open eyes, and five digits before and behind. In the same place,
Rafinesque establishes another genus, *Geomys*, which is based upon fair characters, though there is nothing in them to prove whether he had a *Thomomys*
or a true *Geomys* in view. The primary reference is, however, to Mitchell's
"Hamster of Georgia" (*G. pinetis*), which fixes the matter. Rafinesque

gives a number of species of each of his two genera. Twelve years subsequently, in 1829, Dr. Richardson discussed Rafinesque's names, coming to the erroneous conclusion that they both represented good genera, in one of which the cheek-pouches opened into the mouth, these being wholly external in the other. He describes several new species of *Thomomys* under the name of *Geomys*, supposing them to all have pendulous pouches; gives the present as *Geomys*? *bursarius;* and refers one *Thomomys* to *Diplostoma*, having satisfied himself of the true state of the case in this instance.

The *Mus ludovicianus* of Ord (1815) is a name which may be supposed to refer to this species, but it is probably not determinable, and in any event is antedated. Dr. Mitchill named the species *Mus saccatus* in 1821. The only late synonyms I have met with are *oregonensis* of LeConte and *breviceps* of Baird. LeConte, indeed, in his excellent sketch of the family, which placed the group upon a far more satisfactory footing than that it had previously occupied, calls it *Geomys canadensis;* but this is merely the restoration of Rafinesque's generic name, coupled with Lichtenstein's specific one, upon the presumption that the faulty *Mus bursarius* of Shaw ought not to be recognized. Dr. LeConte's *oregonensis* is founded upon an animal said to be from Oregon; but this locality is doubtless erroneous, for, as now well known, Townsend collected all the way from the Missouri westward, though his specimens fell in the way of being marked "Columbia River," or "Oregon," with little regard for actual localities where procured. The name *oregonensis*, besides being geographically erroneous in all probability (no *Geomys* is known to occur west of the Rocky Mountains), rests upon characters not in the least incompatible with the now known *G. bursarius.* The types of *G. breviceps* now before me are all smaller than average *bursarius*, but within the range of variation of that species; and I fail to substantiate any tangible characters by which this supposed species may be held to be distinct.

The English name of "gopher," applied to this and other species of the family, is evidently a corruption of the French term "gaufre," given by Canadian *voyageurs.* It re-appears in German as *Goffer.* In the West, where the *Spermophili* are universally called gophers by hunters and settlers, the species of this family are distinguished as "pocket-gophers." The application of the word "salamander" is not so obvious. The German equivalent of "pouched rat" is *Taschenmaus*.

Measurements.

Current number.	Locality.	Sex.	From tip of nose to—				Tail to end of vertebræ.	Length of—		Longest fore claw.	Nature of specimen.
			Eye.	Ear.	Occiput.	Tail.		Fore foot.	Hind foot.		
......	Niobrara River	♂	0.85	1.40	1.90	6.75	2.50	1.50	1.25	0.70	Alcoholic.
7327	Kansas	♂	0.95	1.65	2.00	6.50	3.00	1.50	1.35	0.70	Alcoholic.
1341	Iowa....................	♂	1.12	1.70	......	......	2.15	1.55	1.30	0.68	Alcoholic.
357	Saint Louis, Mo	♂	......	......	......	8.00	3.00	1.60	1.35	0.55	Fresh.
2635	Saint Louis, Mo	......	1.05	1.75	2.20	7.00	2.75	1.50	1.35	0.65	Alcoholic.
2636	Saint Louis, Mo	......	1.20	1.85	2.60	7.50	3.35	1.55	1.35	0.70	Alcoholic.
2633	Illinois	......	1.00	1.45	1.90	5.75	2.65	1.50	1.15	0.65	Alcoholic.
2589	Iowa....................	......	1.95	2.10	2.33	8.90	3.30	......	1.45	0.80	Fresh.
1775	Vermilion River	......	0.75	1.75	2.25	8.00	......	1.75	1.25	0.75	Fresh.
2630*	Louisiana	......	0.90	1.45	......	......	1.75	1.20	1.05	0.55	Alcoholic.

*A type of *breviceps.*

GEOMYS TUZA, (Ord.) Coues.

Hamster of Georgia, MITCHILL, N. Y. Med. Repos. v, 1802, 89; Bewick's Quad. 1st Am. ed. 1801, 525 (mentioned also by Anderson, Meare, Say, Barton, &c.)
Mus tuza, ORD, Guthrie's Geog. 2d Am. ed. ii, 1815, 292. (Based on Mitchill's animal.)
Geomys pinctis, RAF., Am. Month. Mag. ii, 1817, 45 (Georgia).—BRANTS, Muizen, 1827, 173.—DESM., Mamm. ii, 1822, 314 (note).—LESS., Man. 1827, 260.—BAIRD, M. N. A. 1857, 380, pl. 22, fig. 3 a-c.—GESNER, Ann. Rep. Smiths. Inst. for 1860, 1861, 431 (habits).
Saccophorus? pineti, FISCHER, Syn. 1829, 305.
Geomys pineti, LEC., Proc. Acad. Nat. Sci. Phila. vi, 1852, 159.—ALLEN, Bull. Mus. Comp. Zool. ii, 1871, 178.
Pseudostoma floridana, AUD. & BACH., Q. N. A. iii, 1853, 242, pl. 150, f. 1.
Southern Pouched Rat, AUD. & BACH.
Geomys des pins, DESM., LESS., ll. cc.
Gopher; Salamander, VULG.

DIAGNOSIS.—Superior incisors with a main groove dividing the tooth into two unequal portions; the outer obviously the smaller; the inner, larger moiety marked by an extremely fine marginal groove, faint, obscure, or perhaps sometimes obsolete. Tail and hind feet in adult life naked, or nearly so. Otherwise like *G. bursarius.*

HABITAT.—Georgia, Florida, and Alabama

Description (numerous specimens from the above localities, including some mentioned by Audubon, those described by Baird, and various others, dry and alcoholic).—This species, apparently distinct, nevertheless resembles *G. bursarius* so closely, that no general points of difference in size, shape, or color can be adduced for their separation. There are, however, certain tangible characters, not necessarily the same as those given by authors. For instance, Audubon and Bachman dwell upon certain supposed differences in the structure of the pouch; but their observations rest upon bad taxidermy, and have no foundation in nature, the pouches in the two species being identical. These authors and some others speak of the upper incisors as single-grooved. This, if so, would be a strong feature: but it, unfortunately, is not the case; for, in all the numerous specimens I have examined, the upper incisors are double-grooved, as in *G. bursarius*, the fine second groove being perceptible as a delicate line of impression running along the inner margin of the tooth. It is perfectly distint, as a rule; and in no case have I failed to recognize clearly at least a trace of it, though in some instances it is faint, and liable to be overlooked if not closely examined. Baird says that this groove is obsolete in old age, implying that such is the rule: but, while not doubting that such may occur, I must consider it as the exception; for, as just said, I have never yet failed to recognize at least a trace of it. *G. tuza*, therefore, has double-grooved incisors, like *G. bursarius;* the point of dental discrepancy lies elsewhere. In *bursarius*, the main groove bisects what is left of the face of the tooth, after subtracting the portion cut off by the inner groove; and this latter is always distinct. In *G. tuza*, the main groove divides what is left of the face of the tooth, after subtracting the portion cut off by the inner groove, into two unequal portions, whereof the exterior is the smaller; and the inner groove, always slight, may be faint, obscure, or perhaps sometimes obsolete. This is the whole case, as far as the incisors are concerned.

The only other character of *G. tuza* I can appreciate is the nakedness of the tail and feet—especially the former. It is true that in *G. bursarius* the nakedness of these parts is sometimes noticeable; but it seems to be not carried, except perhaps in extreme cases, to the extent witnessed, as a rule, in *G. tuza*. The latter thus corresponds with *G. hispidus* in this respect, though very different in other features. In the best-marked cases, the tail is perfectly naked beyond the enlarged hairy base; the skin may be stuffed out to the calibor of a stout goose-quill, and has then a peculiar bladdery appearance; if the vertebræ be left in, it shrinks tightly around them in drying, displaying not only the joints, but also the shape of the individual bones. The hind feet share this nakedness, but not to the same extent; the instep is nearly bare, but the toes are sparsely pilous with short colorless bristles. The back of the fore feet is in much the same condition. The depilation of the members is not always as complete as here described; but such is the unmistakable tendency in all cases, and such the accomplished result in the majority of examples in adult life. Younger specimens, in the plumbago state of pelage, show as hairy tail and feet as an average sample of *G. bursarius*, and before the incisors have attained maturity, so as to afford fair characters, might readily be supposed to be *G. bursarius*, were locality not taken into account. Of such character is No. 1500, Museum of the Smithsonian Institution, particularly mentioned by Baird, *op. cit.*, p. 382.

My material is abundant for a table of measurements of this species; but it seems unnecessary to prepare one, since it would be simply an amplification of the statement that the animal does not differ at all from *G. bursarius* in size or shape. For the same reason, it is unnecessary to enter into further description after presenting the two characters (particular style of sulcation of incisors and nakedness of tail and feet) in which solely does the species stand apart from *G. bursarius*.

Under these circumstances, it might be held by some that the present is merely a localized race of *G. bursarius*; and I should be the last one to dispute such statement of an abstract fact. This *Geomys* is, of course, an offshoot of the *bursarius* stock; and, for that matter, so are all the rest of the "species" modified descendants of some one stock. It would be only shifting the question a peg to require that the fact should affect the nomenclature. A "permanent variety" is a contradiction in terms. This is the case: Here is a set of individuals differing thus-and-thus (as above described) from another set. The difference is slight, but constant; there is no intergradation, for the simple reason that the two sets of animals now occupy different geographical areas, are completely isolated from each other, and thus cut off from interbreeding; or, in other words, from reproducing offspring in which the characters of both parents are blended. It is quite possible that, in their blind movements under the ground, the two may come together and interbreed;

but we must wait for this to occur, and be attested by intergrading specimens, before we need hesitate to describe *G. tuza* as a "distinct species."

The earliest notice specially referable here appears to be the unmistakable description by S. L. Mitchill of the "Hamster of Georgia," and various allusions are made by other writers to the same animal. The *Mus tuza** of Ord unquestionably belongs here, being based upon Mitchill's animal. A short though expressive diagnosis is given by Rafinesque, with unwonted accuracy, of *Geomys pinetis*. This name, or its emended form *G. pineti*, has been generally applied, excepting by Audubon and Bachman, who, ignoring Rafinesque, rename the animal *floridana*, and refer it to Say's genus *Pseudostoma*. The species puts in the customary second-hand appearance under the supervision of several systematic compilers, few, if any, of whom appear to have had much knowledge of their own upon the subject.

The geographical distribution of the species is remarkably limited. I have no knowledge of its occurrence anywhere excepting in Georgia, Florida, and Alabama. The Savannah River is said to form a complete barrier to its northward extension. Its westward limit is not so precisely defined; but it does not appear to reach to the Mississippi, where the other species is found.

Audubon and Bachman have nothing particular to say of the habits of this species in comparison with *G. bursarius*, beyond the statement that it does not become dormant in winter. The best account of its habits, and particularly of its mode of constructing its underground galleries, is Dr. Gesner's article above quoted.

GEOMYS CASTANOPS, (Bd.) Lec.

Pseudostoma castanops, BAIRD, Stansbury's Rep. Great Salt Lake, 1852, 313.—AUD. & BACH., Q. N. A. iii, 1854, 304.
Geomys castanops, LEC., Proc. Acad. Nat. Sci. Phila. 1852, 163.—BAIRD, M. N. A. 1857, 381.—BAIRD, P. R. R. Rep. x, 1859, Gunnison and Beckwith's Route, Mamm. 8, pl. 10, f. 2.
Geomys clarkii, BAIRD, Proc. Acad. Nat. Sci. Phila. 1855, 332.—BAIRD, M. N. A. 1857, 383, pl. 50, figs. 1a–g.—KENNERLY, P. R. R. Rep. x, 1859, Whipple's Route, Mamm. 13.—BAIRD, U. S. Mex. Bound. Survey, ii, pt. ii, 1859, Mamm. p. —, —.—GERR., Cat. Bones Br. Mus. 1862, 222.
Chestnut-faced, and *Pecos Gopher*, BAIRD, *ll. cc.*

DIAGNOSIS.—Superior incisors with a single median groove bisecting the face exactly. Fore feet shorter, or not longer than hind feet; these and the

---

* Evidently the same word as *tuga, tuza, tucan,* &c.

tail sparsely pilous. Color pale yellowish-brown above, inclining more or less to dull chestnut about the head ; whitish below.   Size of *G. bursarius*, or rather less.   Fur soft, as usual in the genus.

HABITAT.—Texas and New Mexico.

Description (from Baird's types of *G. castanops* and *G. clarkii*, and other specimens).—This remarkable species is immediately distinguished from all others known to me by the combination of a single median groove of the incisors, pale light color, and small size.   In the first-named particular alone, it agrees with *G. mexicanus ;* in both these species, the single groove is central, bisecting the surface, so that, viewed from the front, there appear to be four incisors.   This at once and permanently separates it from *G. bursarius*, with which it is to be compared in other respects.   In size, the five specimens before me average about the same as *G. bursarius*, though none are as large as the largest of the latter I have seen.   The length of the full-grown animal may be about 8 inches, rather less than more ; and some are not much over 6 inches.   The tail, as well as can be judged, is 2½ to 3 inches.   A notable peculiarity of form, in comparison with *G. bursarius*, lies in the relative proportions of the fore and hind feet, which are much as in *GG. mexicanus* and *hispidus ;* the palm, with the length of claws included, being shorter, or, at most no longer, than the sole and claws ; the latter measuring about 1⅓ inches, the former only about 1¼ inches.   The fore claws are, however, well developed proportionally, no difference in this respect from *G. bursarius* being readily appreciable.   The external ears may fairly be called obsolete ; in neither of the specimens can I make out anything more than a thickened rim surrounding the orifice of the meatus.   The hairiness of the tail and hind feet is pretty much as in an average specimen of *G. bursarius* or *G. mexicanus;* they are thinly clothed indeed, but noticeably more so than is ever the case with *G. tuza* or *G. hispidus*.   The pouches are somewhat less ample, apparently, than in *G. bursarius*—a character coördinated in this genus with weaker fore feet, and seen also in *G. mexicanus* and *G. hispidus*.

The coloration merits particular attention, not only as it is the next to the strongest character of the species, but because a casual phase of it was the basis of the original *Pseudostoma castanops*.   It might seem surprising, and certainly it would be contrary to analogy, that a single species of this un-

formly-colored family should exhibit "sharply-defined" or "symmetrically-
subcircular" areas of color; and such proves *not* to be the case. The type
of *Pseudostoma castanops*, now before me, in a good state of preservation,
notwithstanding the vicissitudes of thirty years of museum existence, though
bleached by long exposure to the light, still shows the curious chestnut head-
patches, sharply defined against pale tawny-white surroundings, just as
described at length by Professor Baird. But the animal was shedding its coat
when killed; hence the appearance. The new fur is brightly colored, contrasting with the old faded and worn pelage.* One of the types of "*clarkii*"
has the same color of the head, but this is also diffused with somewhat diminished intensity over the whole upper parts. Other specimens are entirely
similar, with various shading of the main color. This may be described as
a dull, pale chestnut, or almost fawn-color, more or less shaded with the plumbeous basal portions of the fur, which usually show more or less in this genus,
be the fur never so smoothly laid. This tawny or fulvous tone of color is
highly characteristic in comparison with the deeper and warmer chocolate or
muddy browns which *G. bursarius* shows. On the under parts, though the
plumbeous basal portion of the fur shows considerably, the general tint is
whitish—quite white in comparison with the muddy gray of the same parts
of *G. bursarius*. The whiskers are mostly colorless; they are fine and
numerous, the longest about equaling the head. The claws are pale horn-
color; the naked palms and soles show various discoloration, perhaps according to the quality of the soil worked in. The incisors are orange, as usual.

The few specimens of this species known to naturalists were procured
in Texas and New Mexico. The animal would appear to be comparatively
rare, as very few individuals, additional to those described by Professor Baird,
have ever been collected, though we have plenty of the *Thomomys* (*umbrinus*)
of the same region. The written history of the species is brief and precise;
determination of the identity of *clarkii* with *castanops* leaves nothing to be
said on the score of synonymy. *Castanops* is to be retained as the prior name,
and is unobjectionable, though it has proven not particularly pertinent.

---

* Various specimens of *Geomys* and *Thomomys*, changing pelage, show curious sharp wandering
lines where the old and new fur fail to meet and fit exactly; and such lines are often observed when the
pelage appears to be all of an age.

GEOMYS MEXICANUS, (Licht.) Lec.

Ascomys mexicanus, LICHT., Abhand. K. Acad. Wiss. Berl. 1827, 113.—BRANTS, Muizen, 1827, 27.—WAGN.,
    Suppl. Schreb. iii, 1843, 384; iv, pl. 206 A.—CHARLESW., P. Z. S. ix, 1841, 60.—SCHINZ,
    Synop. ii, 1845, 133.
Saccophorus mexicanus, FISCH., Synop. 1829, 305.—EYD. & GERV., Guérin Mag. vi, 1836, 23, pl. 21, f. 5, 6;
    Voy. Favorite, v, 1839, 23, pl. 8, f. 5, 6.—RICH., Rep. Brit. Assoc. vi, 1836, 156.—GRAY, List
    Mamm. Br. Mus. 1843, 150.—GERR., Cat. Bones Br. Mus. 1862, 223.
Pseudostoma (*Geomys*) *mexicana*, AUD. & BACH., Q. N. A. iii, 1854, 309.
Geomys mexicanus, LEC., Proc. Acad. Nat. Sci. Phila. 1852, 160.—BAIRD, M. N. A. 1857, 387.
Geomys (*Saccophorus*) *mexicanus*, GIEB., Säug. 1855, 529.
Tucan of HERNANDEZ.—*Tuça* or *Tuza*, MEXICAN.—*Tugan* apud GERR., *l. c.*
Mexicanische Taschenmaus, GERMAN.

DIAGNOSIS.—Superior incisors bisected by a single median furrow (as in *G. castanops*, which is very different in color). Coloration and general appearance of *G. bursarius* (which has two distinct grooves on the upper incisors). Fur soft, sleek, as in other species of the genus (excepting *G. hispidus*, where it is extremely coarse and harsh). Averaging much larger than any United States species (nearly equaling *G. hispidus*), with proportionally smaller pouches and hands, and weaker claws (these parts being as in *G. hispidus*). Tail and feet clothed (as usual in the genus), not naked as in *G. hispidus* and *G. tuza*.

HABITAT.—Mexico.

Description (No. 3523, Xalapa, *De Oca*, skin).—The general appearance of this animal is so exactly that of an overgrown or overstuffed specimen of ordinary *bursarius*, that I should be at a loss for terms referring to color to precisely characterize it. It is, nevertheless, entirely distinct from this or any other species. It shares, with *G. castanops*, the *single median** furrow of the upper incisors, and some other points of form; but it is much larger, and altogether of a different color. The excellently well-prepared and not overstuffed specimen here described is only equaled in a large series of *G. bursarius* by a single much overstuffed example. The dimensions cannot be given with entire accuracy; but the species probably averages, when full-

---

***G. hispidus* has been described as having a single median furrow; the emphasis here, however, is upon "single," in antithesis to the double furrow of *G. bursarius*, without reference to *exact* position. *G. tuza* is said to have a "single" furrow; but the proper implication is merely obsoleteness of the fine inner second furrow usually seen. In *G. mexicanus*, as in *G. castanops*, the furrow is truly *single* and *median;* in *G. hispidus*, single and internal; in *G. tuza*, apparently single and external.

grown, about 10 inches from nose to root of tail.   Tail about 3 inches from
its apparent base (LeConte gives its length as 5 inches); sole, somewhat
cramped, apparently 1.50; hand, much cramped, estimated to be about the
same, or rather less.   Nose to eye about 1.35.   Girth of body 8 or 9 inches.
The pouches, as well as can be judged from the skin, are smaller proportionally than those of the United States species; in this respect, being like those
of *G. hispidus.*   These two Mexican species further agree in the relative
smallness of the hands and less enormous development of the claws; the fore
member being shorter, or, at most, not longer, than the hinder one.   The
vesture of the feet and tail is much the same in extent as in *bursarius,* and
thus in striking contrast to those parts in either *G. tuza* or *G. hispidus.*   The
orifice of the external ear presents, in the dried state, a mere rim, around
which no flap can be fairly recognized.

It seems preferable thus to describe this species in comparative terms to
bring out the curious interrelations of the animal—a species with the size
and single incisor-furrow of *G. hispidus,* yet the furrow different in position,
and the pelage altogether different.   Agreeing in the points of character of
pelage, its color, and amount of hairiness of tail and feet with *G. bursarius,*
yet at once distinguished by its superior size and single median furrow of the
upper front teeth; exactly like *G. castanops* in this last respect, and in most
others, yet entirely of a different color; disagreeing with all the United States
species in its smaller pouches and weaker hands, and in these points agreeing
with its very distinct Mexican congener.

As regards color: LeConte's animal, "which agrees with Lichtenstein's
and Wagner's descriptions," and is called *"saturate cinereus, suprà nigro-tinctus,
naso brunneo,"* was evidently an example of the "plumbago"-colored variation,
which may occur in any species of this genus as well as in *Thomomys.*   The
specimen before me is of the normal coloration; and this cannot readily be
characterized as anything decidedly different from ordinary *bursarius,* though
there is a purity of the chestnut-brown which contrasts with the muddy brown
(in some cases almost a glaucous shade or "bloom") commonly seen in *bursarius.*   All the fur is deep plumbeous basally, pointed with the warm brown
on the upper parts, and only partially hidden below by muddy gray and hoary
ends of the hairs.   There is a darkness about the auricular region.   The hind

feet and tail are mostly whitish (as is always liable to be the case in *Geomys*). There is some whitishness about the lower jaw, and a small white abdominal and anal patch; these last being of the irregular indeterminate character often seen in and out of this genus. This specimen corresponds exactly with Brants's diagnosis of his var. *β.* of *mexicanus*—"*castaneus, infra canescens, maculis auricularibus duabus nigro-fuscis.*" The same author's var. *γ.* suggests *hispidus;* but it is as well not to strain a point here; for injudicious scrutiny of some of the printed matter extant upon the subject of *mexicanus* might raise synonymatic difficulty with *hispidus.*

Owing to insufficiency of material, I am not prepared to pursue the subject of the characters of *mexicanus* into the details of variation in size and color; but I have no doubt that it corresponds with *G. bursarius* in these respects.

The specimen shows three pairs of mammæ—two of which are inguinal and close together along the inside of the thigh, the third being pectoral, at a considerable distance; I can find none between.

This animal is supposed to be the Tucan of Hernandez, with much probability; and, if so, it was the first of the genus to appear in print. It does not appear, however, to have received a scientific designation, or to have properly entered upon record until many years after "*Mus bursarius*" had become known, when, in 1827, it was called *Ascomys mexicanus* by Lichtenstein. I have met with no specific synonyms, though it has been referred to various genera. As the Tuza or Tuça of the Mexicans, it is treated at some length in the inedited MSS. of Dr. Berlandier, who, after a good description, says that it was supposed by Mocinno and Sessé (ined.) to be the *Mus citillus* of Linnæus, and that it is the *Taupe mexicaine* of which Clavigero speaks. "It is destructive in the fields by riddling the ground . . . . it brings up earth in its pouches, and empties them with its fore feet;" and he adds that it inhabits the cold and temperate regions of New Spain, and that he never saw the Tuza in places where there were squirrels. It is not to be inferred that its habits are in any wise different from those of *G. bursarius.*

GEOMYS HISPIDUS, Lec.

Saccophorus quachil, GRAY, P. Z. S. xi, 1843, 79, ox Coban, Vera Paz, *descr. nulla!*—GERR., Cat. Bones Br. Mus. 1862, 223.

Geomys hispidus, LEC., Proc. Acad. Nat. Sci. Phila. 1852, 158.—BAIRD, M. N. A. 1857, 386, pl. 22, f. 4 *a–d*.

Pseudostoma (*Geomys*) *hispidum*, AUD. & BACH., Q. N. A. iii, 1854, 306.

DIAGNOSIS.—Superior incisors with a single strong deep furrow, lying wholly in the inner half of the tooth.   Tail and hind feet naked, or nearly so; fore feet sparsely hirsute.   Fore feet, including claws, decidedly shorter than the hind feet.   Pouches moderate, scarcely or not reaching beyond the head. Pelage stiff, hispid, and almost lusterless.   Color uniform dull chocolate-brown, merely paler, grayer, or smoky brown below.   Of large size; upward of a foot long; tail short, about 3 inches; sole, 1⅜, &c.

HABITAT.—Mexico and Central America.

Description (from various dried specimens).—The animal indicated in the foregoing paragraph, and about to be described in further detail, agrees perfectly with the accounts given by LeConte and Baird from the same specimen collected some years ago by Mr. Charles Pease, somewhere between Vera Cruz and Mexico City.   The type remained unique until recently, when several well-prepared skins reached the Smithsonian.   These are from Xalapa, Mexico (*De Oca*), and Necostla, Mexico (*Sumichrast*); Costa Rica (*Zeledon* and *Carmiol*); and Guatemala City (*Van Patten*).   Most of these specimens are labeled "mexicanus," as might have been expected under the circumstances.   They agree perfectly with each other, as well as with the above-quoted descriptions, and are unquestionably distinct from the true *mexicanus*.

In the original notices, the character of the upper incisors was not fully indicated, owing to defect of the specimens.   My specimens show that these teeth are unisulcate, as in *mexicanus*, but that the position of the groove is sufficiently different to constitute by itself a perfect specific character.   In *mexicanus*, as has been already said, a single profound groove bisects the tooth; in *hispidus*, there is a similar single groove, but it lies on the inner half of the tooth.   In some specimens, indeed, where the groove is widest, it may encroach slightly upon the median line; but it usually lies altogether to one side, the outer plane surface of the tooth being alone as wide as the groove *plus* the inner plane surface.   This character is unique among the species described in this paper. The teeth of old animals are also of immense size, suggesting a beaver or porcupine; the under incisors sometimes protrude nearly an inch, while the upper ones are exposed for over half an inch.

The next most notable feature is the nakedness of the tail and feet. The tail, in extreme cases, is absolutely bare—not a hair or bristle can be discerned, even on holding the specimen up to the light, except upon the enlarged base In these cases, the hind feet, from the tarso-metatarsal joint outward, are nearly bare, though a few bristly hairs may be observed, especially on the toes. The hands share the same nakedness, but in less degree; their backs are sparsely clothed with bristly hairs, indeed, but not in sufficient quantity to conceal the skin; a slight stiff fringe of hairs overhangs the inner border. Specimens vary in these respects; in some, delicate bristles, scarcely visible except when held up to a light, are scattered over the tail, and more evident ones clothe the instep. But the parts are never fairly hairy, as in *mexicanus*, always presenting a peculiar skinny appearance.

There are additional characters, aside from size and color. The very short tail is less than one-fourth as long as the head and body. Owing, in part, to a less development of the fore claws, the hands are not as long as the feet. The longest third claw before me is only exserted three-fourths of an inch, and it is usually shorter than this. The second and fourth claws are subequal to each other. The whole hand is smaller and weaker than in the *G. bursarius* group, indicating less fossorial nature; and coincidently with this—perhaps in correspondence with it—the cheek-pouches are not so highly developed. As well as can be judged from prepared skins, the sacs do not reach beyond the head—certainly not to the shoulder; their capacity, in an individual nearly a foot long, seems no greater than that of specimens of *G. bursarius* eight inches long, and not more than half as bulky.

The hispid pelage is a remarkable feature; this is so strong a character that the species may readily be diagnosticated in the dark by the "feel" of the fur, and it is instantly noted in comparison with any of the other species, in which the pelage is sleek and soft, much like a mole's. Besides being so coarse and harsh, and almost entirely lusterless, it is longer than usual, and interspersed with still longer and almost bristly hairs. There is no perceptible under-fur different from the general pelage; and the color is uniform to the roots of the hairs. The whiskers are numerous, but short; the longest not equaling the head. There are other lengthened bristles over the eyes, on the cheeks, and elsewhere; but they are not readily discovered amidst the coarse hispid hair of the parts.

There is no occasion to enlarge upon general characters of the muffle, feet, &c., shared by other species. In the best-prepared specimens, the large orifice of the external ear is seen to be nearly surrounded by a small but unmistakable flap.

It is characteristic of all the other species of *Geomys* I know of, those with soft hair, to have plumbeous-colored fur at base, pointed with the particular brown, fulvous, or other shade which determines their appearance to the eye. The case is different with *G. hispidus*, in which the pelage is unicolor from base to tip; and the color, too, is peculiar. It is a dark mahogany-brown, or rather a chocolate, or *café sans lait* color, a little lighter or darker according to age or season, or fortuitously, but in any event uniform over all the upper parts and sides. Underneath the color is the same, but paler and dilute—like *café au lait;* sometimes quite smoky gray, or muddy brown. The under parts, however, frequently show patches of white here and there; these are altogether indeterminate, being as irregular in size, shape, number, and position as the similar white patches on the under side of a mink (*Putorius vison*). It is probable, also, that plumbago-colored individuals occur, as happens to the other species; but I have seen none such. The naked parts appear to have been reddish or flesh-colored; the claws are an indefinite horn-color; the incisors are faced with the usual rodent-red; color of eyes not stated on labels, but probably black.

The size of the species can only be approximately estimated from the dried skins; but it is evidently the largest species of those here treated, somewhat exceeding *G. mexicanus.* Well-prepared skins average about 11 inches in length, with a girth of some 9 inches. The tail, from the extreme base, is less than 3 inches: its naked part hardly over 2. Sole of foot about $1\frac{3}{4}$; palm, including longest claw, less than this. Nose to eye, nearly $1\frac{1}{2}$. A ruler inserted in the pouch measures off about $2\frac{1}{2}$ inches from the bottom of the sac to the snout. The opening of the sac is about $1\frac{1}{2}$ inches long.

In a female, killed during lactation apparently, I find, after diligent search,

31 COL

only three pairs of teats—two pairs inguinal, and one pair, *longo intervallo*, pectoral. These are very conspicuous, on naked scabrous spaces, and the thin coarse fur would hardly, I think, hide others if they were present. In some species of this family I have distinctly recognized *six* pairs. I observe no sexual peculiarities in size or color.

The geographical distribution of the species has been already indicated as far as my present materials go. I am in possession of no information respecting its habits, which, however, may be presumed to be the same as those of its congeners; though the weaker feet and proportionally smaller pouches may indicate that the fossorial character is not pushed to such an extreme as is the case with *G. bursarius.*

The written history of the species is brief and precise; the name having been only introduced in 1852. Audubon and Bachman's account is from Le Conte, and Baird redescribes LeConte's type. It is quite possible, and, indeed, probable, that this second Mexican species has figured at times under the name of *mexicanus*, but it would only tend to obscure a matter now clear to drag any such point to light. Now that we know of two perfectly good species in Mexico, the less said about the Tucan of Hernandez, or any similar subsequent uncertainties, the better.

A *Saccophorus quachil*, from Guatemala, was named by Dr. Gray in 1843, though I cannot find that the species was ever described. But through the kind offices of Mr. R. B. Sharpe, who, with the assistance of Mr. Gerrard, examined the type still in the British Museum, at my request, I am informed that it is the animal first described, though subsequently named, by Dr. LeConte.

———

The foregoing pages include all the species of *Geomys* with which I am acquainted, and account probably for all the names which have been introduced excepting one, *G. heterodus*, recently described, from Central America, by Professor Peters, of which I know nothing. ("Uber neue Arten der Säugthier-Gattungen *Geomys*, Haplodon und Dasypus." < Monatsberichte Acad. Wissensch. Berlin, 1864, Mar. 17, pp. 177–180.)

Genus THOMOMYS, Maxim.

Oryctomys, pt. EYD. & GERV., Mag. Zool. vi, 1836, 23.
Thomomys, MAXIM., N. Act. Acad. Cæs. Leop. xix, 1839, 383.

(In addition to the foregoing, all the synonyms of *Geomys*, *q. v.*, have been applied to this genus.)

The readiness with which the species of *Geomys* may be recognized and defined, is a measure of the difficulties encountered in the genus *Thomomys*, where, with the exception of *T. clusius*, the several forms into which the genus has become differentiated are not yet sufficiently stable to permit of positive, precise determination. After bringing to bear upon the subject an unusually protracted study, in the course of which I have critically examined a hundred or more specimens, I am forced to the conclusion that not a single one of the six or eight currently recognized species is susceptible of satisfactory diagnosis. No descriptive formula can be devised to mark off the characters of any one set of specimens, so completely is the whole series linked together. Nevertheless, it is easy to recognize three extremes of variation (*i. e.*, of differentiation), selected specimens of which would not be confounded by the most careless observer; and it would be as unscientific to ignore these various phases of the genus, as to force them unnaturally apart in an attempt to ignore the still extant links by which they are bound together. There is an unmistakable average of characters, which serves for the recognition of three climatic or geographical races, conspecies or subspecies, which may be described in terms perhaps covering 75 per cent. of existing individuals; but the remainder cannot be thus disposed of. In other words, the causes which have been operative in modifying an original *Thomomys* stock have been only incompletely effectual in the formation of species. We clearly observe the tendency of those modifying influences to which the genus has been subjected; but we note with equal clearness the incompleteness, up to the present time, of the result. Nor is this by any means an exceptional case; on the contrary, positive diagnosis of forms, or specific distinctions in the proper sense, become impossible, *in perhaps a majority of cases*, when sufficient series of specimens are examined. As I have frequently remarked before under different modes of expression, the ability to define species satisfactorily is a very good gauge of our ignorance of the whole truth.

But naturalists practically work, for the most part, upon the surface of the subjects presented to their examination, not necessarily concerning themselves at all times with what lies hidden underneath. There are occasions to speculate and theorize, and there are other times when a naturalist may legitimately ignore underlying principles, and properly content himself with statement of certain observed facts. Working on this plane, as I am in the present instance, it is my business to render an exact account of what I find the case of *Thomomys* to be, without reference to abstract questions involved; and to sum the statement in such nomenclatural terms as I may judge most suitable to express the relationships believed to subsist between the several differentiations which the genus has undergone. In describing the several forms of *Thomomys*, I waive the question of species; no harvest would be garnered if the laborers waited till they learned how the grain grew. In studying my specimens, I find that one of them differs from all the rest to such a degree that its characters are totally irreconcilable with those of any others. My description of it is merely an amplification of this statement. I give it a name, and call it a species, conventionally, simply in recognition of this fact, and for the usual purpose of readily indexing the items of information the specimen affords. I find, furthermore, that all the other specimens collectively present a varying sum of characters, according to difference in the emphasis of each one of these characters common to all; and that their interrelation or intergradation is so intimate and complete that no lines of precise distinction can be drawn; but that, nevertheless, an average difference in *three* directions may be readily perceived and described intelligibly. It is an undoubted fact, furthermore, that these three differentiations are related in some way to certain geographical areas, for the simple reason that all the specimens of one style are produced in certain portions of the country, and all of the rest in certain other regions; and that the *Thomomys* existing on the confines of the several areas share each others' peculiarities. It is, once again, within the experience of those who have studied such subjects in their general bearings, that the aspects of the case presented by *Thomomys* tally exactly with those determined in a great many other cases.

Not to pursue this subject to the extent of further allusion to laws fairly deducible from such premises, it is a logical inference from what has been said that there is but one "species" among all these specimens. This "species" is modified by some unknown means, evidently related in some way to the climate, soil, vegetable productions, or other peculiarities of certain geographical areas, yet not to the extent of severing the links which bind all its individuals together. This species, in the course of time, by the continued operation of the same influences, may or may not be resolved into three or more species in the current acceptation of the term ; but at present such is not the case. It is my intention, in the following pages, to describe these variations in detail. In so doing, I consider it advisable, for convenience' sake, to give them each a name ; and, in so doing, I shall adopt a formula of nomenclature which I consider best suited to suggest the intergradation which I find to exist, without reference to Linnæus or to the British Association.

It may tend to take the edge off the imputation implied in the remark made above, that six or eight species admitted by naturalists of high repute must be reduced to one, to briefly review the written history of *Thomomys*. The literature of the subject is unusually brief, and it is somewhat surprising how much of it is pure compilation, which has no actual bearing upon the case. Eydoux and Gervais, and Maximilian, each described a species, and Waterhouse and Brandt have both handled the general aspects of the case ; but, with these exceptions, almost no original work appears from foreign authorities. Fischer, Schinz (whose one new species was a self-confessed synonym), Wagner, Giebel, and doubtless other systematists, have treated of a number of species of *Thomomys*, but entirely at second hand. Such authorities may be passed over in respectful silence, having no weight whatever. The very slight knowledge from abroad will seem the less remarkable when we find how little has been done by the naturalists of this country. Rafinesque's animals appear to have been all *Geomys*. Godman had nothing to say upon the subject. Bachman's descriptions of two species, in 1839, were upon Richardson's MSS. DeKay enumerated some species at second hand. Audubon and Bachman's accounts of several species add positively nothing to what was already extant upon the subject. When LeConte monographed the family in 1852, he knew but a single species, giving compiled indications only of several others. Woodhouse described a new species in 1853. Various naturalists of the Pacific Railroad Surveys furnished field-notes of observation, but their determinations, to state a well-known fact, were not upon their own authority. In fact, the literature of the whole subject, so far as original work in determination of species is concerned, focuses only in two authors—Richardson, 1829, and Baird, 1857.

No species of *Thomomys* having apparently been described before 1829, the history of the genus may be considered to begin at that date. The eminent author of the Fauna Boreali-Americana gave five species of "Geomys" and "Diplostoma." One of these is a true *Geomys;* the four remaining ones (*douglasii, bulbivorum, talpoides,* and *umbrinus*), to which a fifth (*borealis*) was subsequently added, are all *Thomomys.* These accounts of Richardson's remained for many years the principal, and, in some cases, the whole, source of what has been written upon the determination of species; and they include every form of the genus known up to this date (every subsequent name proposed having proven a synonym). I hardly know where to look for the parallel of this curious case. Two points strike one in reviewing Richardson's work : First, he had a wholly erroneous idea that there were two distinct genera, "Geomys" and "Diplostoma," in one of which the pouches, opening into the mouth, dangled naturally as sacks on each side, and in the other of which the pouches were as we know them to be. This radically wrong premise vitiated all his work, and led him to the length of describing one and the same species as "Geomys douglasii" and "Diplostoma bulbivorum." Secondly, the minute descriptions consist mainly of the repetition, under varying forms of expression, of generic characters, common, of course, to all the species. When sifted of their generalities, there is very little left; though, fortunately, such was this author's habitual accuracy, the residuum suffices, when coupled with the indications of locality, for the identification of all his species.

As already stated, there was little real change in the state of the case from 1829 to 1857, when Professor Baird reviewed the subject, with considerably more material and much more other information than Richardson appears to have possessed. "Diplostoma" had meanwhile been effectually disposed of; but to this author is due the credit of having first actually identified with specimens several of Richardson's species, which, though often re-appearing by name, remained names only, with copied or compiled accounts attached. Professor Baird's only compilation was in the case of *Thomomys* "talpoides," which he did not claim to recognize. He examined the Philadelphia types of "borealis" and "townsendii," which Dr. LeConte had already satisfactorily located. He referred "Diplostoma bulbivorum" to the Californian form, remarking upon its close affinity to *T*. "douglasii," and established the identity of "umbrinus" with the New Mexican form. He adopted as distinct species the *T. rufescens* of Maximilian and *T. fulvus* of Woodhouse, and added a new one, *T. laticeps*. His descriptions are like those of Richardson's in their minuteness and accuracy, which leave no doubt of his meaning, and the continual recurrence of comparative expression favors recognition of the discriminations made; but, as in the former case, they include much repetition of generic characters. It is a significant fact, however, that in this article the author omits the admirable antithetical tables he usually gives, and throughout seems to have rather undertaken the identification and description of the species currently recognized at the time, than a critical revision of the subject. Alluding to his lack of adequate material, he frankly characterizes the article as "a very unsatisfactory account." I have only to add to this, that, as is well known, the tendency at the time Professor Baird's article was written was to push specific discriminations beyond a point now usual.

Under such circumstances as this sketch of the history of the genus shows to have existed, it would be singular if some combination of currently-recognized species were not required. The reduction I find necessary, and propose to make, is after all not a violent one. Holding for the moment the three forms I shall describe as geographical races to be species—and they would be so regarded by any one working upon a moderate number of specimens—the following are the only combinations required:

BAIRD, 1857.		COUES, 1875.	
1. *Thomomys bulbivorus* .. ⎫			
2. *Thomomys laticeps*..... ⎬ Pacific coast region .... ⎰ BULBIVORUS ..			
3. *Thomomys douglassii* .. ⎭			
4. *Thomomys ?borealis*. .. ⎫			
5. *Thomomys rufescens* ... ⎬ Northern Interior........................ .... ⎰ TALPOIDES....			
6. *Thomomys "talpoides"*. ⎭			
7. *Thomomys umbrinus* ... ⎫			
8. *Thomomys fulvus*...... ⎬ Southern Interior and Lower California........ ⎰ UMBRINUS			

As well-marked geographical races of one species not completely differentiated.

Of these eight species which Professor Baird gave, one, "talpoides," is not really indentified by him, as he only copies Richardson's account; and another, *borealis*, he says himself he failed to recognize satisfactorily. This leaves only six which he actually indorsed "Borealis" had already been identified by LeConte with *rufescens;* and the animal I describe as "talpoides" is the same as his under another name, resulting from the identification with it of Richardson's species. Another name is thus diposed of. That Woodhouse's "fulvus" is an absolute synonym of what Baird called *umbrinus,* I have satisfied myself by inspection of his type-specimen. Respecting the Pacific-coast form, it is perfectly easy to trace the complete intergradation between the northern (*douglasi*) and southern (*bulbivorus*) extreme. Of "laticeps," no second specimen is known; some of the external characters are altered, apparently, by skinning and drying after immersion in alcohol.

In accounts of the species of this genus, much stress has been laid upon size and shape as distinguishing marks, even by those who are fully aware, not only of the high normal variability in these respects, but also of the peculiar susceptibility to overstuffing, and to various distortions of parts. Nowhere else, perhaps, has bad taxidermy made such a break; it is responsible for different genera, to say nothing of various species. The skin of the whole body, like that of the pouch, is extremely distensible, and *several* inches may be added to the stature of any individual by overstuffing, without leaving any very obvious trace. The peculiar configuration of the body at the base of the tail renders nice measurement of that member very difficult. The feet, particularly the fore feet, shrink and cramp in drying, so that neither their size nor their shape can be appreciated. Upon removal of the skull, the mouthparts infallibly lose all semblance of nature in drying. In *Geomys*, it is the same; but there the species are so well marked that the worst taxidermy can hardly obscure them. After careful examination of many specimens, fresh, alcoholic, and dried, the following is the full extent of the discriminations I have been able to make:

Size.—The Northern Interior form and the Pacific-coast form are of the same size; the Southern Interior form averages an inch or two less in total length than the other; but large specimens of the latter, and small examples of the two former, overlap each other in stature.

Form.—The Northern Interior race and the Northern styles of the Pacific-coast race have larger fore claws than the Southern style of the Pacific-coast race or than the Southern Interior race. The difference is sufficient to make the whole hand of the former about equal to the foot, while, in the latter, the hand is usually shorter than the foot. But this is only true as a rule; there are many exceptions. In all three of the forms, the tail, measured from its true base, ranges from one-third to one-half the total length of head and body, though only rarely reaching either of these extremes. Nothing can be predicated on this score.

Color.—The Northern Interior race is a rat-colored animal, hoary-gray underneath, with white tail and feet, much white about the mouth, and no sooty-blackish there. The Pacific-coast race is a rich dark-brown animal, muddy-bellied, with dusky tail and feet, wholly or in part, and sooty about the mouth. The Southern Interior race is usually a rich tawny or fulvous animal, with partly dark tail or feet, or both, sooty mouth-parts, and white pouches. This race is particularly variable in color; and, in every respect of color, all the races show much variation, and, moreover, intergrade completely.

The various forms under which the genus *Thomomys* is exhibited may be discriminated, as far as it is possible to do so, by the following characters:

A. Large. Hind foot an inch or more long. Tail at least one-third as long as head and body. Above brown, reddish, &c. Below gray, brown, reddish, &c. (not white). Ears in a blackish area well developed..... 1. TALPOIDES.

    a. Six to eight inches long; fore claws highly developed (0.45 to 0.55 long), making the hand about as long as the foot. Color of the house-rat, with white tail and feet, and usually white about the mouth and throat; no contrasts of dark color about the mouth. Northern Interior... *a. talpoides.*

    b. Seven to nine inches long; fore claws less developed, usually under 0.50, leaving the hand shorter than the foot. Reddish-brown, the belly muddy-brownish, feet and tail usually not entirely white; mouth-parts dark, contrasting with white of the pouch-lining. Pacific coast..... *b. bulbivorus.*

c. Smaller on an average ; usually six to seven inches
long. Fore claws about 0.40 or less, leaving
the hand decidedly shorter than the foot. Rich
fulvous, or even fawn-color, the same below but
paler, variously obscured on the back with
dusky ; tail and feet usually dark ; face and
mouth-parts sooty-blackish, sharply contrasting
with white pouch-lining. Southern Interior
and Lower California...................... c. *umbrinus*.

B. Small ; decidedly less than six inches long. Hind foot
about 0.75 ; fore foot still less. Tail scarcely one-
fourth as long as the head and body. Above, pallid
yellowish-gray, with a shade of light-brown ; below,
entirely white ; feet and tail white. Ears minute, not
in a blackish area. Nose blackish. Bridger's Pass,
Rocky Mountains.............................. 2. CLUSIUS, *n. s.*

THOMOMYS TALPOIDES, (Rich.) Baird.

Cricetus talpoides, RICH., Zool. Journ. iii, App. 1828, 518. (Plumbago-colored.)
Geomys talpoides, RICH., F. B. A. i, 1829, 204 ; Rep. Brit. Assoc. for 1836, v, 1837, 157. (Same as the pre-
    ceding, but "Florida" assigned wrongly as a locality.)—DEKAY, N. Y. Fn. 1842, 92. (Com-
    piled from Richardson.)—SCHINZ, Synop. Mamm. ii, 1845, 137. (Compiled from Rich-
    ardson.)—LECONTE, Proc. Acad. Nat. Sci. Phila. vi, 1852, 162. (Compiled from Richardson.)
Saccophorus talpoides, FISCH., Synop. Mamm. 1829, 588 (marked "388"). (Compiled from Richardson.)
Ascomys talpoides, WAGN., Suppl. Schreb. iii, 1843, 399. (Compiled from Richardson.)
Pseudostoma talpoides, AUD. & BACH., Q. N. A. iii, 1853, 43, pl. 110. (Compiled from Richardson ; figure
    from the type-specimen.)
Geomys (Thomomys) talpoides, GIEBEL, Säug. 1855, 530. (Compiled from Richardson.)
Thomomys talpoides, BAIRD, M. N. A. 1857, 403. (Compiled from Richardson.)
Geomys borealis, RICH., Rep. Brit. Assoc. for 1836, v, 1837, 156. (Named, not described. "Saskatchewan.")—
    BACHM., Journ. Acad. Nat. Sci. Phila. 1839, 103. (Originally described from Richardson's
    type, "Columbia R.," marked "*Pseudostoma borealis*, Rich.")—DEKAY, N. Y. Fn. 1842,
    92. (Compiled from Bachman.)—SCHINZ, Synop. Mamm. ii, 1845, 136. (Compiled from
    Bachman.)
Ascomys borealis, WAGN., Suppl. Schreb. iii, 1843, 391. (Compiled.)
Saccophorus borealis, GRAY, List Br. Mus. 1843, 149 ("Canada ;" mere mention, with some wrong syno-
    nyms).—MURIE, P. Z. S. 1870, 80 (as host of *Œstrus*).
Pseudostoma borealis, "RICH. MSS."—AUD. & BACH., Q. N. A. iii, 1853, 198, pl. 142. (Description and fig-
    ure apparently from the original specimens.)
Thomomys borealis, BAIRD, Mamm. N. A. 1857, 396, pl. 22, figs. 2a-c. (Account from types of "borealis" and
    "townsendii," in Mus. Phila. Acad., with which a Californian specimen is considered prob-
    ably identical.)—NEWB., P. R. R. Rep. vi, 1857, 59 (rests on the Californian specimen just
    mentioned.)

Geomys townsendii, "Rich. MSS."—Bachm., Journ. Acad. Nat. Sci. Phila. 1839, 105. ("Columbia R." Described as distinct from "borealis," with much hesitation, entirely in deference to Richardson.)—Rich., Zool. Voy. Blossom, 1839, p. 12*.—DeKay, N. Y. Fn. 1842, 92. (Compiled from Bachman.)—Schinz, Synop. Mamm. ii, 1845, 137. (Compiled.)

Ascomys townsendii, Wagn., Suppl. Schreb. iii, 1843, 391.

"*Geomys unisulcatus*, Gray, Br. Mus."—Gray, *l. c.*

Thomomys rufescens, Maxim., Nov. Act. Acad. Cæs.-Leop. xix, pt. i, 1839, 343; Arch. f. Naturg. 1841, pt. ii, 42; *ibid.* 1861, —; Verz. Säug. N.-Am. Reise, 1862, 149, pl. 4, f. 5 (penis-bone). (In the last quotation, the generic name is spelled "Tomomys.") (Missouri region.)—Schinz, Synop. Mamm. ii, 1845, 134 (exclusive of the synonym *Oryctomys bottæ*, Eyd. & Gerv.). (Compiled from Maximilian; California erroneously assigned as the locality.)—Baird, Proc. Acad. Nat. Sci. Phila. vii, 1855, 335; M. N. A. 1857, 397. (Redescription of specimens from "Nebraska," *i. e.*, Dakota; Forts Pierre, Randall, and Union.)—Baird, P. R. R. Rep. x, 1859, Gunnison's and Beckwith's Routes, Mamm. p. 8, pl. 10, f. 1 (the same).—Stevenson, U. S. Geol. Surv. Terr. for 1870, 1871, 462 (Wyoming).—Ames, Bull. Minn. Acad. i, 1874, 70 (catalogued upon presumption of its occurrence in Minnesota).—Allen, Proc. Bost. Soc. xvii, 1874, 43 (Yellowstone River); Bull. Ess. Inst. vi, 1874, 56, 61, 65 (rather supposed than known to be this species).

Geomys rufescens, LeConte, Proc. Acad. Nat. Sci. Phila. vi, 1852, 161. (Redescribed from types of "borealis" and "towusendii," in Philadelphia Academy, *marked* "Columbia River.")

Ascomys rufescens, Wagn., Suppl. Schreb. iii, 1843, 387.

Geomys (Thomomys) rufescens, Giebel, Säug. 1855, 530.

Thomomys "fulvus", Merr., U. S. Geol. Surv. Terr. for 1872, 1873, 665. (*Nec* Woodh.—Err. test. specim. ipsis.)

DIAGNOSIS.—Coloration almost exactly that of the house-rat (*Mus decumanus*)—sometimes assuming a more reddish phase, occasionally blackish-plumbeous; tail and feet white, and much of the chin, throat, and breast white in irregular patches, where the fur is white to the base. No sooty-blackish about the mouth-parts; no obvious distinction in color between the pouch and its surroundings; no strongly-pronounced reddish-brown on the under parts; general tone of coloration never decidedly tawny. Ears set in a small blackish area. Length 6 to 8 inches; tail 3 inches or less, decidedly less than half the length of head and body; fore and hind feet (claws included) approximately equal to each other, about 1.25; longest fore claw little less than the length of the rest of the hand, about 0.50.

HABITAT.—Supposed to occur in the Interior of North America, from "Hudson's Bay" to the "Columbia River", and to occupy about the northern half of the United States west of the Mississippi, exclusive of the Pacific-coast region; being replaced, to the west, by *T. bulbivorus*, and, to the south, by *T. umbrinus*. Undoubted specimens seen from Selkirk Settlement, British America; from Minnesota westward along the parallel of 49° N. to the Rocky Mountains, and from Idaho, Wyoming, Utah, and Nevada.

Description (from a series of skins taken by myself along the northern

border of Dakota—the details of external form checked from alcoholic specimens from Fort Bridger; in the latter respects, the account represents an
amplification of the generic characters, and serves as a standard of comparison for the other species, in the account of which these full details need not
be repeated).—So close is the general resemblance of this animal to *Geomys
bursarius* that, when the incisors are not examined, a second glance is required
to distinguish them. The most obvious points of difference are the much
smaller and weaker fore claws, altogether less mole-like (spade-like) hands,
and the decided though small external ears. The cheek-pouches are ample—
if anything, more capacious than in *Geomys bursarius* or *tuza*, and very
decidedly larger than in other species of that genus. They extend fairly past
(over) the shoulders to a point about opposite the elbow, when the fore limb
is in a usual position. In comparison with species of its own genus, there are,
in *T. talpoides*, absolutely no decided points of difference in form. With very
little modification in some details, one description is equally applicable to them
all, excepting *T. clusius*, in which there are tangible distinctions.

The general arrangement of the mouth-parts is as in *Geomys bursarius.*
Beneath the whisker-patch, on each side of the muzzle, about half-way from
nose to eye, the fold of skin arises and curves loosely around, to subside again in
the common integument over the posterior angle of the under jaw. In a full-
grown animal, the slit is an inch and a half long; the "slack" of the edge of the
pouch may be pushed an inch or more away from the check; the amplification
of the sac is here at a maximum—it reaches past the shoulder, as already said,
and, in a full-grown animal, two fingers may be inserted to the second joint.
The arrangement of the immediate mouth-parts is such that, as in *Geomys*, the
mouth appears to be a vertical fissure instead of a horizontal one, bounded on
either side by thick, fleshy, and hairy lips. This, however, is only the vestibule of the mouth; the buccal orifice proper being small, closing horizontally
of course, as usual, remote from the upper incisors, which are shut out completely by a long, vaulted, hairy interval. The mucous membrane of the checks
only fairly reaches the edge of the lips in a small patch on either side, and
just in advance of the under incisors. Besides the general hairiness of the
buccal vestibule, there are longer and more bristly hairs, depending like a
fringe around the roots of the incisors, and margining the false lips for some

distance.* The upper incisors are smoothly convex on their front face, with a very fine line of impression running immediately along their inner margin. This groove, always delicate and liable to be overlooked, is sometimes obsolete, or, at any rate, fails to run the whole length of the tooth. The inferior incisors are similar, but longer, narrower, and with no sign of a groove. The blunt, tumid snout is entirely hairy, excepting a small nasal pad, strictly confined between the nostrils. The whiskers are very numerous, very fine and soft bristles (mostly colorless), and the longest of them do not equal the head in length. A few slight straggling bristles grow over the eyes and elsewhere about the head. The eyes are situated about midway between the nose and ears; they are small, only about an eighth of an inch in diameter, with rather tumid lids. A notable peculiarity of the species of *Thomomys*, in comparison with *Geomys*, is the presence of external ears, about which there is no question. In *Geomys*, the mere rim of integument warrants use of the terms "rudimentary" or "obsolete." In *Thomomys*, there is a very evident auricle, which rises behind, something like a quarter of an inch above the head; nor is it a mere rim even of this decided dimension; it tapers to quite a point behind, and the lower border of the conch shows a slight folding, which represents a rudimentary lobule. The cavity of the auricle admits the end of my pen-holder; the external meatus itself would admit a pigeon-quill.

In the general shape of the body, there is nothing but what is shared by all the species of the family. The amplitude of the pouches is such that the width across them is much the greatest diameter of the body. The next greatest girth is around the belly; the chest-measure is a little less than this. The fore and hind feet are as nearly as may be of the same length; either may slightly exceed the other, the difference being mainly due to varying development of the fore claws. These, though decidedly fossorial (a family-character), are not so enormously developed as in *Geomys bursarius*, being decidedly less than half the total length of the hand. The digits have the same relative lengths, taken either with or without their claws: the 3d is longest, with the largest claw; the 2d is next; the 4th next, being about as much shorter than the 2d as this is less than the 3d; the 5th is abruptly much shorter, the tip of its claw scarcely or not reaching the base of the 4th claw; the 1st is shorter still, a mere stump, with a little knob for a claw.

---

* No idea whatever of the true configuration of the mouth-parts in this family can be gained from dried specimens from which the skull and teeth have been removed.

The longer claws are much compressed, moderately curved, acute, falcate, or sharp-edged underneath, except at the end, where the sides separate with a slight excavation. The back of the hand is moderately pilous, with short, soft hairs; the toes being fringed with rather longer and more bristly ones. The perfectly smooth and naked palm ends behind in an immense protuberance (as elsewhere in the family), which consists, in effect, of an exterior and an interior callosity, united by a slightly-constricted isthmus. This wrist-bulb is overhung by a special tuft of short, bristly hairs. The sole is naked like the palm, but much narrower and longer (the equality in total length of hand and foot being brought about by the length of the fore claws); it contracts regularly from before behind, ending in a prominent but narrow calcaneum. The upper surface of the foot is hairy like the back of the hand. The 3d digit is longest; the 2d and 4th are subequal to each other, and the tips of their claws reach about to the base of the middle claw. The 1st and 5th are again about equal to each other, but abruptly much shorter than the others; the tips of their claws hardly or not attaining the base of the 2d and 4th digits. The hind claws are of the same character as those of the hand, but very much shorter.

The tail, as in other species of the family, is surrounded at base by a conical enlargement—a prolongation of the body, haired like the rest of the frame, which, in the rutting-season, becomes highly tumid underneath, rendering it still more difficult to say where the tail actually begins. Measured from its true base, as well as this can be ascertained without dissection (from the true base as far as external form is concerned), the tail is more than one-third, but decidedly less than one-half, of the length of head and body together—say about two-fifths. In an average specimen, 7 inches long, the tail may be about 2.75. Measured from where the long hair of the body ceases, or from its apparent base, the tail is about one-third of the length of head and body. This member is somewhat quadrangular, the flattening being especially noticeable underneath; it gradually tapers to an obtuse tip, and is pilous throughout, being clothed with short, soft hairs like those covering the hands and feet.

In the male as well as in the female, the genital aperture is immediately in front of the anus. In the rutting-season, the enlargement of the parts is chiefly post-anal; there being a great swelling behind the anus, which carries the anus away from the apparent base of the tail. The os penis is a slender, sharp spicule, clubbed at base, tapering and slightly curved, nearly three-quarters of an inch long. In a female, I have distinctly made out twelve mammæ, of which two pairs are inside the thigh, two pairs on the chest, and two pairs axillary.

Few, however, if any, of the foregoing points are diagnostic of the species; nor will the *ensemble* serve to distinguish it infallibly from its congeners, excepting *T. clusius*. As to form, the single character I notice is the greater average development of the fore claws, bringing the length of the hands up to about that of the feet. Some points of color about to be noticed are the most reliable distinctions. The animal is as nearly as possible like the house-rat (*Mus decumanus*). The whole upper parts are of a uniform grayish-brown, generally quite pure, though occasionally warming into a more reddish-brown. But, in the most reddish specimens, the tint is uniform, without the peculiar mottling or lining of a dark-brown with a reddish-brown which constitutes the richer color of the Pacific-coast *bulbivorus*. The only departure from the uniformity of the upper parts is a small blackish patch, usually very evident, in which the ears are set. On the sides of the body, the color gives way gradually to the lighter tint of the under parts: here we find the plumbeous of the roots of the hairs as a background to a hoary-grayish, resulting from the tips of the hairs. This hoary is usually quite pure, but it sometimes takes on an appreciably muddy-brown tinge, still never equaling, as far as known, the richer fulvous-brown which tones the under parts in the coast form. The tail and feet are white in every specimen I have seen; and, besides this, there are usually patches about the mouth, cheeks, throat, and breast, where the fur is pure white to the roots. But these white markings are wholly indeterminate in extent, as well as inconstant in appearing at all; in many cases, the parts are concolor with the rest of the under surface. Perhaps the strongest color-mark of the species is the absence from any part of the head of sooty-blackish or even dusky areas, there being no noticeable contrasts of color between the mouth-parts and pouches; whereas, in *T. bulbivorus*, and, still more so, in *umbrinus*, these parts are dusky, or even coal-black, contrasting sharply with the pure-white linings of the pouches. The whiskers are mostly colorless; the claws are colorless, though usually stained with extravasated blood.

Northern Dakotan and Minnesotan specimens may be taken to represent the extreme of this race as above described, characterized by the purity of the gray and brown shades, absence of any decided reddish cast, and pure-white feet, tail, and throat. Specimens from Selkirk Settlement and the Assiniboine region are identical. Others, from Idaho, Nevada, and Utah, are too nearly similar to admit of any intelligible noting of differences; though, as might be expected, there is a slight tendency to the characters of *bulbi-vorus.*

A few specimens before me from Southern and Western Dakota, being those that Baird referred to "rufescens," with one from California, which he placed under "borealis," and one lately received from Fort Benton, Montana, are more decidedly reddish-brown than any of the above. They are unquestionably exactly what Maximilian called "rufescens." They are all considerably smaller than average *talpoides;* and, if I could satisfy myself that they were full-grown, something more would have to be said upon the subject. As it is, however, I can make out no satisfactory distinctions from ordinary *talpoides.* There are only five or six of these small rufous specimens before me; fuller series may indicate some tangible distinctions.

The following measurements indicate the average dimensions, and, to some extent, the variation, of this species:

Current number.	Locality.	Sex.	From tip of nose to—				Tail to end of vertebra.	Length of—			Nature of specimen.
			Eye.	Ear.	Occiput.	Tail.		Fore foot.	Hind foot.	Longest fore claw.	
11515	Souris River, Dakota ..	✕	1.00	1.60	1.75	7.00	2.50	1.25	1.25	0.55	Fresh.
11517	Pembina, Dakota	♀	0.75	1.40	1.60	6.25	2.75	1.15	1.25	0.55	Fresh.
11518	Pembina, Dakota	♂	0.90	1.60	1.70	7.50	2.50	1.20	1.20	0.50	Fresh.
11520	Pembina, Dakota	♂	0.90	1.50	1.90	7.25	2.75	1.25	1.20	0.45	Fresh.
11522	Pembina, Dakota	♂	0.95	1.60	1.80	7.00	2.60	1.25	1.20	0.55	Fresh.

NOTE.—The foregoing specimens, all adult, taken the same season (June to September, 1873), were carefully measured in the flesh by myself. Other specimens, from the same region, not measured in the flesh, carry the limits of total length from about 6 to about 8 inches, with a corresponding range of variation in other parts. The tail is taken from its true base—it appears about half an inch shorter in the dried state. The weight of these specimens ranges from 6 to 7 ounces. The girth of the chest is about 5 inches; of the belly, 6.50. No. 11517, ♀, has 12 teats—2 pairs axillary, 2 pairs pectoral, 2 pairs inguinal. When fully distended, in the fresh state, the width across the cheek-pouches is the greatest diameter of the body.

Distribution.—The most northern specimen I have seen is from the Assiniboine River; the species is supposed to range from Hudson's Bay to the Rocky Mountains in British America (northern limit unknown). In the United States, I have specimens from Minnesota, Dakota, Montana, Idaho, Nebraska, Wyoming, Nevada, and Utah. The southern limit is likewise unknown, but inferred to be somewhere along the middle of the United States. Its range, probably, does not inosculate with that of *T. umbrinus;* at any rate, I have seen nothing intermediate in character from anywhere in the Interior. The approach to *umbrinus* seems to be only made in the Pacific province, through *bulbivorus*. *Talpoides* exists fairly westward of the main chains of the Rocky Mountains; but no *Thomomys* of this style is known from immediate Pacific slopes. It meets and inosculates with the Northern style of *bulbivorus* ("douglasi") in the Columbia River region.

Synonymy.—The name "talpoides," coupled with various generic terms, is of frequent appearance in works on natural history; but, so far as I know, everything relating to it is pure compilation, the species never having been hitherto actually identified. The sole advance upon Richardson's original accounts is Audubon's figure of the type-specimen. A difficulty in the way of identifying Richardson's animal seems to have been an expression he used with regard to the number of digits. But it is morally certain that no such difference exists in the genus *Thomomys.* In some other cases, as in *Muridæ* and *Sciuridæ*, strict interpretation of Richardson's remarks in this regard would throw his species out of the question; for he speaks more than once of four perfect digits, and a rudimentary one, as in this very case. The diagnosis in the Fn. Bor.-Am. is: "grayish-black, with white chin, throat, and tail, and only four *perfect* toes on the hind feet." The expression "cinera-scenti-niger" is no obstacle; for here, as in the genus *Geomys*, there is a plumbago-state of pelage. The "white chin, throat, and tail" are diagnostic, in fact, of the animal I here describe, and inapplicable to any other. These facts, especially when coupled with the locality assigned (Hudson's Bay), leave no doubt in my mind that this is the species indicated by Richardson. Furthermore, Audubon's figure from Richardson's type is an unusually faithful representation. I consider this point established.

The next names in point of date are "borealis" and "townsendii," both

33 COL

described, in 1839, by Dr. Bachman, from Richardson's MSS., upon specimens in the Philadelphia Academy, said to be from the "Columbia River." These two names may be treated together, as they are unquestionably the same. These specimens, apparently, were figured by Audubon; the plate is too highly colored, the richness of the tint there represented being only matched in strong cases of *umbrinus;* but exactly the same wrong tawny coloration is on the same author's plate of "douglasii," and need not stand in the least in the way of the identification which I make. The same original specimens were taken by Dr. LeConte as the basis of his *Geomys rufescens,* and were examined by Professor Baird, who failed to see any decided difference from "douglasi." I have not taken occasion to handle these specimens myself; but Dr. Bachman's original description gives nothing incompatible with the characters of the present species, and the balance of his account inclines here. From the locality, it is most likely that these specimens are more or less intermediate between pure *talpoides* and "douglasi." It becomes, in fact, a matter of indifference whether we allocate the quotations of "borealis" here or under the next head.

Respecting the *T. rufescens* of Maximilian, I have nothing to add to what has been already said. "Geomys unisulcatus" of Gray, apparently only a museum-name, is here assigned by the author himself. The specimens collected by the United States Geological Survey of the Territories, catalogued by Mr. Merriam as "fulvus," belong here, as I ascertain by inspection.

THOMOMYS TALPOIDES BULBIVORUS, (Rich.) Coues.

Diplostoma ? bulbivorum, RICH., F. B. A. i, 1829, 206, pl. 18 B (lettered *douglasii* by mistake).—RICH., Zool. Voy. Blossom, 1839, pp. 9 and 13.*

Ascomys bulbivorus, WAGN., Suppl. Schreb. iii, 1843, 387. (Compiled.)

Geomys bulbivorus, DEKAY, N. Y. Fn. 1842, 92. (Compiled from Richardson.)—SCHINZ, Syn. Mamm. ii, 1845, 135. (Compiled; quotes *D. "bulbiferum"*; gives wrong locality).—LECONTE, Proc. Acad. Nat. Sci. Phila. 1852, 162. (Compiled from Richardson.)

Pseudostoma bulbivorum, AUD. & BACH., Q. N. A. iii, 1854, 337. (Compiled from Richardson.)

Geomys (Thomomys) bulbivorus, GIEB., Säng. 1855, 530. (Compiled from Richardson)

Thomomys bulbivorus, BAIRD, M. N. A. 1857, 389, pl. 50, f. 3 *a–g,* and pl. 52, f. 1 *a–g.* (Identifies the common Californian animal with this species of Richardson's, and minutely describes it.)—BAIRD, P. R. R. Rep. x, 1859, Williamson's Route, Mamm. 82. (Tejon, Cal.)—KENNERLY, P. R. R. Rep. x, 1859, Whipple's Route, Mamm. 13, pl. 11. (California.)—GERR., Cat. Bones Brit. Mus. 1862, 223. (California.)

Oryctomys (Saccophorus) bottæ, EYD. & GERV., Mag. de Zool. vi, 1836, 23, pl. 21, f. 4 (teeth); Voy. Favorite, v, 1839, 23, pl. 8, f. 4 (same).

Thomomys bottœ, LESS., Nouv. Man. R. Anim. 1842, 119. (Compiled.)—BAIRD, Proc. Acad. Nat. Sci. Phila. 1855, 335.* (Subsequently identified the same with *bulbivorus*.)
Geomys fuliginosus, SCHINZ, Syn. Mamm. ii, 1845, 136. (Based on *douglasi*; name altered for no good reason.)
Thomomys laticeps, BAIRD, Proc. Acad. Nat. Sci. Phila. 1855, 335; M. N. A. 1857, 392. (Humboldt Bay.)— KENN., P. R. R. Rep. x, 1859, Whipple's Route, Mamm. 13, pl. 12, f. 1 (by error marked "2" in text). (Same as the foregoing.)
Geomys douglasii, RICH., F. B. A. i, 1829, 200, pl. 18 C, ff. 1-6 (skull); Zool. Voy. Blossom, 1839, 9. (Near mouth of Columbia; Fort Vancouver.)—LECONTE, Proc. Acad. Nat. Sci. Phila. 1852, 162. (Compiled from Richardson.)
Geomys douglasi, DEKAY, N. Y. Fn. 1842, 92. (Compiled from Richardson.)
Ascomys douglasii, WAGN., Suppl. Schreb. iii, 1843, 392. (Compiled.)
Pseudostoma douglasii, AUD. & BACH., Q. N. A. iii, 1853, 24, pl. 105 (altogether too brightly colored). (Mainly compiled from Richardson.)
Geomys (Thomomys) douglasi, GIEBEL, Säng. 1855, 531. (Compiled.)
Thomomys douglassii, BAIRD, M. N. A. 1857, 394. (Minute description of specimens from Washington and Oregon Territories.)—SUCKL., P. R. R. Rep. xii, 1860, pt. ii, pp. 100, 126.

DIAGNOSIS.—Coloration heavier than in the foregoing; general cast reddish-brown, lined with dusky on the back; the head usually darker than the rest of the upper parts; on the sides, the color giving way to a clearer tawny-brown, which occupies the belly also, there overlying the plumbeous roots of the fur as a strong wash. Face and mouth-parts dusky, or even sooty-blackish, contrasting with the white lining of the pouches. No pure white on the under parts. Tail and feet usually incompletely whitish, or quite dusky. If anything averaging rather larger than true *talpoides*. Hand rather shorter than the foot, owing to less development of the claws, which are only about 0.40 long.

HABITAT.—Pacific coast and slopes of the United States, from Washington Territory to Southern California.

Description (from San Francisco specimens).—Having already sufficiently insisted upon the fact that there is no decided difference in size or shape between this form and the last, beyond an average less development of the fore claws, there is little to be said by way of description, except to amplify the foregoing points of coloration. The extreme of the *bulbivorus* branch of this species is readily recognized by a warmth and intensity of coloration not known to occur in specimens from the Northern Interior. The color varies a great deal in different specimens, but is never like the clear mouse-gray seen in *talpoides*. It is in reality an intimate mixture of yellowish-brown and dark-brown or blackish. Above, the pointing of the fur conceals the plumbeous bases of the hairs; below, this plumbeous shows, overlaid with a strong wash of tawny or muddy-brown, quite unlike the hoary-gray of the same parts of *talpoides*. The under surface is not known to be varied with patches of white, nor is there any white about the mouth, excepting the immediate border of the lips. On the contrary, the mouth-parts are sooty or dusky, contrasting with the white which lines the check-pouches. This is very much as in *umbrinus*, and quite different from *talpoides*. The hands and feet are sometimes white, as in *talpoides*, but oftener merely whitish, and not seldom dusky. I have not seen the tail pure white; it is generally dark-colored for the most part, often wholly so. The fore claws average about 0.40—rather less than more.

Such is the typical manifestation of this form, which I have only seen from California. We have next to trace the change by insensible degrees into both *talpoides* and *umbrinus*. Proceeding up the Pacific coast, we find an animal still like *bulbivorus* in the general tone of coloration (warm-brown above and muddy-bellied), but in which the mouth-parts have nearly or entirely lost their sootiness. Here, also, the fore claws enlarge somewhat, and from this state it is but a step to the grayer true *talpoides*, which joins with *douglasi* in the interior of Oregon and Washington. In the interior of California, the opposite modification begins, tending toward *umbrinus*, which becomes fully established in Arizona and New Mexico. Here the dark mouth-parts are preserved and even intensified, but the color grows richer till a decidedly tawny or fulvous cast is the result. Various specimens from Fort Crook and Fort Tejon, and from Provo, Utah, are of this ambiguous sort, and exhibit among themselves such variations that their labeling becomes a matter of indifference. Some of the browner ones are not separable at all from *bulbivorus*, while the ruddiness of others matches that of true *fulvus*. The gradation of the two forms in this region is demonstrably complete. Some other specimens from Fort Crook are absolutely identical with Steilacoom ones in respect of color; the only difference I can note being the somewhat weaker claws. To the southward, on the coast, the same gradation occurs, becoming established about San Diego. In Lower California, pure *umbrinus* prevails.

A San Franciscan specimen lately received at the Smithsonian is a perfect albino—snow-white all over.

Little further discussion of the synonymy of this form is required than is implied in what has already been said. Professor Baird appears to have first satisfactorily identified the *Diplostoma bulbivorum* of Richardson with the animal subsequently described as *Oryctomys bottæ* by Eydoux and Gervais. Preceding authors' use of the name had been altogether compilation. Schinz's name is a synonym upon its face, being a mere renaming of the same animal. The *T. laticeps* was based upon the individual peculiarities of a single specimen, the characters of which are more or less obscured by drying after immersion in alcohol.

THOMOMYS TALPOIDES UMBRINUS, (Rich.) Coues.

Geomys umbrinus, RICH., F. B. A. i, 1829, 202; Rep. Brit. Assoc. for 1836, v, 1837, 157. "Cadadagnios, Southwestern Louisiana"—more likely Texas.*—WATERH., Charlesw. Mag. N. H. iii, 1839, 596, f. 71 (skull).—DEKAY, N. Y. Fn. 1842, 92. (Compiled from Richardson.)—SCHINZ, Syn. Mamm. ii, 1845, 137. (Compiled from Richardson.)—LEC., Proc. Acad. Nat. Sci. Phila. 1852, 162. (Compiled from Richardson.)

Ascomys umbrinus, WAGN., Suppl. Schreb. iii, 1843, 389. (Compiled.)

Pseudostoma umbrinus, AUD. & BACH., iii, 1854, 307. (Compiled from Richardson.)

Geomys (Thomomys) umbrinus, GIEB., Säug. 1855, 530. (Compiled from Richardson.)

Thomomys umbrinus, BAIRD, M. N. A. 1857, 399 (redescribed from numerous New Mexican specimens).— BAIRD, U. S. Mex. B. Survey, ii, pt. ii, 1859, Mamm. p. —.—GERR., Cat. Bones Br. Mus. 1862, 228.

Geomys fulvus, WOODH., Proc. Acad. Nat. Sci. Phila. 1852, 201 (San Francisco Mountains, Arizona); Rep. Expl. Zuñi and Colorado R. 1853, 51, pl. 5 (the same).

Pseudostoma (Geomys) fulvus, AUD. & BACH., Q. N. A. iii, 1854, 300. (Copied from Woodhouse.)

Thomomys fulvus, BAIRD, M. N. A. 1857, 402. (Describes Woodhouse's type, and other specimens, from California.)—BAIRD, U. S. Mex. Bound. Surv. ii, pt. ii, 1859, Mamm. p. —.—KENN., P. R. R. Rep. x, 1859, Whipple's Route, Mamm. 14, pl. 12, f. 2.—COUES, Am. Nat. i, 1867, 394 (habits).—COUES, Proc. Acad. Nat. Sci. Phila. 1867, 135 (Fort Whipple, Arizona).

DIAGNOSIS.—Averaging decidedly smaller than either of the foregoing. Length of head and body about six inches, rarely seven. Fore feet averaging decidedly less than the hind feet; longest claw oftener under than over 0.40. Color variable, from a nearly uniform rich fawn-color all over, or even intense reddish-chestnut, to various tawny-brown shades, with or without a blackish dorsal area. Belly merely a paler shade of the color of the upper parts, or much as described under *bulbivorus*. Occasionally quite gray, much as in typical *talpoides*. (Variety: lustrous coal-black all over.) Mouth-parts, and often whole face, blackish, except sometimes immediately around the lips,

---

* The probability is heightened by the Spanish appearance of the name, as if a corruption of *Ciudad de Aguas*, "City of the Waters." The locality is now unknown. "Louisiana" was formerly a vague term.

strongly contrasting with the white lining of the pouch. Tail usually more
or less like the body.

HABITAT.—South Colorado, Southern Utah and Southern Nevada, Western Texas, New Mexico, Arizona, and Lower California to Cape Saint Lucas.
Southward extension into Mexico undetermined. "Louisiana."

Description (from extensive series from the above localities).—No other
form of the genus varies so much in color as this one. With the increase in
intensity and richness of coloration of the genus to the southward, there is
a corresponding ratio of variation to or from what may be held the normal
mean. Selecting average samples, as, for instance, some I collected at Fort
Whipple, Arizona, in 1864–'65, we observe a very rich tawny or fulvous
pelage, more or less obscured on the back by a blackish area. The under
parts are of the same color, paler or of about equal intensity, with the deep
plumbeous bases of the hairs showing. The ears are set in a small blackish
area; the face, and, to a less extent, the top of the head, are blackish, with
or without white spots on the lips or chin, contrasting strongly with the
white lining of the pouches. The feet are indifferently whitish or dusky;
and more or less of the tail is usually colored.

Other specimens, by the extinction of the blackish dorsal area, become
nearly concolor all over, and of so rich a hue as to almost bear the term
golden-brown. There is a great similarity in many cases to the coloration
of *Jaculus hudsonius* or *Arvicola aureola*. The best-marked samples of this
style before me are from Southern Arizona and Cape Saint Lucas, where this
appears to prevail. Dr. Woodhouse's type of "fulvus" is entirely of this color
above, with nearly white belly. Specimens from the Colorado Valley exhibit
another style of coloration in their extreme pallor, from the bleaching of
fulvous into a pale brownish-yellow, and with whitish belly. A specimen
from "Sonora" (rather Southern Arizona, as now bounded) is dark-cinnamon
or chestnut-red, with blackish dorsal area. More northerly specimens tend
to grayer tints; but this grayishness has a plumbeous cast, and is suffused on
the sides with tawny. The belly in these cases is as purely hoary-gray as in
typical *talpoides;* and one specimen, from Fort Massachusetts, is exactly rat-
colored, and indistinguishable from pure *talpoides*, except in being smaller,
though it is apparently very old. In this specimen, too, the characteristic

markings of the mouth-parts and pouches are much obscured, and the fore claws are fully as long as in some northern examples of *talpoides*. Half-grown specimens, as elsewhere in the family, are lead-colored, merely paler below.

A melanistic specimen from Cantonment Burgwyn, New Mexico, is a uniform, intense, lustrous plumbago color (almost like anthracite coal), with white lips and pouches.

In this form, which exhibits such variation as well as intensity of color, we observe more clearly than elsewhere the changes produced in the shedding and renewal of the pelage. It seems to be the rule in this genus, as in *Geomys*, that the hair is cast from before backward by a regular progression. As already hinted, the animals appear to grow gray with age; but, besides this, each annual or seasonal coat seems to lose its richness of coloration toward the time that it is to fall off, and the fresh coat comes out more heavily tinted. It results from this, in connection with the peculiar mode of shedding, that patchy specimens are of frequent occurrence, with a sharp line of demarkation between differently-colored areas (*Geomys castanops* is a notable case of this). Some examples before me are, in fact, strong "umbrinus" in front and very fair "bulbivorus" behind. Season, as well as age, doubtless influences the color of the pelage, but exactly to what extent I am unable to say, owing to the usual oversight of collectors in neglecting to date their labels.

The geographical distribution of the species, as far as now known, is indicated in a preceding paragraph. The original locality given for *umbrinus* has not been checked by subsequent accounts, and is probably somewhat out of the way; Texas or New Mexico being more likely the source of the type-specimen described by Richardson. I see no occasion to question Baird's identification of the species, with which the *Geomys fulvus* of Woodhouse is indisputably identical.

THOMOMYS CLUSIUS, Coues, *nov. sp.*

SP. CHAR.—Smallest known species of the genus. Length (♀, *adult*) about 5 inches. Feet remarkably small; sole of hind foot 0.75; palm of hand, including longest claw, 0.65. Fore claws small, weak, little curved, the longest under 0.30. Incisors as usual in the genus. Muzzle almost entirely hairy, with a very small naked pad confined between the nostrils. Pouches ample, about 1.75 deep (measured from the beginning of the fold of skin at the side of the snout). Tail extremely short; under 1.50 in length from the true base, and little over 1.00 from the end of the conical enlargement at base; the thinly-haired portion being thus less than one-fourth the total length of head and body. Ears minute. Color above pale yellowish-gray, with a slight light-brown shade; the fur plumbeous at base, as usual Below, nearly pure white, the fur being mostly of this color to the very base. No dark auricular area. Feet and tail white. Extremity of snout blackish Claws and whiskers colorless. Incisors faced with orange.

HABITAT.—The single specimen of the species at present known, No. 3051, Museum of the Smithsonian Institution, was taken at Bridger's Pass, Rocky Mountains, July 28, 1857, by Dr. W. A. Hammond.

With only one specimen to go upon, there is little to be added to the foregoing diagnosis. That the small size is not due to immaturity is evidenced by the fact that the specimen is a female, with functionally-developed teats, which had been in use. As well as I can determine from the dried skin, there are twelve mammæ,* situated as in *T. talpoides.* In its present state, somewhat stretched, the skin measures about $5\frac{1}{2}$ inches from nose to root of tail. The general dimensions, as well as the relative and absolute length of tail and the proportions of the feet, are all quite beyond the utmost limit of variation determined for any other form of *Thomomys.* It may give an idea of the smallness of the feet to say that the hind ones are no larger than those of the white-footed mouse (*Hesperomys leucopus*); they are a trifle broader, but not quite so long. The fore feet are decidedly shorter than the hinder ones, owing to the slight development of the slender weak claws. The ears are minute—scarcely larger, comparatively, than in a *Geomys,* though the tiny auricle has the recognizable shape of *Thomomys,* instead of being a mere tumid rim. The tail, as well as can be guessed from the present dried state, is less than a fourth as long as the head and body, measured from its apparent base. All these characters are utterly incompatible with any variety

---

* This appears to be the normal number in this genus; but, in an alcoholic specimen of *talpoides,* with the fur all gone from the belly, completely exposing the parts, I can find but eight; the two axillary pairs being wanting.

Figure 80.—THOMOMYS CLUSIUS, *Couce*. Natural size.

of *talpoides* and its conspecies I know of. The color is equally diagnostic. We miss the peculiar blackish area in which the ears of all other *Thomomys* are set, and we find instead a blackish snout. The pallid yellowish-gray of the upper parts is as different from any of the interminable variations of color of other *Thomomys* as that of *Geomys castanops* in comparison with *G. bursarius*. The whiteness of the fur to the very roots, on the under parts, is a striking character.

The specimen was procured in a region where the true *talpoides* is also found in abundance.

It seems to be the fortune of monographers who have found it necessary to reduce various species previously established to geographical races or mere synonyms, that they should have at the same time new ones of their own to propose. But I see no help for this. New species are not, to me, the altogether desirable things they seem to some; and my growing dislike to find them out keeps pace with my increasing knowledge of our ignorance respecting old species; nevertheless, there is no escape from them·at present, at frequent intervals, and of course the sooner they are all indexed binomially the better. Having no material for the further elucidation of the characters of *Thomomys clusius*, I may close with the remark that, if the unique specimen is not a pure "sport," it is a perfectly good species.

The name chosen for this species commemorates a peculiar trait of the whole family *Geomyidæ*—their remarkable and not generally known habit of plugging up the numerous openings of their extensive subterranean tunnels. This name, in connection with several others, completes a sort of epitome of the history of the family. They are underground animals (*Geomys*) that throw up heaps of earth (Θωμος, a pile—*Thomomys*) and close the entrances of their excavations (*clusius*); they are mole-like in many respects (*talpoides*); they are peculiarly provided with pouches (*bursarius*); and they feed on roots (*bulbivorus*)

34 COL

ADDENDUM A.

THE CRANIAL AND DENTAL CHARACTERS OF GEOMYIDÆ.

[*Reprinted, with some modification, from the Bulletin of the United States Geological and Geographical Survey of the Territories, 2d series, No. 2, pp.* 81–90, *published May* 11, 1875.]

$$\text{I.}\frac{1-1}{1-1};\ \text{C.}\frac{0-0}{0-0};\ \text{M.}\frac{4-4}{4-4};\ =\frac{5-5}{5-5}=\frac{10}{10}=20.$$

In its massiveness and angularity, the skull of the *Geomyidæ* differs altogether from that of the *Saccomyidæ*, in which the cranium is singularly papery and bullous, with few angles; and it quite closely resembles an arvicoline type. The jaws are remarkably strong; the incisors immense; the zygomata flaring; the occipital region is extensive; the palate proper is contracted and at the same time prolonged downward; there is a long arched interval between molars and incisors. On a plane surface, the skull without the lower jaw rests level upon the molars and incisors; no other points touching the support. The molars are all rootless and perennial. The inferior incisors traverse the whole jaw. The superior incisors are semicircular. No anteorbital foramen occupies a usual site. The complex temporal bone is inordinately enlarged in all its elements, but especially the squamosal, which represents most of the cerebral roofing at expense of the reduced parietals. The malar is merely a short splint; there is an osseous tubular meatus auditorius. There are no orbital processes; the interorbital constriction is narrower than the rostrum; the latter is more than a third of the length of the whole skull. Such are some of the general features, from which we may proceed to details—first of configuration of the whole, afterward of characters of individual bones.

Viewed from above, rather less than the posterior two-thirds of the skull presents a subquadrilateral figure, from which the rostrum protrudes in front. The greatest width is opposite the fore part of the zygomata in most cases;

though specimens differ in this respect, owing to a variable curve of these parts. In adult *Geomys*, the case is as stated, the zygomata converging a little backward in a nearly straight line, so that posteriorly their width apart is little if any greater than the intermastoid diameter of the skull. In *Thomomys*, there is a more decided outward convexity of these arches, and their greatest width apart is nearly at their middle—if anything, posterior to this, and at any rate the width here decidedly surpasses the intermastoid diameter. In front, the zygomatic plates of the maxillaries start out at nearly a right angle with the long axis of the skull; behind, the zygomata curve rather abruptly into the squamosal. There is a deep abrupt emargination behind the posterior root of the zygomata, between this and the postero-lateral corner of the skull; in the recess, the tubular bony meatus auditorius appears protruding in this view. The lambdoidal crest, forming the posterior boundary of the skull, is a slight curve, more or less irregular; most of it is squamosal, for the occipital bone rises to this crest for only a short distance. The narrowest part of the skull is between the orbits, where the width is less than the diameter of the rostrum. The irregularly pyriform figures, circumscribed by the zygomata and walls of the cranium, are of large size; no orbits proper are defined in the general orbital space, owing to deficiency of both pre- and post-orbital processes. The dome of the cerebral cavity is but little inflated; its sides seem somewhat pinched, there being a decided though shallow concavity just above the zygomatic spur of the squamosal; and a slight bulging anteriorly on each side at the usual site of post-orbital processes. The median line of the cerebral roof, in an old *Geomys* skull, is a ridge; this ridge bifurcates anteriorly to send a curved leg forward and outward to the orbital margins; and behind enlarges a little to receive a small interparietal. In various *Thomomys* skulls of different ages, the squamosals leave a rectangular interval occupied by small, narrowly linear parietals; and, instead of a single median ridge, there are two parallel ridges, with a depressed interval. The sides of the rostrum are straight and parallel, the edge being the swollen track of the superior incisors. The end is vertically truncate; the tips of the nasals and intermaxillaries and the faces of the incisors being all about in one perpendicular plane. The width of the rostrum is rather more than half its length.

Viewed in profile, the skull shows an almost perfectly straight dorsal outline from the occipital protuberance to a point just in advance of the orbits. Here is the highest point of the skull, whence the profile of the rostrum slopes gently downward, ending abruptly by vertical truncation. Likewise, the posterior or occipital outline is straight, or nearly so, and at a right angle with the superior surface. Likewise, again, the inferior surface of the skull, in all that part lying behind the pterygoids, presents a nearly straight and horizontal profile, at right angles with the occipital plane. Neither bulla ossea nor paroccipital nor condyle is sufficiently developed to interfere with the straightness of outline and rectangularity which all the back part of the skull presents to the side view. The rest of the under outline of the skull consists of the palatal profile as a whole. This consists anteriorly of a deep (semi-oval) concavity; there is an abrupt rise from the incisive alveolus, and then a long gradual curve sloping far backward and downward to the molar alveolus; while the strong obliquity of set of the anterior molars protracts this same curve to the tips of the teeth. The molar alveolar border is very short, and rather oblique, being lowest behind. The enormous arched inter-val between the incisors and molars is highly characteristic, as is also the low position of the molars—the teeth dip below a line drawn from the tips of the incisors to the foramen magnum. Behind the palate, flange-like pterygoids slope up to the basi-occipital plane. In this view, the zygomata are seen to dip but slightly downward. Their point of greatest deflection lies high above a line drawn from the incisive alveolus to the occipital condyle—in fact, even above a line from the end of the nasal bones to the same point; at their low-est point, they are still on a level with the meatus, and they scarcely dip more than half-way from the top of the skull to the level of the molar crowns. For the rest, notable points of the profile view of the skull are the small size and peculiar position of the "anteorbital" foramen, here situate low down and far forward in the maxillary, near its antero-inferior angle; a deep pit, but not perforation, behind the zygomatic plate of the maxillary; extensive lacerate. foramina of exit of nerves entering the orbit from the brain; similar fissured vacuities between the bulla ossea and the squamosal. The foreshortened tubular meatus is seen in the deep recess between the posterior root of the zygoma and the postero-inferior angle of the squamosal.

Viewed from behind, the occipital surface is seen to be nearly plane and vertical, with some beveling of the lateral (mastoid) portions. The most remarkable feature is the extent of this surface which is formed by the mastoid. In *Geomys*, at any rate, the mastoids take as much part in the occipital surface as the occipital bone itself. The upper border of this surface is a nearly regular arch from one squamosal angle to the other. The lower outline is likewise a curve, with its convexity downward, but its regularity is broken by the nick of the foramen magnum in the middle, the protuberance of the condyles next, similar paroccipital processes next, and after a little interval the mastoid processes. Barring these irregularities of detail, the general occipital surface is elliptical in shape. In the middle, and nicking the lower limb of the ellipse, is the foramen magnum, nearly all of which is vertical, and consequently not foreshortened in this view.

Viewed from below, the general contour is substantially like that presented from the opposite inspection, and we need only attend to details. The first feature is the incisive foramina—very small slits lying wholly in the intermaxillary bones, yet nearer to the molars than to the incisors, so great is the production of the rostrum The palate proper,* *i. e.,* the intermolar portion, is extremely contracted, its width anteriorly being no greater than that of one of the molars. It widens a little backward. It is deeply twice furrowed, having a strong median ridge separating the furrows, and strong alveolar ridges on either hand. Posteriorly, there is a pair of deep pits extending to opposite the penultimate molars, and divided by a strong ridge. The palatal plate upon which these pits are constructed reaches considerably back of the molars in *Geomys;* less so in *Thomomys.* The general resemblance of the parts to some *Arvicolinæ* is strong. The pterygoids are thin, vertical, and somewhat circular plates, divaricating a little posteriorly, and abutting against the tips of the bulla ossea They appear like a bifurcation of the median palatal ridge just mentioned. The post-palatal parts being contracted, like the palate itself, and compressed into small space, it is not easy to fully appreciate the conformation of the parts, and still less so to describe it. Moreover, the lamellar pterygoids are often broken off in care-

---

* The long upward-sloping anterior part of palate is not "palate" at all. In life, it is altogether outside the mouth, like the superior incisors, and covered with furry skin.

less preparation of the skull, and in such a way that scarcely a suggestion of their former presence is left. Behind the pterygoids, the conspicuous bullæ ossæ appear convergent anteriorly to touch the former, prolonged into a tube exteriorly. Between them, the basi-occipital space is cuneiform (especially in *Thomomys*—more nearly quadrangular in *Geomys*), with a median ridge and lateral depressions, nicked behind by a small portion of the foramen magnum. The skull finishes behind by an irregular curve, substantially the same as that described in speaking of the occipital plane.

In all but the oldest animals, the following sutures, or, at any rate, traces of them, persist: internasal, naso-intermaxillary, maxillo-intermaxillary, fronto-nasal, fronto-intermaxillary, and fronto-maxillary; maxillo-malar, squamo-parietal, squamo-malar, squamo-mastoid, occipito-mastoid, occipito-petrosal; basi-occipito-sphenoid; and there is fissured separation of the petrosal and tympanic from the squamosal. The various intricate relations of the palatals, and of the "sphenoid" as a whole, are inappreciable in the adult skull. Detailed relations of such of the individual bones as can be made out from the material before me here follow:

The nasals reach back to a point opposite the anterior root of the zygoma, but extend little, if any, in the other direction, beyond the intermaxillaries. For two-thirds their extent they are narrow and approximately parallel in the examples of *Geomys* before me, and then rapidly expand. In all the *Thomomys* I have seen, they widen regularly from the base to tip. They are flat at first, but toward the end become somewhat volute or scroll-like. They remain permanently distinct from the intermaxillaries, and have failed in no case to show me separation from each other.

The intermaxillaries run up on the forehead farther than the nasals—to or beyond the back instead of front border of the zygomata. being received in a deep emargination of the frontal. Below, similarly, they run far down on the false palate, ending opposite the back end of the incisive foramina. Their course around the side of the rostrum (maxillo-intermaxillary suture) may usually be traced as a strongly convex curve between the upper and lower points just mentioned, the most forward portion of the curve lying nearly midway between zygoma and incisors. The lateral surface is thrown into a curved elevation, denoting the track of the incisor within. A strong alveolar plate dips down between the front teeth. The maxillary ends anteriorly in the curve just described; its other boundaries are obscured in adult life. The side is flat; it suddenly rises in a broad, thin, zygomatic plate, flush above with the general level of the top of the skull, there abutting (as shown by a long persistent suture) both with frontal and intermaxillary. This plate stands away nearly at a right angle with the axis of the skull, but very oblique to the other two planes. It circumscribes the orbit anteriorly; is excavated in the lachrymal region; its upper border is widened to a sharp-edged surface, and slopes gently outward, downward, and backward; its thin under margin rises to nearly meet the upper, finishing the laminar portion, and continuing to the malar bone as an angular process. A lachrymal bone is plainly indicated at the upper back part of the plate, but its extent and relations are not appreciable.

The frontal is much contracted, especially across the middle, having a somewhat hourglass-like superior outline, though both ends are angular. In front, it sends a rectangular median process abutting against the nasals, and inclosed between the intermaxillaries, and an acute lateral process on each side, entering a recess between intermaxillary and maxillary. These sutures seem persistent. Behind, the fronto-parietal and fronto-squamosal sutures are commonly obliterated; when appreciable, the bone is seen to unite with the extremely narrow parietals by a directly transverse straight line, and with the squamosals by an oblique line on each side. These sutures persist longer on top of the head than in the orbital region.

The malar bone is a mere splint, reduced coincidently with the great extension of the zygomatic spurs of both squamosal and maxillary. It is somewhat clubbed anteriorly and overrides its support; behind, it is itself overlapped.*

The parietals, as already hinted, are singularly reduced in this family. In the skull of an old *Geomys*, the squamo-parietal suture is obscure or inappreciable, and the squamosals appear to meet each other at the above-described ridge on the median line; careful inspection, however, usually reveals a very irregular and much overlapping squamo-parietal suture, defining

---

* Although the zygoma in this family is a good stout arch, this reduction of the malar prepares us for the delicate thread-like condition of the parts in the next family, *Saccomyidæ*.

the parietals externally. These are of indeterminate shape, but tend to be narrowly rectangular; and, in *Thomomys*, a pair of pretty regular linear parietals is usually evident. There is constantly an interparietal—squarish or pentagonal in *Thomomys*; rather triangular in *Geomys*.

With such state of the parietals, there is a corresponding overdevelopment of the temporal bone, especially of its squamosal element, though not to the extraordinary extent witnessed in *Saccomyidæ*, where the whole bone is blown up like a bladder. The squamosal roofs over most of the cranial cavity, and alone forms (with the exception of a little place occupied by the interparietal) the whole occipital or lambdoidal crest. The mastoid, which persists distinct from both squamosal and occipital, though usually fusing with the petrosal, is immensely developed, its superficies lying mostly in, and representing about half of each side of, the occipital surface. It develops a moderate " mastoid process", lying against the postero-external corner of the squamosal, and looking like a duplicate of the paroccipital process that lies against its opposite extremity. The petrosal does not share this unusual development, the bullæ osseæ being, in fact, smaller than they are in *Arvicola*, for instance; they swell but little below the baso-occipital plane. The tympanic develops into a tubular meatus, set quite free from its surroundings in a deep recess of the squamosal. The petrosal likewise is fissured away from the squamosal, but, in adult life, the tympanic, petrosal, and mastoid are consolidated.

The upper and lower parts of the occipital bone are at right angles with each other; the basi-occipital is horizontal upon the floor of the skull, while the superior and lateral elements are perpendicular behind. The supra-occipital is squarish, with rounded corners; the ex-occipitals develop into moderate obtuse processes. Nearly all of the foramen magnum is vertical; the condyles are rather small, and widely divergent superiorly.

The suture with the basi-occipital, which persists for some time, is ordinarily the most conspicuous of the sphenoidal relations which may be appreciated in examination of adult skulls. Close inspection, however, shows the squamo-sphenoid suture just inside the glenoid fossa; the alisphenoid barely misses taking a part in the mandibular articulation (as in some marsupials);

35 COL

the orbito-sphenoid, lining the orbit behind, rises nearly to the top of the skull.

The mandible remains for consideration. This is eminently characterized by its massiveness and the emphasis of its various ridges and angles. Nevertheless, the symphysis, though extensive, is incomplete. Instead of an edge below, the bone presents a broad, smooth, flattened area, bounded on the sides by a ridge indicating the limit of masseteric muscular attachment. The angle of the jaw is strongly exflected in a peculiar way. An oblique plate (the "descending process" in many rodents) arises from the inner side of the body of the bone, and curves strongly backward and outward, ending far exterior to the main part of the bone as a strong laminar process. Just inside of this, between it and the condyle, there is a strongly-marked, smooth, upright protuberance. This is where the root of the incisor pushes up from the inside. To the inner side of this knob, again, rises a third protuberance; it is the condyle, rather small, and of no noteworthy features. (It appears particularly small when compared with the glenoid cavity, which, as I should have remarked before, is of unusual width.) Thus the mandibles, viewed from behind, present the curious appearance of three prongs—condyle, incisor-knob, and exterior process. The appearance of trifurcation is best marked in *Thomomys*, where the tooth-knob is most prominent, and separated by deepest notches from the processes between which it stands. In addition to all these prominences, a slender, falcate, acute coronoid rises in front, and overtops the rest, being separated from the condylar ramus by a deep notch. There is a deep excavation between the thin laminar basis of the coronoid and the molar alveolus. The foramen of the inferior maxillary nerve appears on the inner side of the root of the condylar ramus.

The dental formula has been already given. The molar dentition appears weak and slight in comparison with the enormous incisors. The under incisors, as already said in effect, run the whole length of the jaw, and push up a knob of bone behind. They are of the ordinary scalpriform construction, quite flat-faced, with converging sides, and beveled to an edge behind. The superior incisors describe nearly a semicircle through the intermaxillaries, and far into the maxillaries, to below the root of the zygoma. They are of distinct character in the two genera, furnishing the most ready means of diagnosis, not only of the genera, but of the species of *Geomys*, as already fully given in the body of this paper.

The molars are perennial rootless prisms, as in *Arvicolinæ* and many other hard gnawers, but are small and of a very simple structure—at least in comparison with the complicate character which obtains in many rodents. The whole molar series is scarcely one-seventh of the length of the skull. They are implanted very obliquely to suit the peculiar conformation of the parts. The axis of the anterior upper molar slopes backward at an angle of about 45°, and the rest succeed with regularly-diminishing obliquity. The relation is reversed in the lower jaw, where the back molar slopes forward, the rest becoming successively more nearly perpendicular. There is the same number of teeth in both jaws, and they are quite similar in construction. The anterior molar in each jaw is a double prism; the others are single and simple, elliptical in cross-section, the first being a pair of ellipses laid together like a short broad figure-of-eight, and the last approaching a cylindrical figure. The relation of the molars to each other is somewhat singular. Their roots are all widely diverging, but their crowns come into close contact. This is effected by the curve in their axis. Thus the front upper molar is curved with the convexity posterior; the rest are curved successively more and more, with the convexity anterior. Similar characters mark the under molars, though less strongly; and there is seen in these teeth, especially in the anterior ones, a lateral as well as fore-and-aft curve. This shape appears to be forced upon the teeth by the peculiar conformation of the alveoli. The molars are quite similar in the two genera, and scarcely afford diagnostic characters, especially since there is some change in the details of the molar crowns with age and wear of the teeth. On the whole, however, it may be observed that in *Geomys* the molars—the immediate ones, at any rate—are more perfectly elliptical than they are in *Thomomys*, where a pinching-together of the exterior portion of the ellipses tends to result in a pyriform contour.

The principal cranial and dental characters of the two genera which compose the *Geomyidæ* may be shortly contrasted, as follows:

GEOMYS.

Superior incisors deeply channeled along the middle, with or without a fine marginal groove.

Crowns of intermediate molars truly elliptical.

Root of inferior incisor but little protuberant on outside of base of condylar ramus; end of mandible thus only two-pronged, with a knob between.

Zygomata widest across anteriorly, thence contracting; the width behind little, if any, greater than the intermastoid diameter of the skull.

Parietals ridged along their line of union with each other.

Interparietal triangular.

Nasals approximately parallel-edged part way, then suddenly widening.

Superficies of mastoid bone occupying nearly half the occipital surface of the skull on each side.

Bullæ osseæ less inflated, quite acute anteriorly.

Basi-occipital, in the middle, about as broad as the width of the bulla at the same point.

A pair of broad deep pits on the palate behind, extending forward to opposite the penultimate molars.

THOMOMYS.

Superior incisors without median sulcus, but with a fine marginal groove (sometimes obsolete).

Crowns of intermediate molars acute-edged exteriorly.

Root of inferior incisors causing a protuberance on outside of base of condylar ramus nearly as high as condyle itself; end of mandible thus singularly three-pronged.

Zygomata regularly convex outward, with a sweeping curve; their breadth across posteriorly decidedly greater than the intermastoid diameter of the skull.

Parietals ridged externally near the squamo-parietal suture.

Interparietal rather pentagonal.

Nasals widening uniformly from behind forward.

Superficies of mastoid bone restricted to less than a fourth of the occipital surface on each side.

Bullæ osseæ more inflated, quite obtuse anteriorly.

Basi-occipital, in the middle, much narrower than the bulla at the same point.

A pair of slight pits on the palate behind, not extending beyond the ultimate molars.

Pterygoids —–? (will be found differ- · Pterygoids appearing like a bifurca-
ing appreciably from those of *Tho-*   tion into two thin diverging plates
momys).   of a single median vertical palatal
                                             plate.

In like manner, we may proceed to compare some of the principal cranial
characters of *Geomyidæ* and *Saccomyidæ*. Notwithstanding the unquestionably close affinity of these two families, which must stand next to each other
in the system, their crania are curiously different in general appearance and
details of contour. The discrepancies are, however, of a superficial character, resulting mainly from the extraordinary molding of the parts in *Saccomyidæ*. In other words, it is a matter of mere *shape*, for the most part.
There are, however, some curious and more essential features, of which the
enormous inflation of various elements of the temporal bone and peculiar
zygomatic relations posteriorly are the most remarkable. Probably, going
into details, a hundred actual differences between the skulls of *Geomyidæ* and
Saccomyidæ might be enumerated. I shall content myself with tabulating a
few of the more important of these. The comparisons are made between
Geomys bursarius and *Dipodomys ordi;* it should be remembered, however,
that the latter presents an extreme case, the average characters of the *Saccomyidæ* being less different from those of *Geomyidæ*.

GEOMYIDÆ.	SACCOMYIDÆ
Skull massive, angular, in general like that of *Arvicola*, &c.	Skull thin and papery, the corners rounded off; the resulting general shape peculiar.
Interorbital space the narrowest part of the skull—narrower than rostrum.	Interorbital space expanded, very much broader than the rostrum.
Occipital region approaching a plane surface, without median emargination.	Occipital region formed chiefly of enormous bulging mastoids, with deep median emargination.
Nasal bones not produced beyond	Nasal bones produced far beyond in-

vertical plane of incisors; rostrum broad, parallel-sided.

Parietals small, linear, remote from the orbits.

Occipital of an ordinary character, not attaining top of skull.

Temporal bone, though of great extent, not remarkably inflated.

Squamosal roofing most of the cerebral cavity.

Zygomata of an ordinary character, with the usual connections.

Tympanic, a contracted tube.

Petrosals discrete from each other, in contact with basi-occipital.

Mastoid excluded from roof of cerebral cavity.

Zygomatic process of maxillary a plate with merely thickened upper border.

Palatal outline strongly ascending

---

cisors; rostrum attenuated, tapering.

Parietals large right-angled triangles, together as broad as the frontal, reaching orbits.

Occipital reduced and of peculiar shape; a part of it mounting the top of the skull.

Temporal bone unique in its enormous size and inflation, being blown up like a bladder; the swollen mastoids forming most of the occipital plane; the two temporals larger than all the rest of the skull together.*

Squamosal restricted to the orbit.

Zygomata thread-like in most of their extent, and greatly depressed in position; *the malar bone abutting against* the tympanic.

Tympanic, an inflated vestibule.

Petrosals in mutual contact at their extremities, and fissured away from basi-occipital.

Mastoid roofing most of cerebral cavity.

Zygomatic process developing into a shield over much of the orbital space.

Palatal profile nearly straight and

---

* If the sense of hearing of *Dipodomys* be co-ordinated with the osseous development of the auditory apparatus, it must be extraordinarily acute.

and arched anteriorly; molars far below level of zygomata.

Incisors large, parallel-edged, scarcely converging.

Anterior molar, a double prism.

Root of inferior incisor protuberant posteriorly.

Large erect falcate coronoid, overtopping condyle.

&c., &c.

horizontal; molars on a level with the zygomata.

Incisors small, acuminate, convergent.

Anterior molar, a single prism.

Root of inferior incisor not prominent posteriorly.

Minute prickle-like sloping coronoid, far below level of condyle.

&c., &c.

ADDENDUM B.

NOTES ON THE "SALAMANDER" OF FLORIDA (GEOMYS TUZA).

[Communicated to the author by Prof. G. Brown Goode.]

One of the most interesting mammals of the Southern Atlantic States is the species of *Geomys* known in Florida and Georgia as the "Salamander." The name of "gopher," by which the various representatives of this genus inhabiting the Upper Mississippi Valley are known, would seem very appropriate for this animal. It appears to be a corruption of the French "gaufre", and to refer to the manner in which the soil is honey-combed by the pouched rats.

Local usage, however, has appropriated this name to a kind of land-tortoise, *Xerobates carolinus*, (Linné) Ag., which is common in Georgia and Florida, and which also excavates a burrow, a habit to which, perhaps, it owes its name. I have never heard an explanation of the name "salamander" in its application to *Geomys tuza;* but it occurs to me that it may allude to the safety enjoyed by these little animals in their subterranean abodes at the time of the devastating fires which sometimes consume the pine-forests. After such a conflagration has passed over their heads, destroying every other kind of life, they are seen at work among the ashes, very good types of the salamander of fable, which passes unharmed over burning coals, and

> " with her touch
> Quenches the fire, though blazing ne'er so much."

Although the species was not scientifically described until 1817, it was noticed by several among the earlier writers. William Bartram, an English naturalist, who visited the Southeastern States in 1773, speaks of a large ground-rat, which he observed in the vicinity of Savannah, which was more than twice the size of the common Norway rat, and which in the night threw out earth, forming little mounds or hillocks.*

---

* Travels through North and South Carolina, Georgia, East and West Florida, the Cherokee Country, the extensive territories of the Muscogulges or Creek Confederacy, and the country of the Chactaws. * * * —By William Bartram.—Dublin.—1793. p. 7. [Orig. ed. Philadelphia, 1791.]

A brief description of the species, under the name of the Hamster of Georgia, was published in the New York Medical Repository in 1802, and afterward in an appendix to the American edition of Bewick's Quadrupeds. On this description was founded the name *Mus tuza*, cited in the list of American mammals published by Ord in 1815,* a name which antedates that of Rafinesque by about two years, and which has been adopted by Dr. Coues.

Notwithstanding their great abundance, it is extremely difficult to obtain specimens of the salamanders. Their acute sense of smell gives them an early warning of the approach of danger, and they easily make their escape in the maze of tunnels. Should one even be driven into a blind passage, it would find little difficulty in baffling its pursuer, for it can burrow faster than a man can follow with a spade; and, since it obliterates its track by throwing the soil behind, it leaves scarcely more trace of its passage in the loose sand than a fish swimming through the water. It is thought quite impossible to dig them out. Occasionally, they are shot, when they come to the surface to throw out sand; but they remain in sight only an instant, and the marksman, to be successful, must have his gun bearing upon the opening at which the animal is expected to appear, with finger on the trigger, and be ready to pull the moment the head is sighted.

By the patient use of steel-traps, while in Florida this spring, I obtained a number of specimens, some of which I succeeded in keeping for several weeks, thus having an excellent opportunity of studying their habits.† They may easily be confined in a wooden box, with sides eight or ten inches high, having dry sand two or three inches deep on the bottom. No cover is necessary; I have never seen one look up from the earth, and have rarely known them to attempt to escape. They require no water, and no food except sweet-potatoes. A single potato of moderate size will feed a salamander for three days.

The senses of sight and hearing seem in them to be very dull. An object may be held within a short distance of their eyes without attract-

---

* Guthrie's Geography, 2d American edition, ii, 1-15, p. 292.

† Two of them, which I sent to the Zoological Society of Philadelphia, may be seen in the garden at Fairmount Park.

ing their attention; but the moment one is touched, he turns with a jump, snapping fiercely, much to the detriment of fingers which may be near. If two are confined in the same cage, the one does not seem aware of the presence of the other, unless they accidentally come in contact. Their eyes are small, dull, and without expression. Their sense of smell I judge to be very delicate, from the manner in which they approach the hills of potatoes. Their motions are surprisingly quick and energetic; their activity never ceasing from morning to night.

They are very pugnacious, and a rough-and-tumble combat between two vigorous males would seem terrific, if their size could be magnified a few diameters in the eye of the spectator. Every muscle of their compact, elastic, stout bodies is brought into action, and they plunge and bite with wonderful ferocity. A battle is usually followed by the death of one or both. I have examined them after death, and found the whole anterior part of the body bruised almost to the consistency of paste, the bones of the legs crushed in four or five places. When two come together in the cage, their salutation is a plunge and a bite.

I watched their burrowing with much interest. They dig by grubbing with the nose and a rapid shoveling with the long, curved fore paws, assisted by the pushing of the hind feet, which remove the dirt from beneath the body and propel it back with great power a distance of eight or ten inches. When a small quantity of earth has accumulated in the rear of the miner, around he whirls, with a vigorous flirt of the tail, and joining fore paws before his nose, he transmutes himself into a sort of wheelbarrow, pushing the dirt before him to a convenient distance, and repeating the act until the accumulation is removed, then resuming his mining. Any root or twig which blocks his way is quickly divided by his sharp chisel-teeth. I have never seen a salamander place sand in his cheek-pouches, though I have watched their burrowing hour after hour. It is, of course, impossible to observe them when at work under ground, but I incline to believe that most of the refuse earth from the burrows is transported in the manner just described. The negroes told me that they had seen the salamander appear at the mouth of its hole for an instant and "spit out" the sand which it carried in its pouches, aiding the act by inserting the fore paws *into* the pockets. I have never met any one who could tell *exactly* what the salamander does at the instant he appeared, his motions being so quick that one cannot be quite sure; the general impression, however, is, that they are unloading their cheek-pouches. This is not at all improbable, for we know that they carry their food in these receptacles, and it seems a very natural way for them to bring their refuse sand to the surface, since they often have to transport it a distance of several feet. Still it is quite desirable to have other and more careful observations; for observers are apt to be deceived by their own eyes, especially in the light of preconceived opinions.

The subterranean labyrinth constructed by this clever army of sappers and miners penetrates the pine-barrens and cultivated fields in every direction. An energetic salamander, with a slight knowledge of engineering, would find little difficulty, I suspect, in making an underground journey through Florida from the Atlantic to the Gulf of Mexico. The direction of the burrows may easily be traced by the loose hillocks of white sand which are thrown up along the line at intervals of three or four feet. These are the "dumps" made by the burrower in throwing out his refuse accumulations. Each consists of about a peck of loose sand, and, by the casual observer, might easily be mistaken for an ant-hill. No opening is visible, but by digging under the hill a hole is found, the mouth of the adit to the main tunnel, which may be three feet below the surface if made in cold weather, but perhaps not more than six inches if in summer. One of these mounds is thrown up in a very few moments; I have seen thirty raised in a single night on the line of one tunnel; this would represent nearly one hundred feet of tunneling. I have seen one hundred and fifty in one continuous row raised in about two days; this would make between four and five hundred feet of burrow completed in that short time apparently by one little animal, an amount of work which may seem incredible to one who has not watched the restless movements of these animated plows, which are seemingly as well adapted for piercing the sand as birds are for cleaving the air. The burrows are about two and one-half inches in diameter, barely large enough to admit a man's hand, and, as has been stated, are at various depths below the surface. They meander in all directions, except in straight lines; their builders being guided apparently only by their whims or their olfactories. They, no doubt, intersect each other at many points, and one tunnel serves as a passage for a community, though fierce battles must often ensue when two rival claimants meet in a common highway. The nests are large chambers, one or two feet from the main tunnel, with which they are connected by side-passages, which leave nearly at right angles. Here the miners lay up a supply of provisions, and the chambers are often found to contain a half-bushel of sweet-potatoes cut up into chunks as large as peach-stones, and of convenient size to be carried in the pockets. The salamander is a liberal provider. In this region, cellars are unknown, and sweet-potatoes are stored in heaps at the surface, covered with straw and sand. The salamanders are cunning enough not to throw up sand-heaps in the vicinity of these potato-heaps, but remove the loose earth into their old tunnels. When they once get access to the "tater-hake," they quickly remove its contents, and the owner wakes up the some morning to find his *cache* a hollow pretense. In these side-chambers, the salamanders rear their young, building a nest of grass, pine-needles, and live-oak leaves. I found them breeding in April.

The color of *Geomys tuza* is quite constant, light reddish-brown above, darker along the back, and lighter yellowish-brown beneath. One specimen was caught for me which showed a decidedly melanistic tendency, being nearly black. The measurements of a very large male are as follows: Nose to eye, 1⅜ inches; nose to ear, 1⅞; nose to root of tail, 11½; tail from root to end of vertebræ, 3; arm, fore foot to end of claws, 1¾; leg, hind foot from heel to end of claws, 1¼; muzzle to bottom of cheek-pouch, 3; circumference of expanded mouth of pouch, 5; distance from tip to tip of the longest toes of the fore feet, when stretched apart at right angles with the body, 7¾; same measurement applied to hind feet, 6½; girth of body behind shoulders, 5; distance from eye to eye, ¾; distance from ear to ear, 1¼.

The contents of one of the cheek-pouches in sand filled an old-fashioned silver tablespoon, heaped full. The contents of the pouch of an ordinary salamander will fill a dessertspoon in the same way.

INDEX.

37 COL

○